CONTENTS

EDITORS' PREFACE

Longman Revise Guides are written by experienced examiners and teachers, and aim to give you the best possible foundation for success in your course. Each book in the series encourages thorough study and a full understanding of the concepts involved, and is designed as a subject companion and study aid to be used throughout the course.

Many candidates fail to achieve the grades which their ability deserves, owing to such problems as the lack of a structured revision strategy, or unsound examination technique. This series aims to remedy such deficiencies, by encouraging a realistic and disciplined approach in preparing for and taking the examinations.

The largely self-contained nature of each chapter gives the book a flexibility which you can use to your advantage. After starting with the background to the courses and details of the syllabus coverage, you can read all other chapters selectively, in any order appropriate to the stage you have reached in your course.

Geoff Black and Stuart Wall

ACKNOWLEDGEMENTS

I would like to thank the Associated Examining Board for permission to reproduce the examination questions, glossary of terms, and marking guidelines used in the 'A' and 'AS' examinations.

My thanks also go to Geoff Black for remaining patient and supportive throughout the writing of this book, Paul Humphreys, Alison Wadeley and Anthony Curtis for their critical comments and helpful advice, and the management and players of Marine Football Club for staying at the top of the Northern Premier League while writing this text!

Most of all I am indebted to the support and friendship of my children, Chris and Alex Cardwell, and it is to them that I humbly dedicate this book.

Michael Cardwell

A-LEVEL
AND AS-LEVEL

LONGMAN
REVISE
GUIDES

£1

PSYCHOLOGY

Mike Cardwell

Longman

LONGMAN A AND AS-LEVEL REVISE GUIDES

Series editors:
Geoff Black and Stuart Wall

Titles available:
Accounting
Art and Design
Biology
Business Studies
Chemistry
Computer Science
Economics
English
French
General Studies
Geography
German
Modern History
Mathematics
Physics
Sociology
Psychology

Longman Group Limited,
Longman House, Burnt Mill, Harlow,
Essex CM20 2JE, England
and Associated Companies throughout the world

© Longman Group Limited 1994

First published 1994

ISBN 0582 226546

British Library Cataloguing in Publication Data
A catalogue record for this book is available from the British Library.

Set by 6QQ in 10/12pt Century Old Style

Printed by William Clowes Ltd., Beccles and London

THE SYLLABUSES AND EXAMINATIONS

GETTING STARTED

Using this book

Let me first say that this is a revision text. In other words, it should not be used in place of a course textbook. It is intended as a tool for revision suitable for students taking the 'A' and 'AS' level Psychology examinations of the AEB, NEAB and Oxford & Cambridge examining boards. The book offers a review of selected areas of these syllabuses, but, particularly with the AEB syllabuses, this selectivity is far from random. In the AEB 'A' level, from the 1994 examinations onwards, candidates are guaranteed one question per subsection for each option. If none of this makes any sense to you, you should get hold of a syllabus and you will see that for each option (excluding Perspectives and Research Methods) there are four subsections. In the examination, you will have a choice from four questions in each option, one per subsection.

So, some subsections have been left out completely (I apologise if they were your favourite ones) so that the other subsections could be treated in more detail.

How should this book be used?

Each chapter is divided into a number of different sections.
The major issues associated with that syllabus area are presented in the first part of the chapter. Note that because of the nature of psychology there is no such thing as the one definitive correct way to approach a particular aspect of human behaviour. The topic content you may be familiar with from your own textbook or your class notes might be completely different. Don't worry about this, simply use the 'new' material to add another perspective to your understanding of the topic.

The second half of the chapter is more concerned with assessment of that material. A selection of examination questions is presented. You might like to attempt some of these, using the previously presented material in conjunction with your own notes. A set of answers is provided, either in outline form, with suggestions how the questions might be answered, or in essay form. One essay in each chapter is written by the examiner, and one by a student so that you can take advantage of the comments made by the examiner when marking it. Note that the examiner essays (called Tutor's answer) are meant as sample answers, not model answers. Student essays are given an 'A' level grade so that you can have some idea of the level of competence displayed in each one. The grades awarded should not be taken as an indication that examiners mark with particular 'A' level grades in mind (or even impressions of pass and fail for that matter). The grade that you eventually receive is determined by many things, including your coursework.

Each chapter ends with a set of Review sheets, so that you can review your knowledge of key points from that chapter.

STUDYING PSYCHOLOGY

TOPICS AND SYLLABUSES

THE EXAMINATION AND ASSESSMENT PATTERNS

KNOWLEDGE AND ABILITIES TO BE TESTED

GLOSSARY OF TERMS USED IN AEB EXAMINATIONS

MARKING GUIDELINES

EFFECTIVE EXAMINATION PERFORMANCE

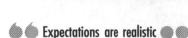

STUDYING PSYCHOLOGY

ESSENTIAL PRINCIPLES

Psychology has grown enormously as an 'A' level subject in the last five years, and this is reflected in the many different ways that students choose to study it. Many students take the subject as part of a part-time course over one year. Whilst it is the case that the examining boards can make no allowances for this in their assessment, it is also worth noting that all boards mark at the level of the *notional 18 year old*. Examiners bear this in mind during their marking, which means that 18 year old students are not being compared unfavourably against older students who might have a much more sophisticated grasp of many of the topics they are writing about.

●● Expectations are realistic ●●

TOPICS AND SYLLABUSES

Table 1.1 shows the chapters which are relevant to the various syllabuses.

Table 1.1 analysis of examination syllabuses by topic and chapter.

EXAMINATION SYLLABUS

Topic	Chapter number	AEB A	AEB AS	NEAB A	Ox & Cam A	Ox & Cam AS
Methodology	2	/	/	/	/	/
Ethics	3	/	/	/	/	/
Perception	4	/	/	/	/	/
Memory	5	/	/	/	/	/
Information processing and selective attention	6	/	/	/	/	/
Affiliation, attraction and prejudice	7	/	/	/	/	/
Pro and antisocial behaviour	8	/	/	/	/	/
Attitudes	9	/	/	/	/	/
Social influence	10	/	/	/	/	/
Animal evolution	11	/				
Animal learning	12	/	/	/	/	/
Experimental design and research methods	13	/	/	/	/	/
Early socialisation	14	/	/	/	/	/
Cognitive development	15	/	/	/	/	/
Social behaviour	16	/	/	/	/	/
Adulthood	17	/	/	/	/	/
Abnormality	18	/	/	/	/	/

●● A useful quick-check ●●

Table 1.1 shows which syllabuses offer which topics, and where you can find the topic in this book. Note that each board adopts a slightly different approach to the material. The AEB requires content and process skills (Skills A and B, more of this later), the Oxford & Cambridge syllabus also embeds this material within a number of specified core studies.

THE EXAMINATION AND ASSESSMENT PATTERNS

In this section we briefly look at the examination and assessment requirements for each syllabus.

Table 1.2 AEB 'A' and 'AS' comparison of methods of assessment.

Method of assessment	AEB 'A'	AEB 'AS'
Essays		
'Split' questions	/	/
Research methods stimulus material	/	/
Number of examination papers	2	1
Total length of papers in hours	6	3
Pieces of coursework and % marks	5 (20%)*	3 (20%)**
	* 4 (20%) from 1995	** 2 (20%) from 1995

Table 1.3 Oxford & Cambridge Board 'A' and 'AS' comparison of methods of assessment

		Duration	Assessment weighting A Level	AS Level
PAPER 1	The core studies 20 short answer questions (40%) 2 stimulus questions (60%)	3hrs	40%	80%
PAPER 2	Coursework folder 2 pieces of structured practical work (50% each)	—	10%	20%
PAPER 3	Specialist Choice Assignments (course work) (a) Project (b) Assignment (50% each)	—	10%	—
PAPER 4	Research Methods (Paper given one week before exam)	$1\frac{1}{2}$ hrs	10%	—
PAPER 5	Specialist Choices 3 stimulus—response structured essays 2 questions on specialist choice	3hrs	30%	
			100%	100%

Table 1.4 NEAB scheme of assessment ('A' level)

	Duration	Weighting
PAPER 1 Section A: One compulsory question on statistics and design	45 mins	10%
Section B: Part (i) Three questions on Section 1 of the syllabus (cognitive and linguistic development) Part (ii) Three questions on Section 2 of the syllabus (acquisition of knowledge and skills)	$2\frac{1}{4}$ hrs	30%
PAPER 2 Section A: As Section A above	45mins	10%
Section B: Part (i) Three questions on Section 3 of the syllabus (development of social behaviour) Part (ii) Three questions based on chosen option	$2\frac{1}{4}$ hrs	30%
PRACTICAL		20%
		100%

KNOWLEDGE AND ABILITIES TO BE TESTED

Check these terms in the 'glossary' below

All three syllabuses award marks proportionally for different abilities. The NEAB weights Knowledge and Understanding (50%) and Analysis, Evaluation and Expression (50%). The AEB weights Knowledge and Understanding (Skill A) and Analysis and Evaluation (Skill B) the same on a straightforward 25 mark essay question. You can earn up to 16 out of 25 for either skill alone or the full 25 for both skills. If that sounds a bit illogical, have a look at the AEB mark guidelines to see how this is possible. On the 'split' questions (e.g. (a) 10 (b) 15), it is possible to earn up to 16 for Skill A alone, but less for Skill B alone.

An example:

(a) Outline the main features of two theories of learning. (10 marks)
(b) Describe and evaluate the applications of these theories in either clinical or educational psychology. (15 marks)

In this question, part (a) is entirely Skill A (note the instruction 'outline', which is a Skill A term) , and part (b) is partly Skill A (Describe) and partly Skill B (Evaluate).

Using this rule and the glossary of terms that follow, try to identify the Skill A requirements and the Skill B requirements of past questions. Note that although most past questions do tend to conform more or less to this glossary, it is not a formal work ing document until the AEB 1994 examination.

GLOSSARY OF TERMS USED IN AEB EXAMINATIONS

Make sure you know what you are being asked to do

Skill A terms

CONSIDER: Requires the candidate to demonstrate knowledge and understanding of the stipulated topic area.

DEFINE: Requires the candidate to explain what is meant by a particular term such as one used to identify a particular concept.

DESCRIBE: Requires the candidate to present evidence of his/her knowledge of the stipulated topic area.

EXAMINE: Requires the candidate to present a detailed, descriptive consideration of the stipulated topic area.

EXPLAIN: Requires the candidate to convey his/her understanding of stipulated topic areas and to make such an explanation coherent and intelligible.

OUTLINE/STATE: Requires the candidate to offer a summary description of the stipulated topic area in brief form.

Skill B terms

ANALYSE/CRITICALLY ANALYSE: Requires the candidate to demonstrate under-standing through consideration of the components or elements of the stipulated topic area.

ASSESS/CRITICALLY ASSESS: Requires the candidate to make an informed judgement about how good or effective something is, based on an awareness of the strengths and limitations of the information and argument presented. The candidate is required to present a considered appraisal of the stipulated topic area.

CRITICISE: Requires the candidate to critically appraise/evaluate the strengths/ weaknesses of the stipulated topic areas.

EVALUATE/CRITICALLY EVALUATE*: Requires the candidate to make an informed judgement regarding the value of the stipulated topic area, based on systematic analysis and examination.

JUSTIFY: Requires the candidate to consider the grounds for a decision, for example, by offering a supportive consideration of the logic behind a particular interpretation.

Skill A + B terms

COMPARE/CONTRAST*: Requires the candidate to consider similarities and/or differences between the stipulated topic areas (e.g. psychological theories or concepts). This may involve critical consideration of points of similarity and differentiation.

CRITICALLY CONSIDER: As 'consider' (above), but in addition the candidate is also required to show an awareness of the strengths and limitations of the material presented.

DISTINGUISH BETWEEN: Requires the candidate to demonstrate his/her understanding of the differences between two stipulated topic areas (e.g. theories). Such a differentiation may be achieved at the levels of both descriptive and critical contrasting.

DISCUSS: Requires the candidate both to describe and evaluate by reference to different if not contrasting points of view. This may be done sequentially or concurrently. Questions may instruct the candidate to discuss with reference to particular criteria, for example, by the use of the phrase '... in terms of...'.

*These two terms are used interchangeably, with examiners being more likely to use the latter one when, given the nature of the question topic, they believe that it is useful to remind candidates of the need to be critical and evaluative.

Other terms

APPLICATIONS: Actual or possible ways of using psychological knowledge in an applied/practical setting.

CONCEPTS: An idea or group of ideas. These are often the basic units of a model or theory.

EVIDENCE: Material (empirical or theoretical) which may be used in support or contradiction of an argument or theory.

FINDINGS: The outcome or product of research.

INSIGHTS: Perceptions which facilitate an understanding or conceptual reappraisal.

METHODS: Different ways in which empirical research is and may be carried out.

MODEL: Often used synonymously with 'theory' (see below) but, strictly, less complex/elaborate and often comprising a single idea or image meant as a metaphor. Explanation is often by analogy.

RESEARCH: The process of gaining knowledge and understanding via either theory construction examination, or empirical data collection.

STUDIES: Empirical investigations providing evidence which, through reference to investigator's name and/or details of investigation/outcome, should be recognisable to the examiner.

THEORY: A (usually) complex set of interrelated ideas/assumptions/principles intended to explain or account for certain observed phenomena.

THE MARKING GUIDELINES

AEB

The AEB use a set of general marking guidelines in the 'A' and 'AS' examinations. An extremely abbreviated version for a 25 mark essay question is given below. Note that for each mark band, marks in that band can be earned *either* by giving Skill A alone, *or* giving Skill B alone, or giving a combination of Skills A and B at the level of the previous band. It makes clear sense then, to make sure that all your answers address *both* skills. Putting it another way, with a coursework mark of 80% (16 for each piece of coursework) and a mark of 16 (i.e. *limited* A + B) for all eight questions over the two papers, that would have been enough to get a grade A in the 1993 examination.

This gives you an idea of the break-down of marks

MARK BAND	BAND DESCRIPTION
0–3	Little psychological content
4–7	Basic A or B or Very basic A + B
8–12	Limited A or B or Basic A + B
13–16	Good A or B or Limited A + B
17–20	Slightly Limited A + B
21–25	Good A + B

Note that in order to gain marks above 16 out of 25, the answer does not need to show evidence of higher quality material, merely a better balance of skills A and B.

EFFECTIVE EXAMINATION PERFORMANCE

One of the things that tends to let even the brightest students down in the examination is that they are not effective in examination situations. This problem is often caused by poor revision strategies which inevitably makes it harder to perform effectively in an examination.

REVISION

1. **Revise carefully**. Don't simply try to learn one essay per topic and then try to reproduce that in an examination. Use the syllabus to check the sort of things that examiners might ask you to do. Remember that Chief Examiners can only ask you questions that are on the syllabus. In the AEB examination, the guidance notes on the right hand side of the syllabus give you a good idea about the particular ways that the topic might be assessed. Don't just rely on your teachers to tell you what to do. Be active, read the syllabus, get hold of past papers (the more recent the better), and practice working out the skill requirements in the question.

Look at syllabuses and past papers

2. **Revise actively**. Sometimes it is a helpful exercise to plan your material on 'mind maps' which link together central ideas, and the necessary evidence and evaluation within topics. These are an active form of revision, and have the added advantage of being visual images that are normally quite easy to remember in examinations. Another effective way of preparing material for an examination answer is to work on an average of 7 or 8 paragraphs and to decide what will go into each of those paragraphs. This way you can control the balance of your answer, ensuring that you are addressing both skill clusters, and that you are answering all parts of the question. Having decided on the division, try not to go outside of those constraints too much, because, as you have seen, you can earn more marks for balanced answers than you can for excellent treatment of just one skill or one part of the question.

'Mind maps' can help

Think of the 7 or 8 key points and use a paragraph for each

For example, a question which asks you to discuss theories of moral development might plan something like this:

1. Psychoanalytic
2. Evaluation
3. Social Learning
4. Evaluation
5. Cognitive-Developmental
6. Evaluation
7. Comparing and Contrasting these theories

Try this approach yourself on the questions presented at the end of each chapter *before* the sample answers.

3. **Be organised**. Make sure that you organise your time so that you are not panicking because you've left revision too late. One of the awful things about revision under anxiety states is that the effectiveness of the revision is minimal.

Plan your revision time

Make a timetable for revising *all* your 'A' and 'AS' Level subjects, perhaps early in the calendar year in which you sit the exam. For Psychology itself, break your revision down into topic areas and revise these systematically, going over the ideas, studies, questions relating to each topic area. If you *know* what you are going to do in a revision period you will not waste valuable time each day *thinking* about what you should do.

If you don't have an up-to-date textbook (other than this one) you should try and get hold of one. There are a number of excellent texts available e.g:

Psychology: The Science of Mind and Behaviour, (2nd edition) by Richard Gross (Hodder & Stoughton 1992)

Foundations of Psychology by Nicky Hayes (Routledge 1994)

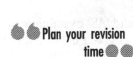
Use your books actively

Whatever book you use, use it *actively*. Highlight important points and make notes from it. You can obtain a copy of the current reading list for your syllabus by writing to the examination board concerned.

THE EXAMINATION

Don't be put off by others

1. **Relax.** If you stress yourself up before the examination by trying to find out what others have learned, it will only make you anxious about your own revision. Take time to unwind in the examination room, and also between questions.

Do what is required

2. **Read the questions and the rubric.** In other words be clear about what is required (number of questions you have to answer, how many from each section etc.) and also what is being asked in each question. Sometimes you can miss topics you have prepared simply because you don't recognise the topic in the wording of the question.

Think before you start

3. **Think carefully about each question.** Although you may have prepared a particular topic, can you address the *specific* requirements of the question as set? Sometimes it is better to go for another question simply because you can show *all* the skills required by that question, rather than just some in the previous one.

Answer the question set

4. **Don't regurgitate prepared answers if they don't fit the question as set.** Many candidates lose marks every year simply because they insist on answering some other question than the one actually in front of them. Examiners can only credit material that is directly relevant to the examination question, and cannot give you marks simply because you are showing scholarship in some other completely different area.

Attempt all the questions

5. **Plan your time.** Don't spend too long on any one question. You will inevitably earn more marks by writing four reasonable answers than three good answers. You may be surprised at how easy it is to get the first 7 marks on an essay compared to the last 7 marks.

Have a clear structure to your answer

6. **Plan your answer.** As mentioned in the revision section earlier, it is a good thing to plan what you are going to write because it lets you organise material in advance, and gives you a visual image so you can check that all points are being covered, and all skills are being addressed. There is no need to cross out this plan, because examiners may use it to find some extra credit for material that you have not managed to fit into the essay. Examiners practice *positive marking*, which means that they do not deduct marks for what might be wrong (it is simply ignored) but rather they add marks for what is right.

Use the ideas and evidence of your subject, Psychology

7. **Try to be psychological.** Although your own personal opinion is a much valued commodity, it is less valued in a psychological essay. The examiner is looking for evidence of *psychological* knowledge and understanding, and the ability to offer critical discussion of the material presented.

Try to avoid anecdotes and long rambling descriptions of studies. Try to be concise and logical, and make sure that you are constructing a psychological argument, not a personal one.

Evaluate the evidence

8. **Try to be critical.** All of the major examining boards award a large percentage of the marks available for *critical evaluation* of material. Many textbooks (particularly some of the more general introductory texts) do not emphasise the critical stance that 'A' level examinations require of their candidates. All is not lost. As well as the critical evaluation of material you will find in this book, there are a number of other ways that you can 'think on your feet' when searching for appropriate evaluation of a theory or a piece of research. Some points you could consider are as follows:

Some hints in evaluating

- Did the study, or studies that a theory is based on take place in a laboratory or in the natural environment ? (Think: what are the advantages and disadvantages of these methods and how might that undermine the conclusions? Remember, a lot of social psychological studies are criticised for their lack of *ecological validity*)
- Who were the participants? Quite apart from references to Freud and his Viennese women, most American social psychology experiments use American undergraduates as participants.
- How were the participants collected? *Ora* (1965) tells us that volunteers are unrepresentative, and the BPS tell us that coercion of individuals to take part in a study is ethically wrong.

■ Might a study or theory be subject to social or historical factors? A lot of the work on conformity was carried out during a period of American history when conformity was highly desirable (the era of McCarthyism) and Kohlberg's theory of moral development became very popular at the time of the American war in Vietnam.

Don't be afraid to link together points from other areas of the syllabus, thus showing the skill of *eclecticism*. For example, if you were writing an essay on play, you could link it to gender role development, moral development, enrichment, maternal deprivation even to dominance hierarchies in play groups! So long as these points tie in explicitly with your argument, they will earn marks.

2

METHODOLOGY IN PSYCHOLOGY

GETTING STARTED

The **methods** used in any particular psychological enquiry will be determined by a number of factors; opportunity, aims, nature of the participants, need for control as opposed to ecological validity, and so on. There is no one *best* method, but rather an *appropriate* method given the aims and circumstances of the investigation.

A key issue in psychological enquiry is whether psychology can claim to be 'scientific'. This is not, perhaps, the central problem that it used to be. Rather, we might consider whether the methods traditionally associated with scientific enquiry would be appropriate in the study of human behaviour. This chapter explores the nature and use of the scientific method in psychology, and the investigative methods that make up this scientific approach in the study of human behaviour. Allied to this are the problems associated with experimental study of behaviour and the advantages and disadvantages that might be experienced in the move away from experimental and/or laboratory study of behaviour. Material in this chapter will also be relevant in the evaluation of theories and studies across the whole of psychology. It could be argued that any theory or piece of research is only as good as its underlying methods.

The major themes involved in questions on this topic arc:

- Description and evaluation of the scientific methodology applied to human behaviour.
- Description and evaluation of experimental methods in psychology.
- Description and evaluation of non-experimental methods and a critical comparison with the experimental methods.
- Critical discussion of laboratory and non- laboratory investigative methods in psychology.

THE SCIENTIFIC METHOD

EVALUATION OF THE SCIENTIFIC METHOD

THE EXPERIMENTAL METHOD

NON-EXPERIMENTAL METHODS

LABORATORY VS NON-LABORATORY METHODS

ESSENTIAL PRINCIPLES

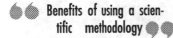

THE SCIENTIFIC METHOD

The **scientific method** refers to an attitude that scientific psychologists have towards *the way* that data is collected and also *the manner* in which theories are constructed, tested, and constantly refined. There is no one definitive scientific method; what makes a method more or less *scientific* is the degree to which it satisfies the criteria that follow.

The **laboratory experiment** is normally seen as the most scientific of the psychological methods simply because it is the clearest example of a method that does fulfill these criteria. You should refer to the description of the laboratory experiment on the next page. Note that other methods (e.g. field experiments, naturalistic observation) can also be considered scientific. Their status as scientific mehtods is determined by the degree to which their data are collected in an objective manner and how that data is used to create and test scientific theories in the manner outlined below.

The criteria or standards used to denote a **scientific methodology** involve the following aspects:

●● Criteria expected in a scientific method ●●

1. **Objective data collection**. This may be achieved by;
   - ■ control (of extraneous variables),.
   - ■ operational definitions (which aids precision of terms used in research),
   - ■ replicability of research (which increases confidence in research findings)

2. **The use of theory**. Objective data collection (induction) gives rise to the development of a theory which can then not only *explain* those findings, but also generate new hypotheses which can be tested empirically and therefore further refine the theory. Thus, scientific theories are;
   - ■ able to explain observable phenomena,
   - ■ testable (and therefore refutable),
   - ■ able to generate new hypotheses.

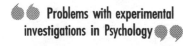

EVALUATION OF THE SCIENTIFIC METHOD

Advantages

●● Benefits of using a scientific methodology ●●

1. The scientific method is a preferred method compared to other routes to knowledge such as the 'method of authority' and the *a priori* method in that knowledge is established and built upon through the collection of data by systematic and empirical methods rather than by passive acceptance of facts.
2. Because scientific procedures allow for empirical and public data, old theories which no longer fit the facts can be refined or abandoned. This means that scientific knowledge is self-corrective.
3. Because scientific investigations are based on a belief in determinism, then the causes of behaviour can be established through examination of data which is both empirical and replicable.

Criticisms

The definitive example of a 'scientific' method in psychology is the **laboratory experiment**. This method is the most appropriate way to realise the goals of science, but is subject to a number of biases (known collectively as 'The Social Psychology of the Experiment') which limit the validity of its findings.

●● Problems with experimental investigations in Psychology ●●

1. **The influence of the situation**. The nature of the experimental situation may alter participants' behaviour in such a way that it cannot be taken as an accurate indication of how they might behave normally. *Orne* (1962) referred to the fact that participants often react to cues in the situation, and adjust their behaviour accordingly. He called these cues 'demand characteristics.'
2. **The influence of the participant**. Participants in psychological research can influence the results of that research in two main ways.

●● Participants might not be representative and might role-play ●●

(a) *Non-representative sample*. As a sample used in research, they may be considered *non-representative*. *Tedeschi* (1985) discovered that the majority of social psychological research used college students as participants. As science is concerned with the establishment of general laws, the use of a restricted sample range will preclude such generalisation.

(b) *Role-playing*. Participants may also influence the outcome of the investigation by adopting any one of a number of *different roles* (negativistic, cooperative, etc.) which limits the likelihood of their behaviour being a natural response to the issues being investigated.

3. **The influence of the experimenter**. Experimenters may influence the research by virtue of their biosocial features (age, race, etc.), their psychosocial features (friendliness, etc.) or by their expectation of results such that a hypothesis becomes self-fulfilling.

Philosophical criticisms of the scientific method

Some philosophical criticisms of the scientific method

1. Because of the nature and subject matter of psychological enquiry, it may not be possible to retain complete objectivity in the observation and recording of data.
2. *Thomas Kuhn* (1962) suggests that psychology lacks the unifying paradigm ('super theory') that characterises the physical sciences. He claims that until psychology attains such a paradigm, it can best be described as 'pre-scientific', and, as such, the use of the scientific method is inappropriate.
3. Humanistic psychologists reject the use of scientific methods in psychology, as they reject the deterministic view of human behaviour. If behaviour is not subject to the laws and regularities implied in scientific investigations, then predictions become impossible using the statistical models which result from such research. Human beings, they argue, are unique, and research techniques should reflect this.

THE EXPERIMENTAL METHOD

Independent and dependent variables

An **experiment** involves the manipulation of some aspect of a situation, and observing the effects this has on a particular behaviour. In technical terms, the former is the **independent variable** (IV), and the latter the **dependent variable** (DV). Note the use of the word *manipulation*, an investigation which does not involve manipulation of the independent variable is not an experiment. Experiments can be broadly divided into three main types:

THE LABORATORY EXPERIMENT

The independent variables are the ones which are varied, one at a time, other things being kept equal

A control group can help to establish the effect of the IV

In a **laboratory method**, the *independent variables* are systematically varied (one at a time, where possible) whilst other *extraneous variables* are kept constant. The main emphasis in a laboratory experiment is that of *control*. The experimenter tries to eliminate or control any other variables that might interfere with the *purity* of the experimental relationship between the IV and the DV. Subject variables can be controlled through the use of experimental designs; task and environmental variables can be controlled through the use of *standardised* procedures and conditions. To enable the experimenter to make an effective and accurate assessment of the effect of the IV, the experiment involves either a *control* group for comparison, or different levels of the IV under study.

Advantages of the laboratory experiment

Some benefits from laboratory experiments

■ Because of better opportunities for the control of extraneous variation in the laboratory, the experimenter is better able to draw conclusions about the causal influence of the IV.
■ The laboratory enables the experimenter to measure behaviour with a greater precision than would be possible in the natural environment.
■ Because of the high degree of operational precision possible in a laboratory, it makes the research much easier to *replicate* (see earlier section on the scientific method).

Disadvantages of the laboratory experiment

Some problems with laboratory experiments

■ Because behaviour is being studied in a contrived situation, there is a risk that participants' behaviour may be artificial, and not valid to real life situations.
■ Participants do not passively respond to psychological stimuli during the experiment, but react to the situation in a number of active ways by adopting roles (cooperative, negativistic, etc.) or by trying to adjust their behaviour to what they feel is appropriate within the experimental paradigm.

- Because the laboratory experiment makes extensive use of volunteers, and research has established that volunteers react differently to non-volunteers (*Ora*, 1965), it becomes possible that atypical participants are being used. Experiments that use animals experience their own problems of interpretation and relevance (see Chapter 3).
- The laboratory experiment is potentially fraught with ethical problems. These too are covered in Chapter 3.

THE FIELD EXPERIMENT

A **field experiment** is where the study is carried out in the natural environment rather than in the controlled conditions of the laboratory. Some degree of control is possible, but obviously not to the degree possible in the laboratory. The experimenter still manipulates the IV and observes its effect in the more natural setting.

There is less control in field experiments

Advantages of the field experiment

- Compared with non-manipulative observation, the field experiment has the advantage of *economy*, in that rather than waiting for the conditions of interest to occur naturally, the experimenter can create them and observe the results.
- As the investigation is taking place within a more natural setting, results are more likely to be *relevant* to real life behaviour. Field studies are thus described as having a degree of *ecological validity*.

Field experiments do bring some benefits

Disadvantages of the field experiment

- What the field experiment gains in ecological validity, it loses in operational control. It is, for example, less easy to control the nature of the people taking part, and it is also harder to obtain the same degree of precision in behavioural measurements. Thus, it is harder to make accurate statements of cause and effect, and research carried out in this way becomes harder to replicate (due to difficulties involved in replicating exactly the conditions under which the study was carried out).
- If participants are unaware that they are part of the investigation, this creates ethical problems such as deception, invasion of privacy and so on.

Field experiments also bring some problems

THE NATURAL EXPERIMENT

A **natural experiment** refers to an experimental situation where the independent variable is not manipulated directly by the experimenter, but is manipulated *fortuitously* by some outside agency. Natural experiments are used to explore research questions of high natural interest, but where practical realities or ethical concerns prevent the possibility of manipulation by the research psychologist.

Natural experiments are largely outside the control of the scientist

Advantages of the natural experiment

- Because of the high degree of ecological validity in natural experiments, they enable psychologists to explore issues of high natural interest which may have important practical implications.
- There are fewer ethical problems (due to lack of experimenter manipulation) in these methods *but* these methods are not without their own ethical problems (see Chapter 3).

Disadvantages of the natural experiment

- Because the experimenter has little or no control over the variables under study, questions of cause and effect become increasingly speculative.
- Because participants' behaviour may be influenced by so many variables over which the experimenter has no control or maybe has no knowledge of, the conditions of natural experiments are extremely difficult to replicate.

NON-EXPERIMENTAL METHODS

The problems inherent in the experimental method – distortion of behaviour, manipulation and dehumanisation etc., have meant that it is not necessarily the most appropriate method for the study of all aspects of human behaviour. A range of **non-**

experimental methods have been developed, which, whilst not possessing the rigour of the experimental method, are more ecologically valid, and potentially more relevant to the behaviours under study.

 **Extremes of control**

Observation in psychology takes place along a continuum of control. At one extreme, the rigour and systematic control of the laboratory experiment, and at the other the ecological relevance of naturalistic observation. Two examples of the non-experimental methods used by research psychologists will be discussed here.

NATURALISTIC OBSERVATION

There are two primary characteristics associated with **naturalistic observation**.

a) It is concerned with naturally occurring phenomena.
b) The investigator does not attempt to intrude or manipulate behaviour in any way.

The essence of naturalistic observation is that the observer does everything possible to remain unobtrusive. This is normally accomplished in a *non-participant* context although, in certain circumstances, the investigator might become a part of the situation which he/she is studying (*participant observation*). Although these methods are used for different types of investigation, the aim is still to prevent possible participant *reactivity* which might accompany more intrusive investigations (i.e. participants might *react* to the presence of the observer and change their behaviour from how they would normally behave).

Advantages of naturalistic observation

Benefits of observation

■ As participants are observed unobtrusively in their own environment, their behaviour is not distorted or artificial.
■ It can be used where it would be considered unethical to carry out manipulative investigations or where it is impractical to question participants directly.
■ In participant observation, the study tends to be of a length where trust and involvement yields far richer data than would be available from other methods.
■ Naturalistic observation cannot, by itself, lead to the establishment of cause and effect relationships, but can generate hypotheses for later testing in more controlled circumstances, and also as a *ecological testing ground* to validate results from contrived laboratory settings.

Disadvantages of naturalistic observation

Problems with observation

■ Naturalistic observation methods suffer from their own ethical problems, deception (particularly in participant observation), and invasion of privacy.
■ In a truly naturalistic setting, the observer has no control over the multitude of variables that may be influencing the behaviour, therefore causal statements are speculative.
■ Observers themselves are a source of bias. The more unstructured, the more open to subjective bias is the material obtained from it.

CASE STUDIES

Most case studies involve individuals

The **case study** can be seen as a variant of the longitudinal method where developmental data is collected on an individual over an extended time period. Ordinarily, the unit of study is an individual rather than a group of participants, and the purpose of the study is to shed light on some problem of adjustment for which diagnosis and therapy might be required. This requires the accumulation of data from a wide diversity of sources. The focus of study in this kind of investigation is the unique growth pattern of a single individual rather than the developmental trends characterising children in general.

Advantages of case studies

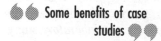 **Some benefits of case studies**

■ Case studies allow for a rich and detailed analysis of individuals that would not be possible using other methods.

■ They also allow psychologists to explore examples of unique or unusual behaviour which might bring new insights into the study of behaviour.
■ As case studies are based more on descriptive and qualitative data, they are less likely to miss aspects of behaviour that would be masked by quantitative measurements.

Disadvantages of case studies

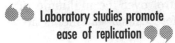 Some problems with case studies

■ The *idiographic* emphasis of the case study is clinically useful, but tends to make it less amenable to statistical analysis. As 'scientific' psychology is *nomothetic* in its emphasis, case studies are more useful in the generation of hypotheses or the illustration of a particular theoretical viewpoint.
■ As the case study focuses on the single case as a unit of analysis, it is impossible to tell whether the finding from a particular study is indicative of a general trend, or restricted to that individual.
■ When data is drawn from retrospective reports, possible distortion of memory makes data obtained less reliable. The advantages or disadvantages of a particular methodology must always be viewed in the context of the research aims and objectives. Sometimes, the need for rigorous control and the establishment of cause-effect relationships outweighs the more ecologically alluring advantages of naturalistic observation and case studies. The researcher decides on the relative importance of each consequence and effect, and determines the most appropriate methodology accordingly.

LABORATORY VS NON LABORATORY RESEARCH

It is a common error to confuse this area with the problem of experimental versus non-experimental research. Whilst it is true that most laboratory studies *are* experimental, this is not always the case. In *describing* non-laboratory research, you should bear this in mind.

Coolican (1990) provides a useful summary of the laboratory as a research setting. He sees the **advantages** of the laboratory setting as threefold.

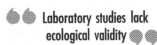 Laboratories enable the researcher to exercise control

1. It enables the researcher to observe behaviour in a way which is both controlled (in terms of extraneous variables) and accurate (in terms of recording and measuring of behaviour).
2. The results of many controlled laboratory investigations have been valuable in their social applications. Whilst is is arguable whether Milgram's study of obedience (*Milgram*, 1963) was ethical and/or valid (see chapters on Ethics and Social Influence), it did have an enormous impact on social psychology, and produced results that took even the researchers by surprise.

Laboratory studies promote ease of replication

3. Laboratory studies lend themselves to *replication* (because of the points outlined in 1. above). This is a fundamental requirement of the scientific method, and is more easily achieved in the laboratory than outside of it.

Coolican makes reference to two major **disadvantages** of the laboratory as a research setting.

Laboratory studies lack ecological validity

1. The laboratory is seen as providing only a narrow focus for the study of behaviour. Behaviour as it occurs in the laboratory may not be seen as ecologically valid. In Chapter 6, this problem is discussed with reference to the phenomenon of selective attention, which some critics believe is simply an artefact of the contrived and unusual simulation in which it is studies.

Subjects may react to the situation

2. Laboratory settings may create a range of *subject effects* such that their behaviour becomes more influenced by their perceptions of the situation than their reactions to the variables under study (you should refer to criticisms of the laboratory experiment earlier in this chapter). Non-laboratory methods may include field and natural experiments as well as the more usually quoted naturalistic observation and case studies.

You might like to try classifying methods into various categories such as experimental/non-experimental and laboratory/non-laboratory. Note that some experimental studies take place outside of the laboratory, therefore might have the advantages of an *experimental* study but the disadvantages of a *non-laboratory* study.

EXAMINATION QUESTIONS

1. Discuss the use of the scientific method in psychology.   *(25)*

2. There are several alternatives to the experimental method in pursuing psychological investigations. Describe and discuss two such alternatives.   *(25)*
   (AEB 1991)

3. Describe what is involved in the experimental method as it is used in psychology and discuss its limitations.   *(25)*
   (AEB 1989)

4. (a) Compare the experimental method with any one other method used by psychologists.   *(10)*
   (b) Critically contrast the relative strengths and weaknesses of these two methods.   *(15)*
   (AEB 1992)

5. Among the core studies there are several that use the case study method or some method that is similar to a case study. Included in this group are Hodges and Tizard, Sperry, Thigpen and Cleckley, and Freud. Using these studies to illustrate your essay, evaluate the use of the case study method in psychology.   *(30)*
   (Oxford and Cambridge sample question)

ANSWERS TO EXAMINATION QUESTIONS

OUTLINE ANSWERS TO QUESTIONS 3 AND 4

Question 3

This question is quite clearly asking you to do two main things.

Firstly, it is asking you to *describe* the nature and use of the experimental method in psychology, and secondly, it is asking you to *discuss* its limitations.

An outline of the experimental method should mention the following:

1. The experimental method involves the *manipulation* of some aspect of a situation and the *observation* of the resulting change in behaviour.
2. Experimental methods require an IV and a DV and at least two ways or levels of manipulating the situation in order to make a comparison.
3. Experimental situations are *controlled* (through the use of experimental designs and standardised procedures) so causal inferences can be made.
4. Experiments are not restricted to the lab, they may be field or natural as well.
5. Examples of experiments, and what the study gained by the use of this method.

In discussing the limitations of the experimental method, a number of points could be made:

1. Distortion of behaviour (particularly in the lab).
2. Subject and experimenter expectancy effects.
3. Sampling problems (for example the reliance on the use of volunteers or even animals, and the resultant problems of generalisation of findings).
4. Ethical problems, ranging from general claims as to the *dehumanising* effects of experimentation, to the BPS guidelines for research.

The quality of your answer will be determined by the degree to which you can offer real discussion of these points. For example, is the 'contrived' setting of the lab actually a good thing in some cases, and are experiments any *more* unethical than their non-experimental alternatives?

Question 4

When this question was answered in the 1992 AEB 'A' level exam, many, if not most candidates found it very difficult to disentangle what was appropriate for the first part of the question and what was appropriate for the second.

(a) The simplest way to do this is to describe the main characteristics of each method (e.g. its emphasis on the individual or the group, the degree of manipulation, the context of the study and so on). It is then a reasonably simple exercise to look for similarities (or indeed differences) in terms of these characteristics.

(b) Having resisted the temptation to unload all that juicy evaluation in part (a), you can now do a similar exercise, but now you describe the strengths *and* weaknesses of these two methods. You can then *contrast* these, e.g. a strength of the lab experiment is the high degree of control. This tends to be absent in naturalistic observation.

A couple of points are worth making here. Firstly, only 10 marks are available in part (a) so the majority of the marks can be earned for part (b). Secondly, this is quite a difficult question to do full justice to. Under the terms of the AEB marking scheme, the compare and contrast injunctions are the *Skill B* terms, everything else is *Skill A*. It is therefore very important to address *all* the requirements of the question in order to gain high marks.

TUTOR'S ANSWER

Question 1

The scientific method refers both to the attitude that scientists share about the nature of knowledge and also the techniques for attaining it. It differs from other methods in its reliance on empirical, public and self corrective knowledge. The *a priori* method, by definition, does not involve testing of assumptions about behaviour, and the *method of authority* does not involve first hand empirical evidence. This need for empirical data obtained by careful and systematic observation puts the scientific method at an advantage over the other methods of acquiring knowledge. Such nonscientific methods are often based on casual observations and cannot, therefore, be considered as valid as information obtained by direct observation under controlled conditions.

The gathering of data through empirical and public methods cannot be the end result of science. The establishment of a theory provides an explanatory framework which enables the scientific psychologist to explain and predict behaviour. Theories lead to testable predictions, which, through further data collection can be used to support or refine existing theories. In this way, scientific theories are 'self correcting' in a way that knowledge gained from other sources tends not to be. The *method of tenacity,* for example, involves clinging to personal beliefs and prejudices *despite* evidence to the contrary. Scientific enquiries, on the other hand, enable people to form opinions and beliefs on the basis of public and replicable information. Beliefs that do not fit the facts can then be abandoned in favour of new ones. Scientific knowledge, therefore, is transient, it changes as a result of constant testing and development of theories and models of behaviour.

An additional advantage of scientific methods over nonscientific methods is the belief in determinism and order. Scientific psychologists share a belief that behaviour is determined and that, as such, these determinants of behaviour can be established through scientific investigation. Scientific psychology shares with the physical sciences the idea that if events are determined by a known cause, and if such events can be reliably predicted (as a result of established theories), then the determinants of behaviour may be expressed in terms of laws which are then open to empirical, publicly observable checking.

The way that psychology achieves its scientific goals are twofold. Firstly, investigators aim for objectivity in their research. This may be achieved in a number of ways. The definitive scientific method, the laboratory experiment, seeks to establish control over extraneous variables such that their influence over the outcome might be minimised. This is particularly important so the causal relationships can be determined without the results being affected by influences outside of the experimental design. Objectivity may also be addressed through an emphasis on replication of research. If results can be replicated, then it leads to a greater confidence in the findings and enhances the likelihood of psychologists achieving the scientific goals of prediction and control.

The second way that scientific psychology achieves its goals (of explanation, prediction and control) is by the use of scientific theories. Acting as explanatory frameworks, they enable the psychologist to generate new hypotheses which can be tested empirically, thus providing the opportunity to constantly refine and develop theoretical understanding through empirical means.

Such scientific processes are not always seen as the most appropriate route to knowledge about human behaviour. In experiments, for example, participants are seen as 'passively responding to psychological stimuli. . . they are docile input-output machines' (*Jung*, 1982). It is clear that participants in a research are anything but docile input-output machines. They adopt different roles (cooperative, negativistic, faithful), they make use of available cues in the experimental situation to react 'appropriately' (demand characteristics), and they interact with and are affected by, the biosocial and psychosocial characteristics of the experimenter.

Humanistic psychologists may also place less importance on the scientific process as a route to knowledge as they tend to reject the deterministic view of human behaviour. If our behaviour is not *determined* by forces outside of our personal control, then the pursuit of causal prediction is pointless. This view is in sharp contrast to the major strength of scientific psychology, i.e. it enables a psychologist to establish *laws* of behaviour that would be universal (the nomothetic approach). To a humanistic psychologist, such an aim would be inappropriate given their interest in the individual as a *unique* being (the idiographic approach) rather than a *universal* being.

STUDENT'S ANSWER WITH EXAMINERS COMMENTS

Question 2

Within the realm of observation in psychology exists both experimental and non-experimental methods. The non-experimental methods hold many alternatives that are functionally and structurally different. This essay aims to discuss naturalistic observation and the case study as alternatives.

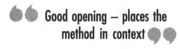 Good opening – places the method in context

Naturalistic observation involves watching and observing activity of both non-human and human species in their natural habitat. It is a fairly unobtrusive method with no intervention on the part of the observer. Behaviour is directly observed , however its advantages are few and its disadvantages many. This method along with the case study has serious flaws when applied to the application of psychology. Superficially it would appear that information that is gained by directly observing and recording behaviour is objective after all. What is seen is what is recorded. However, because the observer has no direct control, the power of interpretation is great. It is virtually impossible to observe all information. Many important or seemingly irrelevant information can be lost. Therefore this method cannot be entirely objective, it is purely subjective in application. The scientific nature of psychology demands a high level of objectivity and shall be further discussed later. Similarly, no generalisations can really be made from naturalistic observation as it does not allow for cause and effect factors.

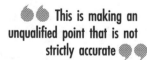 This is making an unqualified point that is not strictly accurate

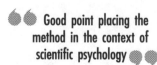 Good point placing the method in the context of scientific psychology

A further criticism exists in this method as having a lack of repeatability; situations observed in one setting do not have a high chance of happening again so that any information that is found is only central to that one situation and cannot be applied more generally.

Case studies on the other hand do provide more scope of investigation. The investigation is lengthy, and is favoured in work into effects of early childhood experience (e.g. Bowlby, Tizard). Case studies are extremely simple to carry out (their simplicity being a major advantage). Similarly, a case study cannot prove much or provide sufficient generalisation. It can disprove a theory easier than any other method, for example the case of H.M. in the investigation into long-term memory. But again, its implication to scientific psychology is limited. It does not allow for generalisations which are the aim of psychology i.e. to predict behaviour by generalised rules and guidelines.

66 Again an unqualified and not strictly accurate conclusion 99

Information is biased in many cases and is not objective for many of the same reasons found in the naturalistic method. Case studies make it impossible for statistical analysis to be carried out.

66 Some repetition here 99

Case studies also embody the distinction between idiographic and nomothetic approaches. A case study is wholly idiographic, that is it relies on the observation of behaviour of an individual, while nomothetic is concerned with group behaviour.

66 Perhaps they are more relevant as clinical tools 99

Humanistic psychologists will argue that idiographic methods are the only method to observe humans are unique and individual. It is therefore impossible to make generalisations about humans. But the scientific method involved in nomothetic approaches is central to the empirical nature of modern psychology. Therefore to the modern psychologists, idiographic methods are irrelevant to psychology as a whole.

At this point we can question the aim of psychology in terms of idiographic and nomothetic approaches. If the aim of psychology is to predict and control behaviour then the assumption applied is that humans do not possess freedom or freewill.

66 Yes, intelligent point to make 99

Heather (1976) and other humanistic psychologists argue that we are in possession of free will because we are all unique and individual and inherently different. If this implication is further expressed, psychology has no place in experimental science. Indeed *Heather* goes on to say that 'psychology has to squeeze human behaviour into laboratory conditions' thus making it an irrelevant context.

66 A bit of a wooly conclusion which adds little to the discussion 99

The implication still remains that non-experimental methods like naturalistic observations and case studies hold no relevant value to the present scientific psychology. However the non-experimental methods have proved productive within their own domain and as idiographic methods, methods which were in the original format of psychology and which have enabled psychology to validate its position as a scientific discipline.

66 This is a very good essay which provides a number of intelligent points relevant to the question. There is ample critical discussion and the answer is characteristic of a grade A candidate 99

REVIEW SHEET

1. What are the two main characteristics of the scientific method?

    _____

    _____

2. Give *three* advantages and three disadvantages of the scientific method as it is used in psychology.

    _____

    _____

    _____

    _____

3. What essential ingredient makes an investigation an experiment?

    _____

    _____

4. Give *two* advantages and two disadvantages of each of the following:
    i) The lab experiment

    _____

    _____

    _____

    ii) The field experiment

    _____

    _____

    _____

    iii) The natural experiment

    _____

    _____

    _____

5. What is meant by *ecological validity* ?

    _____

    _____

6. Give the *two* main characteristics associated with naturalistic observation.

    _____

    _____

7. Give *two* advantages and *two* disadvantages of naturalistic observation.

_____

_____

_____

_____

8. What is a case study?

_____

_____

9. Give *two advantages and two* disadvantages of the case study.

_____

_____

_____

10. What does Coolican see as the *three* major advantages of laboratory studies in psychology?

_____

_____

_____

11. Give *two* disadvantages of studying behaviour in a laboratory

_____

_____

_____

12. Give examples of the different ways of studying behaviour by completing the following table:

EXPERIMENTAL METHODS	NON-EXPERIMENTAL METHODS
LABORATORY METHODS	NON-LABORATORY METHODS

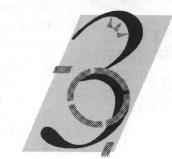

ETHICS IN PSYCHO-LOGICAL RESEARCH AND PRACTICE

GETTING STARTED

Because of the nature of what psychologists study and how they work, they inevitably carry a burden of responsibility which extends to the welfare of the participants in their research, and their clients in psychological practice. You are probably aware of the need for strict **ethical control** over investigations from your own coursework, indeed some boards now assess the ethical content of an investigation directly.

This ethical consideration is a fundamental requirement of all psychological research. In the post war years, the rise of **psychology as science** was accompanied at times by an insensitivity and at times total disregard for the participants used in the research. This is clearly no longer acceptable, psychology cannot take the role of a value–free science, and, as with most other areas of academic enquiry, is now accountable both within the discipline of psychology itself, and also to the public outside of the subject.

This chapter covers three main areas, and prepares you to answer questions relating to the following:

■ **The ethics of psychological research with humans.**
■ **The ethics of behaviour change.**
■ **The use of animals in psychological research.**

As these issues may well raise a lot of contentious points, some of which you may find morally repugnant, it is important to stay objective. Marks in examinations are awarded for the quality of informed psychological discussion, not for the intensity of a particular moral standpoint, no matter how personally important it is to you. This is particularly true in the issues relating to the use of animals in psychology, where students who can find no morally defensible reason for using animals in psychological research, cannot bring themselves to offer more than a condemnation of all animal research.

THE ETHICS OF PSYCHOLOGICAL RESEARCH WITH HUMANS

THE ETHICS OF BEHAVIOUR CHANGE

THE USE OF ANIMALS IN PSYCHOLOGICAL RESEARCH

ESSENTIAL PRINCIPLES

THE ETHICS OF PSYCHOLOGICAL RESEARCH WITH HUMANS

The following guidelines are examples of those issued by the British Psychological Society (BPS).

■ **Ethical implications**. A fundamental requirement of all research is the consideration of the ethical implications and consequences for the research participants.

■ **Informed consent**. Participants should, wherever possible, be given the opportunity to give their informed consent before taking part in the research.

■ **Deception**. Deceiving or misleading participants should be avoided wherever possible.

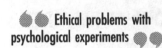 Some important ethical guidelines

■ **Debriefing**. If participants are aware of taking part in the research, they should be fully debriefed when the research is over.

■ **Right to withdraw**. Participants have the right to withdraw at any time in the study.

■ **Protection from harm**. Investigators should take every step to protect participants from physical and psychological harm during or arising from the investigation.

■ **Right to privacy**. In observational studies, participants have the right to privacy, covert observation only being permissible in circumstances where participants would expect to be observed by strangers.

Specific issues (experimental research)

The **experiment** is often criticised for its particular form of ethical problems. Experiments are often described as dehumanising simply because they are not seen as attending to the human needs of the people who participate as subjects. Some of the specific issues are as follows.

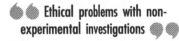 Ethical problems with psychological experiments

■ **Coercion**. Because volunteers may be atypical, (*Ora*, 1965), some degree of coercion may be necessary to obtain participants in an investigation. This is a particularly difficult issue where participants are not in a position to give their informed consent (e.g. children, the mentally retarded, prisoners etc.).

■ **Deception**. This may sometimes be necessary if the design requires it. Alternatives have been suggested, e.g. participants might be informed of the nature of the investigation and then asked to role play the role of naive participants. A sample of participants similar to those being studied might be interviewed prior to the investigation to probe their attitudes to the aims and practices (including deception) of the investigation. Debriefing becomes a vital part of any experimental procedure where deception has taken place.

■ **Costs/benefits analysis**. In line with the ethical requirement to protect participants from harm, it is established practice to consider both the costs of participation against the benefits which might be possible as a result of the study taking place.

Specific issues (non-experimental research)

It is a commonly held belief that ethical issues need only concern the *experimental* psychologist, and that non-experimental research is free from such concerns. There are a number of important ethical problems that beset **non-experimental** investigations.

Ethical problems with non-experimental investigations

■ **Informed consent**. A rigid insistence on informed consent in naturalistic observation is unrealistic. It would create participant reactivity (where participants react to the presence of the observer) and may well result in artificial behaviour. Anonymity and confidentiality of data does, however, tend to minimise the harmful effects of such invasion of privacy. *Westin* (1967) argues that when persons engage in public behaviour, they expect to be observed by strangers, and therefore no breach of privacy is evident.

■ **Deception**. This is particularly problematic in participant observation, where observers must be deceptive about their roles in order to play them successfully. Psychologists disagree about the need to deceive in such situations, although the consensus appears to be in favour of such practices provided such data is used solely for research purposes and anonymity of participants is assured. However, the 'jury-bugging' investigation in Chicago in 1955, despite legal clearance outraged the American public and cast doubt over the professional integrity of research psychologists.

Unethical studies: An example

The most commonly quoted study is that of *Milgram*, (1963). You should consider in what ways this study might be considered **unethical** today;

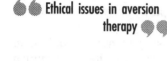
An important case of using unethical techniques

- **Coercion**. 'Prods' were used to pressurise participants into continuing (*right to withdraw*). Milgram, however, argued that as some participants *had* withdrawn, it meant that all *could* have withdrawn had they chosen.
- **Deception**. Participants were told that the experiment was investigating something else, therefore could not give their *informed* consent. Milgram defended this action, stating that both in debriefing and in a follow up of participants, the majority of the participants had not objected to the deception, nor did they regret taking part in the investigation.

BEHAVIOURAL TREATMENTS

THE ETHICS OF BEHAVIOUR CHANGE

Two treatments which are often singled out for ethical criticism are **behaviour therapy** (based on classical conditioning) and **behaviour modification** (based on operant conditioning).

Aversion therapy (a form of behaviour therapy)

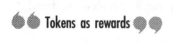
Ethical issues in aversion therapy

Although rarely used nowadays, this treatment involves the use of unpleasant stimuli to bring about behavioural change. Its use is often associated with attempts to change 'anti-social' or 'deviant' behaviour. This raises a number of associated ethical issues including consideration of who is the actual client, and why is the treatment taking place? The use of aversion therapy may also be evident in the treatment of children. *Lang and Melamed* (1969) treated a nine month old child who suffered from chronic post-ruminative vomiting. The treatment involved a series of electric shocks to the child's calf, and, as a result of the treatment, the vomiting stopped and the infant, whose life had been in danger, made a complete recovery. How might this example be assessed in terms of costs and benefits?

Token economies (a type of behaviour modification)

Tokens as rewards

This treatment, where plastic tokens are given for desirable behaviour, and which may later be 'swapped' for rewards such as sweets, cigarettes etc., has been successful in a number of institutional contexts including hospital wards, schools and prisons. Its use has been curtailed in the USA, where legal rulings have made some of the rewards a basic human right rather than something to be made contingent upon desirable behaviour. Advocates of the treatment, such as *Paul and Lentz* (1977) argue that such practices may be necessary if the patient is so retarded that other methods are ineffective, and claim that this treatment, as with others, should be viewed in the 'general context of rehabilitation'.

Dehumanisation

Behavioural treatments are often referred to as 'dehumanising'. Whilst this term is rather vague, it may be taken to have two rather different meanings.

a) **Treatment of humans as 'animals'**. By this definition, it would appear that treatment somehow lowers the quality of human life (to the status of animals), but as the fundamental aim of such research is to raise the quality of human life, this criticism would not appear valid.

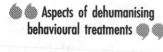
Aspects of dehumanising behavioural treatments

b) **Treatment of humans as 'machines'**. Although still a controversial line of thinking, the essence of the Behavioural view of abnormality is that neuroses have a 'mechanistic' origin, therefore advocates a mechanistic (i.e. unlearning) treatment for them.

Problems relating to coercion and informed consent

Some techniques which might save patients from continuing self injury are especially necessary when the patient cannot realistically be expected to give their informed consent.

ALTERNATIVES TO BEHAVIOURAL TREATMENT

Psychoanalysis

The notion of manipulation through treatment is not an issue confined to behavioural treatments alone. Manipulation, and indeed pain, is present in a number of other therapies. In **psychoanalysis** intense emotional pain may accompany the moment of insight during the analytic session. As with other therapies however, this 'pain' is placed in the context of rehabilitation, as the analyst helps the client construct a healthier attitude to him/herself and to those around them.

> ❝ Not all treatments are behavioural ❞

Psychochemicals

Although generally regarded as a type of 'somatic' treatment, the use of drugs may also have behavioural consequences for the clients that receive them. These **psychochemicals** are more readily accepted by the general public because of the high level of trust in the medical profession that dispenses them, and therefore are potentially a greater source of ethical abuse. Such reductionist levels of intervention (e.g. the use of drugs for the treatment of hyperkinesis) may distract attention away from the real issues of social reform.

Why are animals used?

> **THE USE OF ANIMALS IN PSYCHOLOGICAL RESEARCH**

The first reason is that of *behavioural continuity* which refers to Darwin's assertion that differences between species are differences in quantity rather differences in quality, therefore by studying animals, it is possible to see human behaviour in a simpler form.

A second reason is that of *experimental control*, whereby many of the rigorous procedures necessary in some experimental manipulations, particularly those involving deprivation, would not be possible with human subjects.

> ❝ Reasons for using animals in psychological research ❞

A third reason, *detachment*, refers to the problem of subjectivity when human psychologists study themselves, a problem not faced when studying non-human animals.

A fourth reason for using animals is for the ease of *comparing generations*, so that conclusions might be drawn on the effects of early experience or heredity on behaviour.

A final reason is to establish *cause and effect* relationships where evidence from human studies might only be circumstantial. Harlow's research with primates illustrated a number of consequences which could only be suggested by Bowlby's work with children.

Benefits of animal research to humans

Harlow (1962) showed that infant monkeys who had been deprived of adequate mothering grew up to be mothers who neglected and abused their own offspring. This finding has helped to encourage and guide studies of the origins of human child abuse.

Schanberg (1984) found that, in newborn rats, short periods of separation from the mother could cause deficiencies in growth hormone. Such hormones are normally released when the mother licks the pups, and these conditions can be simulated by stroking with a paintbrush, with a resulting prevention of growth deficits. Schanberg used this knowledge to initiate a programme for premature human babies, where conditions in the incubator approximate those of maternal deprivation. The programme produced significant physical and behavioural improvements over a control group.

> ❝ Human benefits from animal research ❞

Benefits of animal research to animals

Insights into imprinting (*Lorenz*, 1937) have been used to overcome some of the problems encountered when hand rearing endangered species. In species which show sexual imprinting, there is a danger that they will imprint on the human being who feeds them, thus subverting a natural process, and providing them with problems of mate choice later in life. Work with Condors, using glove puppets to feed the Condor chicks has largely overcome this problem. The Wildfowl Trust, working with the NeNe (Hawaiian Geese) have also made use of such knowledge to initiate an imprinting opportunity for incubator reared goslings (*Black*, 1992).

> ❝ Animals may benefit too! ❞

Practical objections to animal research

Critics often raise practical objections to animal research, claiming that as the brain and behaviour of animals is not seen as comparable to that of humans any conclusions drawn from animal studies would be inappropriate. *Green* (1992) criticises this view by offering the observation that the brain physiology (function and structure.) is virtually the same in all mammals, therefore comparisons would indeed be appropriate. Green also points out that the major classes of behaviour (motivational, cognitive and affective) can all be found in the simplest rat. This is in contrast to Koestler's accusation of *ratomorphism* (*Koestler*, 1970) whereby he claims that studies of rats have no part in a science of *human* behaviour.

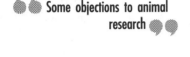 Some objections to animal research

Ethical objections to animal research

These can be broadly divided into two separate issues. The first is that *any* use of animals is wrong on moral grounds, the second is that psychological research using animals is only appropriate if it is of high quality, is properly carried out under guidelines set out in the 1986 *Animals (Scientific procedures) Act*, and makes significant contributions to science or medicine.

The 1986 Animals Act

 An important act regulating animal use

This act set down specific guidelines for the use of animals in scientific research. These include consideration of the needs and habits of animals so that animals may be chosen which will suffer the least distress during the research programme. The act also aims to control any procedures which might cause pain or distress to the animals used by only issuing licences to research programmes where the knowledge obtained justifies the means of obtaining it. This results in alternatives to animal research (e.g. computer simulations) being considered, and trivial research being avoided. A model proposed by *Bateson* (1986) considers animal research on three conditions, the quality of the research, the certainty of medical benefit, and the stress to the animal. He proposes that all animal research should be reviewed along these guidelines. Where the first two are high and the third low, decisions to proceed are fairly straightforward. If all three are high, then such considerations are more complex. *Green* (1992) uses the example of Alzheimer's disease to illustrate the difficulties of this area. Research with elderly laboratory rats has established that the neural dysfunction which is found in sufferers of Alzheimer's can also be found in rats suffering from similar symptoms. Given the similarity of primate brains and brain functioning, this would seem to justify the testing of drugs that might retard the onset of Alzheimer's in human patients. Opponents of this view point to the disasters in assuming that drugs have the same effect on all species. The drug Thalidomide, for example, had clearly different effects in its animal trials than in the humans who eventually had it prescribed to them.

Philosophical objections to the use of animals are more difficult to discuss in the medium of a revision text. However, some points to consider are:

■ The relationship between animal rights and human rights and the need to avoid 'speciesism' (subjugation of one species for the ends of another).
■ The problems with *comparative* psychology. 'It is simple to select facts to fit theories, to slide from animal metaphors to the implication that they contain something basic to human nature.' (*Hinde*, 1984). Here Hinde is suggesting that animals are worth studying in their own right, but we should guard against using the results of such studies for anything other than that.

EXAMINATION QUESTIONS

1. 'The experimental method used in psychology can be unethical and alternative methods of investigating behaviour should be adopted.' To what extent do you agree with this statement?
(25)
(AEB 1990)

2. Discuss the use of animals in psychology and consider the ethical issues raised by such research. *(25)*

(AEB 1992)

3. 'All behaviour is inevitably controlled...the moral question is not whether man's behaviour will be controlled but rather by whom, by what means, and for what ends.' Discuss the ethics of behaviour change. *(25)*

(AEB 1993)

ANSWERS TO EXAMINATION QUESTIONS

OUTLINE ANSWER TO QUESTION 3

The *Skill A* (AEB syllabus) part of this question might take the form of a description of techniques and treatments that bring about behaviour change, and the *Skill B* part would be a critical discussion of their related ethical problems.

Techniques which involve behavioural change include behaviour therapy and behaviour modification, drug treatments and perhaps even psychoanalysis.

It is also relevant to offer an account of other psychological, practices (e.g. manipulation in the experiment) which being about behavioural change. This link should be made explicit, and your answer should not wander off into a prepared answer on something completely different.

It is also perfectly relevant to write about persuasion or any other area of psychology where behavioural change is either an aim or a consequence of intervention. Use this material cautiously, though, and make all your links explicit.

Discussion may include the following points:

1. The need to see all treatment in a 'context of rehabilitation', i.e. the benefits may outweigh the costs.
2. The side effects (e.g. dependency, dehumanization etc.).
3. The effectiveness of the treatment, measured against its ethical problems.
4. Identification of the *client* (i.e. the patient, the family, society etc.).
5. The reductionist nature of some interventions (e.g. the overuse of drug treatments in place of social change).

One final point: As this question contains a quote, you should relate your discussion directly to the information contained in that quote.

TUTOR'S ANSWER

Question 1

It is a common belief that the experimental method in psychology, by virtue of its very nature, is unethical. Critics of the method point to the mechanistic, dehumanizing manipulation which is characteristic of, in particular, the laboratory experiment (*Heather*, 1976). Defendants of experimental methods however, point to the need for a detached and objective view of humankind, and suggest that such methods are the most likely to achieve those aims (*Broadbent*, 1977).

Objections to the experimental method on ethical grounds tend to focus on a number of issues. The experiment may, for example, be seen as an invasion of privacy, yet this problem cannot be overcome by transferring the investigation to more natural settings where the participants may be totally unaware that they are taking part in a psychological study. Central to this argument is the need for *informed* consent, in that participants appreciate that participation is voluntary, they are aware of any potential risk, and are free to withdraw at any time. Again, this may not be seen as appropriate to *non*-experimental situations, where the investigator needs to weigh up the benefits of informing his participants against the possibility of creating artificial behaviour as a result.

One of the hardest practices to justify is the use of deception in experiments. This may be necessary where the design would be undermined by telling participants the true nature of the study. There are alternatives to deception, however. *Kelman* (1967) found that participants who were aware of the true nature of the investigation could often role play the part of the *naive* participant yet without the need for deception on the part of the experimenter. *Berscheid et al.* (1973) proposed the use of a representative sample drawn from the same population in order to assess objections to the aims and practices of the experiment (including deception). In the absence of objections from this group, Berscheid reasoned, it would be reasonable to proceed with the experiment on a similar group of participants. Such dubious practices emphasise the need for full and effective debriefing after the experiment. In this way, participants can be reassured, counselled and informed such that they are no worse off as a result of taking part. The debriefing session can also act as a useful methodological tool where the experimenter can assess the degree to which his or her methodology is effective.

A problem which is often specific to the experiment is the problem of coercion of participants. Although most experiments rely on volunteers to take part, it is possible that volunteers are not representative of the rest of the population (*Ora*, 1965). Children, who may not be in a position to give their informed consent about participation are a particularly vulnerable group. Coercion may be quite subtle; the payment of participants for their 'services' and the use of experimental 'prods' (for example 'You must continue, you have no other choice', *Milgram*, 1963) are prime examples of the pressures which experimenters may exert on their participants.

Having mentioned Milgram, it is worthwhile looking at his research to examine just why it is generally regarded as the definitive unethical study. Despite claims from some critics that Milgram's participants were fully aware that they were not *really* giving shocks, it is evident from Milgram's own reports that many of them suffered extreme distress during the experiment. *Diana Baumrind* (1964) claimed that the benefit to humanity of Milgram's work was not sufficient to justify the anxiety and distress felt by those who took part. Baumrind also claimed that Milgram violated the basic human rights of his participants by exposing them to a potentially harmful experience without first getting their *informed* consent to do so. Milgram's response to these criticisms provided a powerful defence of his actions, showing that although most participants did indeed suffer distress during the experiment, a follow up survey showed that the vast majority were glad to have taken part and some actually volunteered to take part in future research. *Erikson* (1968) wrote of the 'momentous contribution' that Milgram had made, and suggested that the ethical criticisms arose simply because people liked to 'close their eyes to undesirable behaviour.'

In the quote above, it is implied that by adopting alternatives to the experimental method, ethical problems can be avoided. This is obviously not the case. The inappropriateness of informed consent in most non-manipulative investigations has already been mentioned, and indeed, strict adherence to the need for confidentiality and anonymity of data in naturalistic methods does go some way to satisfying the breach of individual privacy. What is more a subject of concern is the use of deception during participant and sometimes non-participant observation. Such deceptive practices are not well received by the lay public and do nothing to enhance the professional integrity of research psychologists.

In conclusion, there is nothing inherently unethical about the experimental method that isn't present in some degree in other non-experimental methods. All research in psychology is subject to the guidelines laid down by the British Psychological Society, and as such is carried out in a way which minimises the ethical concerns which characterised earlier research in psychology.

STUDENT'S ANSWER WITH EXAMINER'S COMMENTS

Question 3

Animals are used in psychological research for two reasons; firstly they are used because they are being studied in their own right, and secondly because humans can't be used for that experiment. When they are studied as a replacement for humans it is done in the belief that their behaviour is similar to human's. This stems from Darwin's theory of evolution; if humans evolved from 'lower species', then the difference in their behaviour must be quantitative rather than qualitative. If this is taken as true then it makes sense to study these 'lower' species such as rats, dogs and monkeys so that from their simpler behaviour we can deduce something of our own more complex behaviour.

Yes, the principle of behavioural continuity

Probably the most famous experiment involving animals was that of *Pavlov* (1927). He experimented with dogs to see how they responded to connected stimuli, i.e. food and another stimulus (e.g. a steady note). Every time he offered them food, he provided the other stimulus, and after a time the dog salivated at the other stimulus without any food. This gave insight into conditioning, which also takes place in humans. *Gardner and Gardner* (1971) adopted a baby chimpanzee and tried to teach her sign language. From the studies of her as she learnt it, much was learned about the learning process as well as about the primate. More frequent, however, are experiments in which the animal is put under a degree of stress or pain. A particularly stressful experiment was that of Brady's executive monkeys (1958). In this, a pair of monkeys were strapped into an electric chair and given electric shocks at regular intervals. One monkey had a lever it could press to stop the shocks. This monkey had 'executive' power over each shock, and soon developed stomach ulceration, similar to stomach ulceration that some executive humans get from their jobs.

The disadvantages with psychological research on animals are significant. Animals are incapable of directly replying to their experimenters so they have to deduce how the animal is feeling or what it is thinking. This means the experimenter must try to deduce from the behaviour of the animal, and this can be very time consuming, and also it is not definitely correct. Another disadvantage is the uncertainty as to whether an animal's behaviour is relevant to a human's. Are a rat's conditioned responses in any way relevant to a human's?

The advantages of researching with animals are great. Animals tend to breed much more rapidly, so the effect of any research on future generations can be much more rapidly observed. *Harlow* (1962) conducted experiments on rhesus monkeys and deprivation of a maternal figure, and how these 'orphaned' monkeys treated their young.

Without faster breeding this would have been impossible; the experiment conducted on humans would have taken over 15 years. Psychologists are also allowed to conduct experiments on animals that would be forbidden on humans e.g. Brady's executive monkey study. Animals are also simpler than humans, this means it is easier to discover what is affected in an animal, and also the cause of behaviour. There is less to affect it from within, i.e. hidden drives.

The big problem with animal research is the problem of ethical objections. Ethical objections arise every time an animal in an experiment suffers, which is almost every time. Brady's executive monkeys were suffering a great deal from the shocks and the ulcers and when that is balanced against the gains from the experiment (medically very little) it is apparent that the experiment is highly unethical. The monkeys' suffering far outweighed any gains. The most common ethically based complaints are about the treatment of rats. Rats are often subjected to food deprivation and/or electric shocks, and most of the complaints are about this. *Gray* (1987) says that these are invalid complaints because the rats are never starved beyond about four fifths of their natural weight, and the electric shocks do not cause extreme pain.

The most powerful anti-animal research argument is that of speciesism. It can be argued that we have no right to put other animals in pain or under stress, or even to breed them for our gain. We are just discriminating against them. The problem with this argument is that it is unarguable; it just can't be backed up with rational argument. The argument is either whether we believe we have the right to discriminate or whether we don't.

The use of animals in psychological research is going to be debated for many years yet, but while it is an important area of research, and while the 1986 Animals Act is enforced, it is acceptable.

REVIEW SHEET

1. Give *four* of the ethical guidelines published by the BPS.

   _____

   _____

   _____

2. Give *two* reasons why Milgram's study would be considered unethical today.

   _____

   _____

3. What is involved in aversion therapy?

   _____

   _____

4. What were the *costs and benefits* of Lang and Melamed's study?

   Costs
   _____

   Benefits
   _____

5. What is a *token* economy?

   _____

   _____

6. Give *two* reasons why it may be considered unethical.

   _____

   _____

7. Why are *medical* treatments seen as more ethically worrying than *psychological* treatments?

   _____

   _____

8. Give *three* reasons why animals are used in psychological research.

   _____

   _____

   _____

9. Give *one* way in which animal research has benefitted humans, and *one* in which it has benefitted animals.

   Humans
   _____

   Animals
   _____

10. What was Koestler's objection to animal research, and what was Green's response?

    _____

    _____

11. Give *two* guidelines from the 1986 Animals Act.

    _____

    _____

12. What are the three criteria of Bateson's model of animal research?

    _____

    _____

13. What is *speciesism*?

    _____

    _____

14. Take any other psychological study with which you are familiar. In what ways might it be considered unethical according to the guidelines discussed in this chapter?

    _____

    _____

    _____

    _____

15. How might that study have been carried out in a more ethically acceptable manner?

    _____

    _____

    _____

16. What were the costs and benefits of that research?

    _____

    Costs
    _____

    Benefits
    _____

4

PERCEPTION

GETTING STARTED

This chapter explores some of the issues connected with **perception**, its nature, its development and its organisation. The chapter is split into those headings to make it easier for you to apply appropriate knowledge to the different areas which appear in examination questions.

What is perception?

Perception refers to the processes by which we interpret information provided by the senses. Explanations of perception tend to differ in the degree to which they attribute analysis to information contained within the sensory stimuli (*bottom-up* theories) or to models and expectations which are generated cognitively and are used to process the information accordingly (*top-down* theories). In the former, perception may be seen as an accurate representation of external stimuli, in the latter as an active process of inference and hypothesis testing.

Two major theories are discussed in this chapter. Richard Gregory believes that perception is indirect, a process of inference. To James Gibson, perception is more direct (he refers to it as 'ecological'). The former theory is an example of a *top-down* theory, whilst the latter is an example of a *bottom-up* theory

The main themes of questions set in this area are:

■ **Sensory systems and how they relate to the processes of perception.**
■ **Theories of perception (e.g. top-down and bottom-up theories)**
■ **Perception as a developmental process.**
■ **Perceptual organization (including space, pattern recognition, movement, constancies and illusions)**

VISUAL SENSORY SYSTEMS AND PERCEPTION

THEORIES OF PERCEPTION

PERCEPTUAL DEVELOPMENT

PERCEPTUAL ORGANISATION

ESSENTIAL PRINCIPLES

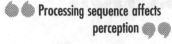
VISUAL SENSORY SYSTEMS AND PERCEPTION

Rods and cones are the **visual receptors** located on the retina which are sensitive to light. *Cones* allow us to see in colour and to make fine discriminative judgements. *Rods* are monochromic, in that they are not sensitive to colour.

Different types of cone are sensitive to different wavelengths of coloured light. The perceived colour of an object is a combination of this sensory information together with any `negativeafterimages` (complementary wavelengths) brought about through extensive viewing of one particular stimulus.

From the retina, information passes down the optic nerve to the optic chiasma, where there is a mixing of information from both eyes. From here, information is passed to the occipital cortex in the brain.

💬💬 Processing sequence affects perception 💬💬

Research by *Hubel and Weisel* (1962) produced evidence for the existence of a hierarchy of processing cells in the occipital cortex. They proposed that **simple cells** were sensitive to stimulation in a particular part of the retina. The output of these simple cells formed complex cells, and the output of the **complex cells** form **hypercomplex cells**. This sequence of processing, argued Hubel and Weisel, formed the basis of form perception. The processing of information in complex cells, for example, could not take place until the processing at earlier, simple cells was complete. Thus, processing was *serial* in nature.

Eysenck (1993), casts doubt on the idea that processing occurred in the simple hierarchical arrangement proposed by Hubel and Weisel. He points out that some complex cells respond to visual stimulation faster than do simple cells, therefore casting doubt on the idea that complex cells merely consist of simple cells and their output.

Eysenck and Keane (1990) also point out that the model of perceptual processing proposed by such **feature analysis** models of perception cannot deal with evidence from neurophysiological studies. This evidence indicates that full feature analysis of objects is not possible from the incomplete information available from sensory systems.

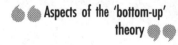
THEORIES OF PERCEPTION

Here is a brief review of some of the theories relating to perception.

GIBSON'S THEORY OF DIRECT PERCEPTION

Frequently described as a '**bottom-up**' theory, Gibson's theory (*Gibson*, 1966) claims that a wealth of information exists in the available sensory stimuli, and this information leads to accurate perception of the world around us.

Main claims

💬💬 Aspects of the 'bottom-up' theory 💬💬

- Light reaching the eye does so in an 'optic array'. This provides unambiguous information about such things as distance, movement and meaning.
- Interpretation is achieved through analysis of the information in this optic array by means of various cues (e.g. optic flow, texture density).
- The meaning of a stimulus is determined by the object's *affordance*, i.e. Gibson claimed that the physical structure of an object gives clues as to its potential use, therefore meaning is directly perceived.

Evaluation of Gibson's theory

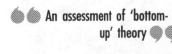
💬💬 An assessment of 'bottom-up' theory 💬💬

- Gibson's emphasis on *direct* perception provides an explanation of the (generally) fast and accurate perception of the environment.
- Although, as Gibson suggests, the environment does provide us with a rich source of information, it seems unlikely that we use this in the simple, direct way proposed. Later theorists (e.g. *Marr*, 1982) cast doubt on the idea that perception could not require information processing from existing cognitive models.
- Gibson's theory cannot explain how perception (e.g. to illusions) is often inaccurate, and although he claimed the illusions used in experimental work constituted extremely artificial perceptual situations unlikely to be encountered in the real world, this dismissal could not realistically apply to *all* illusions.

CONSTRUCTIVE THEORIES

Generally referred to as **top-down** theories, these **constructive** theories share basic assumptions about the perceptual process.

Main claims

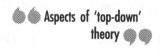

Aspects of 'top-down' theory

- Perception is not seen as a direct representation of the world around us, but rather an active, constructive, search for meaning.
- Perception is the end product of a process of which the stimulus is only one part. Hypotheses, expectations and previous experiences will interact with this stimulus to produce an *inference* about the external environment.
- Because the process involves hypothesis and expectations, perception is occasionally prone to error. *Gregory* (1970) has provided an explanation of how illusions can lead to perceptual error through the inappropriate application of previous knowledge to the stimulus given.

Evaluation of constructivist theories

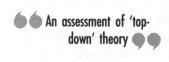

An assessment of 'top-down' theory

- If, as Gregory claims, perception is largely a matter of inference, then it would follow that the perceptual process would be more prone to error than it actually is. As with direct perception explanations, to place undue emphasis on *one* aspect of the perceptual process (*either* the stimulus *or* inference and hypothesis testing) does not appear to fit the facts.
- Gibson's answer to the problem of explaining illusions was to claim that laboratory studies are highly artificial situations that do not relate to the way in which we normally perceive. The fact that illusory stimuli tend to be presented only briefly lends some support to this claim. Brief presentations of stimuli prevent effective analysis and give more scope for interpretation on the basis of past experiences and expectations.

BOTTOM-UP OR TOP-DOWN?

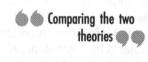

Comparing the two theories

As has been suggested, neither direct nor constructive theories of perception seem capable of explaining all perception all of the time. Gibson's theory appears to be based on perceivers operating under ideal viewing conditions, where stimulus information is plentiful, and is available for a suitable period of time. Constructivist theories such as Gregory's have typically involved viewing under less than ideal conditions. Research by *Tulving et al.* manipulated both the clarity of stimulus input and the impact of perceptual context in a word identification task. As clarity of the stimulus (through exposure duration) and the amount of context increased, so did the likelihood of correct identification. However, as the exposure duration increased, so the impact of context was reduced, suggesting that if stimulus information is high, then the need to use other sources of information is reduced. *Neisser* (1976) has attempted to resolve this issue by suggesting that existing perceptual models (schemata) guide us into sampling particular aspects of the stimulus environment. This tends to involve movement within that environment (a key aspect of Gibson's theory) as we gather information. During this stimulus exploration, if data gathered does not appear to match the relevant schema, then the information in that schema can be modified. Such a theory explains how top-down and bottom-up processes may be seen as interacting with each other to produce the best interpretation of the stimulus.

PERCEPTUAL DEVELOPMENT

This section deals with issues relating to the *development* of perceptual abilities. The **nature-nurture** issue is concerned with whether perception is innate or learned, and the other two sections deal with the development of perception in infancy and beyond.

THE NATURE-NURTURE ISSUE

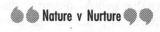

Nature v Nurture

Nativists believe that perceptual abilities are present at birth, or develop gradually through the process of maturation. **Empiricists** believe that perceptual abilities are acquired through experience in the environment.

There are various ways of investigating this issue. Two are described here:

Studies of animals

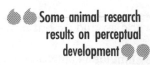

Research has been carried out where animals have been reared in the dark, and then tested for their perceptual ability when first exposed to the light (e.g. *Riesen*, 1947), their perceptual ability is considerably less than that of normal animals. Critics (e.g. *Weiskrantz*, 1956) have pointed out that animals reared in darkness will probably have suffered physiological degeneration of the retina and optic nerve. Later experiments by Riesen using animals reared in unpatterned light to overcome such degeneration discovered some perceptual retardation, but less than that of the dark reared animals. He concluded that light was needed for normal physical development of the visual system, and patterned light was necessary for the development of the more complex perceptual abilities.

Blakemore and Cooper (1970) showed the importance of early visual experience in the specialisation of cells in the visual cortex. They reared cats in the dark, but for a restricted period, they were exposed to an experimental environment which consisted only of vertical stripes. As a result of this exposure, their cortical cells became selectively responsive to vertical lines rather than horizontal lines.

These findings do appear to suggest that the environment is very important in the development of certain kinds of perceptual ability. However, as animals are unable to *tell* us what they see, we can *only* infer what their perceptual abilities are from what they do. A second problem arises from the use of animals in the first place. It is by no means readily accepted within psychology that animals are appropriate in the study of *human* behaviour. Critics of animal research point to the existence of brain and behaviour differences between non-human animals and man, a point challenged by others (see Chapter 3).

Studies of the visually deprived

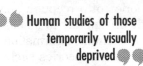

This problem with the use of animals might be overcome by studying human patients who, through their circumstances, have suffered visual deprivation, yet been given sight later in their lives.

Von Senden (1932) reported on patients who had undergone surgery to remove cataracts from their eyes. These adult patients showed basic perceptual skills. They could, for example, distinguish figure from ground, but showed an inability to perform other perceptual tasks such as the identification of familiar objects by sight alone. *Hebb* (1949) claimed that the former skill was an example of *figural unity* which he suggested was innate, and the latter an example of *figural identity* which, according to Hebb, was learned.

Gregory and Wallace (1963) reported the case of S.B., who had his sight restored when he was 52. S.B. *was* able to identify objects from vision if he was familiar with them from touch (unlike the patients that Von Senden reported). However, his other perceptual abilities remained largely undeveloped. He could not, for example, readily identify objects which he was not 'touch familiar' with, even after extensive sighted experience of them.

However, there are a number of problems with these kind of studies. As they involve adult patients (who are humans, and *can* report what they see) these patients have frequently developed a reliance on other sensory modalities, and therefore show less motivation to use their new visual sense. Patients, it appears, were inadequately prepared for the new stimuli. Many of them were extremely distressed by the experience, which could have depressed their desire to use it. Finally, the accuracy of the reporting of Von Senden's patients is questionable by contemporary standards. There appears to be a large amount of difference in the age when the cataracts first appeared, therefore a large variation in the amount of previous visual experience.

PERCEPTION IN INFANCY

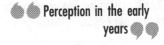

Early research in this area found less evidence of early perceptual skills than is now evident. Classic research by *Fantz* (1961) changed the way that people looked at this problem. Using a visual preference test, he showed that infants as young as four days old showed a clear discrimination for human like faces than other 'less human' stimuli.

Fantz concluded that the infant *sees a patterned and organised world which he explores discriminatingly within the limited means at his command.*

Fantz's conclusions have been criticised, partly on methodological grounds (the *actual* differences in time preference between the faces and non faces were quite modest), and partly on interpretative grounds (it is possible the faces were more pleasing to look at simply because they represented a more symmetrical and a more complex stimulus).

Gibson and Walk (1960) used infants between 6 months and 12 months of age on a *visual cliff.* They found that they would not crawl over to the 'deep' side of the cliff. This, they suggested, showed the existence of depth perception. *Eysenck* (1993) cautions that we are too quick to take this as evidence that depth perception is innate. It is possible that the experiences of the children *before* 6 months were sufficient for depth perception to develop. He also points out that in Gibson and Walk's research, when the children were *placed* on the deep side, 9 month old children's heart rate tended to quicken (suggesting that they perceived the 'drop' and were frightened by it) whereas the heart rate of 2 month old children became slower (suggesting interest in the perceived difference between the stimuli offered by the two sides).

POST INFANCY PERCEPTUAL DEVELOPMENT

Age plays a part in perception

Gibson (1969) reported that perceptual skills increase gradually with age. She also suggested that the *types* of perceptual error change with age. Orientation errors are frequent in young children but rare in older children.

Gibson suggests that the reason for this is that older children are better able to make use of the features of a stimulus (in keeping with James Gibson's theory of direct perception). The developmental process at work here is one of **perceptual differentiation**. The information had always been in the stimulus, but younger children are less able to recognise it. The **perceptual enrichment hypothesis**, a constructivist point of view, suggests that young children simply do not have the knowledge and experience to *enrich* an impoverished visual stimulus. As they get older they can supplement that stimulus for a more complete and accurate interpretation.

Perception Enrichment Hypothesis

As in the analysis of top-down and bottom-up theories of perception, it would appear likely that perceptual enrichment mainly occurs when stimuli *are* impoverished, otherwise, perceptual differentiation is necessary for accurate perception.

GESTALT PSYCHOLOGY

PERCEPTUAL ORGANISATION

Gestalt psychologists believed that perception was determined by innate factors, which predisposed the perceptual system toward particular types of perceptual organisation. The **law of Pragnanz** was the belief that form perception was a question of organising stimuli into the simplest and most uniform pattern that the prevailing conditions would allow. Among the principles proposed were:

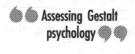
Law of Pragnanz

- The **law of similarity** (similar objects will be grouped together).
- The **law of closure** (missing parts of a figure are 'filled in').
- The **law of proximity** (stimuli which are close together will be perceived as being part of the same figure).

Evaluation of Gestalt psychology

1. Too much emphasis is placed on innate factors in perceptual organisation. This underestimates the importance of experiential learning.
2. The principles and laws of Gestalt are only *descriptions* of perceptual organisation, they do not explain *why* such organisational groupings take place.

Assessing Gestalt psychology

3. It is difficult to apply Gestalt explanations to complex stimuli which do not conform to the ideas of similarity, proximity etc.
4. *Eysenck* (1993) suggests that the processes proposed by the Gestalt psychologists account for the *early stages* of perceptual processing in which important features are identified. He feels that subsequent processing is then far more detailed.

OTHER FACTORS IN PERCEPTUAL ORGANISATION

Movement

Movement may be perceived by:

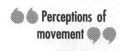

1. **Image displacement**, whereby the stimulus image moves across the retina, thus stimulating different receptors.
2. **Movement against a stationary background**, where the changing position of the object relative to the background is taken as an indication that the object has moved. *Induced movement* may occur when the larger background moves, such that the object in the foreground appears to move.
3. **Ocular pursuit**, brought about by feedback from the eyes which track the object.

Space and distance

When we perceive the world in **three dimensions**, we use the following cues to judge distance:

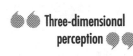

1. **Size**. Objects of known size can be used to judge distance. The smaller the retinal image the farther away it is judged to be.
2. **Height in the visual plane**. Objects which are higher in the visual plane are seen as being farther away.

Additional information is available as the perceiver moves around the perceptual environment. *Motion parallax* is the tendency for images of things that are farther away to move less across the retina than things that are closer to us.

Pattern recognition

The process of **pattern recognition** involves matching information present in the visual stimulus with information stored in our long term memory. Several theories have attempted to explain how this might happen.

1. **Template theory**. This type of theory proposes that we possess copies of previously experienced patterns, and that we match incoming stimuli with these. Apart from the problems with sheer size of the number of templates we would need, this theory runs into problems explaining unusual or inverted presentations of familiar stimuli, which are recognised very easily.
2. **Prototype theory**. These theories propose that every visual stimulus might be grouped in a category of similar stimuli that have similar features. Thus, stimuli can be matched against these generalisations of the class of stimuli. These theories do tend to ignore, however, the context in which perception occurs. This has been found to have significant effects on the nature of the perceptual decision.
3. **Feature theories**. These propose that pattern recognition involves the extraction of key elements of the stimulus (lines, loops etc.) leading to an interpretation of what it might be. *Gibson et al.* (1968) provided support for this approach by showing that letter recognition errors were typically ones in which the letters shared similar features. *Eysenck* (1993) criticises the exclusive use of these theories in explaining pattern recognition, saying that they ignore the important role of experience and context. Proof reading errors, he argues, are very common because peoples' expectations of what will be seen often outweighs what they actually see.

CONSTANCIES AND ILLUSIONS

A *perceptual constancy* is a tendency to experience a stable perception in the face of continually changing sensory input.

An *optical illusion* involves an apparently inexplicable discrepancy between the appearance of a visual stimulus and its physical reality.

Size constancy is the tendency to perceive familiar objects as stable in size, even though their retinal size changes with distance.

Shape constancy helps us to compensate for the distortions we experience in a three dimensional world. A door for example, continues to appear rectangular, even though its retinal registration is quite different.

A lack of cues can lead to errors

If we use information about size and distance to make perceptual judgements, then it follows that if cues relating to one are absent, then errors will be made in the judgement of the other. Familiar objects are seen as maintaining their size, for example, thus their retinal size is used as a cue to distance.

Gregory (1970) suggested that the cues which are so useful in three dimensional space can be misapplied to two dimensional space, causing a misperception. The *Muller-Lyer illusion*, he claims exists because in a three dimensional situation, the outward facing fins are seen as coming toward us, thus the principle of size constancy leads us to believe that the upright line is actually farther away.

Although the Muller-Lyer illusion does appear three dimensional when viewed in a darkened room, (giving credit to the Gregory's explanation), it is still possible to obtain the illusion when the fins are replaced with circles. The misapplied size constancy explanation then no longer applies.

Optical illusions provide support for the view of perception as inference. If we constantly test hypotheses about our perceptional world, then occasionally these hypotheses will be wrong, and we will experience an illusion.

Illusions also demonstrate the importance of context in perception, with factors such as depth cues playing a very important role in our perceptual judgements. The existence of optical illusions reinforces the idea of perception as a subjective process rather than a one to one representation of objective reality

EXAMINATION QUESTIONS

1. Critically consider the processes involved in perceptual organisation. *(25)*

2. (a) Give a definition of perception. *(5)*
   (b) Describe any one theory or model of perception. *(10)*
   (c) Evaluate this theory in terms of its explanation of perceptual processes. *(10)*
   (AEB 1993)

3. 'Perception is a developmental process.' To what extent does psychological evidence support this statement?' *(25)*
   (AEB 1989)

4. 'There is more to visual perception than meets the eye.' Discuss the above statement in relation to theories of perceptual organisation. *(25)*
   (AEB 1992)

ANSWERS TO EXAMINATION QUESTIONS

OUTLINE ANSWERS TO QUESTIONS 2 AND 3

Question 2

(a) The first part of this question asks for a *definition* of perception. This does not have to be a textbook definition, your own would do, as would a range of quite different conceptions of what perception actually is.

(b) The usual theories presented here are either Gibson's theory of direct perception, which sees the stimulus as a rich source of perceptual information, or Gregory's theory which sees perception for an active search for the best interpretation of a stimulus.

(c) The theory should now be evaluated. For example, Gibson's theory fails to explain inaccurate perception, Gregory's fails to explain why perception is usually accurate (i.e. it is a process of inference).

Note that the question only calls for *one* theory, but one may be used in evaluation of the other.

Question 3

This question is concerned with how perceptual processes might *develop* throughout the lifespan of the individual. It essentially asks for the following:

- In what ways does perception develop over time?
- What is the evidence for this?

You should then pay particular attention to the evaluation of this evidence. A suitable approach might be:

1. Studies of neonates. The early appearance of a perceptual ability might be taken as a sign that it was present due to genetic factors rather than experiential ones. There are difficulties in inferring perceptual competence from speechless infants.
2. Animal Studies e.g. *Riesen* (1947). These often show the detrimental effect of deprivation during *critical periods* of perceptual development. There are problems connected with the generalisation from animal studies to humans.
3. Perceptual adaptation studies. People have had to readjust to distorted views of the world. Many of these accounts are subjective and anecdotal.
4. Cross-cultural studies. These provide *natural laboratories* for testing the effects of differing experiences on the development of perceptual processes.
5. Post infancy studies. Perception clearly improves with age. Gibson claims that this is because children become better able to use the information in a stimulus as they get older. Other explanations claim that older children perceive better because their greater experience helps them to supplement an impoverished visual stimulus.

TUTOR'S ANSWER

Question 1

Probably the most famous theory which attempted to explain the processes of perceptual organisation was the Gestalt theory. This theory proposed that our perceptual organisation was determined by innate factors which steered us toward particular types of perceptual decision. The law of Pragnanz suggested that we are 'programmed' to organise material into the simplest and most uniform arrangement that is possible in the visual conditions. *Koffka* (1935) suggested that perceptual organisation would thus tend towards what he described as 'good' form.

The Gestalt approach was characterised by a number of perceptual principles. Among these were the principles of similarity, proximity and closure. The perceiver would thus be guided into making such perceptual judgements by perceptual predispositions which Koffka claimed were innate.

Eysenck (1993) criticises the Gestalt approach on a number of counts. He claims that too much emphasis is placed on innate factors in perception, underestimating the importance of learning and experience. He also claims that the Gestalt principles are only descriptions of perceptual organisation, which fail to explain why organisation might proceed inthe ways suggested. Eysenck goes on to suggest that as the principles suggested might not apply to complex visual stimuli which do not conform to the stimulus arrangements described within the Gestalt approach, it is more likely that the approach deals only with the initial stages of perceptual organisation, where important features are extracted. Later processing would then be responsible for more discriminating perceptual judgements.

Other, more contemporary approaches to perceptual organisation have tended to focus on explanations of specific aspects of organisation. The process of pattern recognition, for example, involves matching the information present in the visual stimulus with information available from long term memory. Earlier template theories proposed the existence of an almost infinite number of templates built up from previously experienced patterns. Incoming stimuli would be matched aginst these templates in order to achieve recognition. The theory does fall into difficulties, quite apart from the sheer number of templates that would be needed, in that it cannot explain why familiar objects (for example, in a letter recognition task) are recognised reasonably easily when they are presented in novel ways. It is possible that these stimuli are somehow corrected before being proceed, but how this might happen is unclear.

Prototype theory proposes that stimuli may be matched against generalisations of visual stimuli which all have similar features. These theories do tend to ignore the context in which perception occurs, This is often found to have very significant effects on the nature of the perceptual decision.

Feature theories propose that pattern recognition involves the extraction of key features of the stimulus which would then lead to an interpretation of what it might be. *Gibson et al.* (1968) in a letter recognition task, claimed that the process of letter recognition could be reduced to twelve main features. He found that recognition errors typically occured when letters shared a high proportion of the same features. Again, these theories might be criticised as being purely **bottom-up** theories, ignoring as they do the expectations and context in which the perceptual judgement is made. *Eysenck* (1993) points to the difficulties of proof reading as indicating that expectation of what is written is a powerful determinant of what will actually be perceived on the page.

An attempt to apply top-down context driven interpretations to the process of perceptual organisation can be found in Gregory's **Misapplied Size constancy theory**. Gregory claims that we use information about the size of an object to make judgements about the distance they are away from us. Familiar objects are seen as maintaining their physical size, therefore any difference in their retinal size is interpreted as a change in the distance between the object and the observer. In illusions, however, some of that information might be missing, or might be manipulated to produce erroneous perceptual judgements. He uses the Müller-Lyer illusion as an example. This is usually perceived in three dimensions. When viewed in two dimensions, the outward facing fins are interpreted as coming toward us, thus indicating that the upright is actually further away. When compared with the 'arrow head' condition, the greater perceived distance of the former is interpreted as indicating its greater size (the retinal sizes of the two lines being the same). Appealing as this interpretation is, when the fins and arrows are replaced by circles or s quares, the illusion still persists.

More recently, *Neisser* (1980) has proposed that perceptual organisation is influenced by both top-down and bottom-up processes, with the former guiding the latter in the selection of information, and the latter guiding the former through modifications as a result of direct experience.

STUDENT'S ANSWER WITH EXAMINER'S COMMENTS

Question 4

It is necessary, in order to discuss the statement, to give a definition of perception. It is generally understood to be the organisation and interpretation of stimuli from the environment. R.L. Gregory states that it is a dynamic searching for the best mental representation of the world.

Since 90% of stimuli is processed visually, then it is not surprising that most psychological research has been carried out in this field. There are four major theorists who give their own very different view of perception. The Gestaltists take the cognitive view, pattern recognition or template matching hypothesis, prototype theory and feature detection.

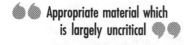 **A bit of confusion here. Theorists or areas of perceptual organisation?**

There are two types of depth cues used in the perception of stimuli. Binocular depth cues are those involving two eyes in a 3D world and of which there are two types. Convergence is the way in which the brain measures the gradient of the inward turning angle of the eye in order to focus. Secondly, retinal disparity is the way a distance judgment can be made by analysing the retinal images received by the brain. Monocular depth cues involve the use of one eye in a 2D world. Such cues are height in the visual plane, convergence of parallel lines, relative size, figure and ground.

In order to perceive a stimulus, the image enters the eye, but the events which take place beyond this stage will be discussed in relation to the four major theories mentioned.

The Gestaltist theorists take the cognitive view with which they put forward the law of Pragnanz or 'best fit'. They say that we look for the best interpretation of a stimulus when we perceive it. Involved in this perception are five principles which help us to perceive an object. Closure is used when an object appears to have gaps, it will be

Appropriate material which is largely uncritical perceived as a whole by filling in the gaps. Proximity is a principle which states that if two things are close together then they will be perceived as a whole. Figure and ground is a final principle which enables us to determine what is in the foreground, which masks whatever is in the background.

The Gestalt theory is criticised by Eysenck as he maintains that the Gestalt theory only explains perception of a 2D stimulus but does not explain that of 3D perception.

Also opposed to the Gestalt view is feature detection of which there are two types. Serial processing involves a stimulus being presented and each individual feature is scanned. When it has been scanned it is either accepted or rejected and then the brain moves on to the next feature, until the whole picture has been built up like a jigsaw. Serial processing was studied by Hubel and Wiesel and an alternative view is offered by Lennie and Spencer. They propose that parallel processing is used in the perception of a stimulus and can occur at the same time as serial processing. However, it is a much more rapid method as it does not involve a sequence of events, only a scanning of the picture as a whole, as each individual feature is analysed as one, therefore perception is much quicker.

The third approach is that of the template matching hypothesis. The hypothesis states that an object is presented and a template or schema already held in the memory is searched for. When the template has been retrieved, a match can be made and perception takes place.

This theory is criticised by Eysenck because it does not explain the perception of totally new objects or stimuli. If we see something for the first time, we will not have a schema or template, so how can perception of new experiences possibly take place? Eysenck offers his own explanation of the prototype theory which states that we have a prototype for everything we see and it is the prototype which is matched with the stimulus and not the template or schema.

Consequently, the brain is constantly trying to make sense of the stimulus it receives despite visual illusions which are deliberate attempts to distort perception. It can also be said that some people are more ready to perceive certain stimuli rather than others because they have perceptual set. Sets can be formed on the basis of expectation, motivation, attention and individual or object value e.g. we may have a perceptual set for money, possessions or our own name.

💬💬 Not strictly accurate. The candidate hasn't really distinguished between templates and prototypes 💬💬

💬💬 Rather glossing over some very important points 💬💬

💬💬 This candidate has centred discussion around a number of different areas of perceptual organisation, which do show some evidence of critical discussion. It is a pity that the answer was not supported by more research evidence. Descriptive skills are more evident here than evaluative skills, but the breadth of discussion might just nudge it into the grade B band. 💬💬

REVIEW SHEET

1. What *two* things determine the perceived colour of an object?

   _____

   _____

2. Eysenck and Keane point out that feature analysis models of perception cannot deal with evidence from neurophysiological studies. Why is this?

   _____

   _____

3. What is the difference between a bottom-up and a top-down theory of perception?

   _____

   _____

4. Give two criticisms of each of Gibson's and Gregory's theories.

   Gibson

   _____

   _____

   Gregory

   _____

   _____

5. How does Neisser resolve the bottom-up/top-down problem?

   _____

   _____

6. Distinguish between nativists and empiricists in their beliefs about perception.

   _____

   _____

7. What is wrong with using animals in perceptual research?

   _____

   _____

8. What was Fantz's main conclusion?

   _____

   _____

9. How could this be criticised?

   _____

   _____

10. State *three* principles of the Gestalt theory of perception.

_____

_____

_____

11. State *three* criticisms of Gestalt theories.

_____

_____

_____

12. What *three* theories were advanced for the explanation of pattern recognition?

_____

_____

_____

13. What did Eysenck feel was wrong with these type of theories?

_____

_____

_____

14. What is meant by a perceptual constancy?

_____

_____

15. Briefly describe *two* types of perceptual constancy.

_____

_____

16. Give *two* reasons why a study of illusions is important for a better understanding of the nature of perception.

_____

_____

_____

_____

MEMORY AND FORGETTING

GETTING STARTED

In this chapter, issues relating to **memory** will be discussed. Most psychologists agree that this area can be conveniently divided into issues related to *storage*, and issues related to *retrieval*. Storage of information has traditionally been associated with the multi-store model of memory, with information passing through a sequence of modality specific stores. Nowadays, the short-term memory is regarded as a multi-component **working memory**. The long-term memory is also most usefully divided into episodic and semantic long term memories. Retrieval of information from long-term memory is governed by a range of factors; the encoding specificity of the retrieval cue, interference, repression, etc. As with other areas of cognitive psychology in particular, you should be prepared to support your discussion with actual research evidence wherever possible. Because of the limitations of a revision text, it is not always possible to provide the depth of research support desired. You should use your supporting texts to provide this.

The main themes of questions set in this area are:

■ **Discussion of explanations of different types of memory, in terms of their characteristics.**
■ **Discussion of the role of organisation in memory.**
■ **Discussion of explanations of forgetting.**
■ **Discussion of practical applications of research in memory and forgetting.**

THE MULTI-STORE APPROACH

WORKING MEMORY

LONG-TERM MEMORY

LEVELS OF PROCESSING

ORGANISATION OF INFORMATION IN MEMORY

FORGETTING

APPLICATIONS OF MEMORY RESEARCH

ESSENTIAL PRINCIPLES

Early distinctions between **short** and **long-term** memory have tended to focus on the evidence from brain damaged patients who demonstrate restricted ability in one of these 'types' of memory whilst apparently remaining unimpaired in the other. Other psychologists have tried to explain the structure and function of memory by adopting various theoretical distinctions that could account for the differential performance of participants in memory research studies.

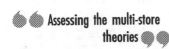
THE MULTI-STORE APPROACH

Atkinson and Shiffrin (1968) proposed the existence of three distinct **stores**, each of which had its own special characteristics.

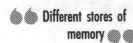
Different stores of memory

a) The **sensory store** holds information for a very short period of time, with visual stimuli going to the *iconic* store and auditory stimuli to the *echoic* store. Material is lost from this store through the process of *trace decay*.

b) The **short-term store** has a very limited capacity, and stores information until displaced by other material. As new material is constantly entering this store, the duration of the trace is very short. The memory trace is retained in this store through *rehearsal*.

c) The **long-term store** has a more or less unlimited capacity. Atkinson and Shiffrin argued that forgetting occurs in this store primarily because of an inability to retrieve the memory trace from similar existing memories.

Evaluation of the multi-store model

Assessing the multi-store theories

One of the advantages of the multi-store model is that evidence does seem to support its main claims, i.e. each of these proposed memory stores differs in terms of its duration of storage, its capacity and the nature of forgetting.

Its greatest problem is its simplicity. Atkinson and Shiffrin proposed that each store acted in a single, uniform manner, yet evidence from *Shallice and Warrington*, where their research subject K.F. displayed greater short term forgetting of auditory stimuli than visual stimuli, challenged this simple unitary explanation.

It is incorrect to think of the Short-term store as having one single capacity limitation. It is more appropriate to see it as comprising a number of different components, each with its own capacity.

A final problem concerns the role of rehearsal. *Eysenck and Keane* (1990) point out that Atkinson and Shiffrin overestimated the importance of rehearsal, which may not have such a vital part in the transfer of material from short term to long term memory in natural learning situations (compared to the artificiality of laboratory tasks).

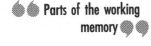
WORKING MEMORY

An alternative to the traditional idea of short-term memory was put forward by *Baddeley and Hitch* (1974), with the idea of the **working memory**. The working memory consists of three parts:

a) A **central executive**, which determines what is and what is not attended to. This is *modality free* in that it deals with both visual and auditory stimuli. The central executive has a limited capacity and deals with tasks which are cognitively demanding.

Parts of the working memory

b) An **articulatory loop**, which is essentially a verbal rehearsal system. It is likely that the capacity of this system is limited to that which could be read out loud in approximately two seconds (*Baddeley et al.*, 1975)

c) A **visuo-spatial scratch pad** which can hold and rehearse visual and spatial information. *Baddeley and Lieberman* (1980) Suggested that the visuo-spatial scratch pad relies more on spatial coding than visual coding.

Evaluation of the working memory model.

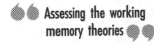
Assessing the working memory theories

The important difference between the multi-store model and working memory would appear to be in the role of verbal rehearsal. In line with research findings which have cast doubt over the importance of verbal rehearsal, its role in working memory is reduced to the articulatory loop only.

The working memory model is able to explain how, in brain damaged patients, selective deficits may occur in short term memory.

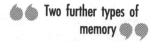 **updated working memory model**

An updated version of the model has been proposed (*Baddeley*, 1986). This sees the articulatory loop as comprising a *passive phonological store* (concerned with speech perception) and an *articulatory control process* (concerned with speech production). This revised model was better able to explain some of the neuropsychological evidence that did not fit the original model

LONG-TERM MEMORY

Episodic and semantic memory

Tulving (1972) draws a distinction between **episodic memory**, which is memory for personal events, and **semantic memory**, which is memories related to knowledge about the world. Evidence for the distinction comes from studies of amnesiacs who still display good language skills (knowledge of vocabulary and grammar) indicative of unimpaired semantic memory, but show impairment of memory of personal events (episodic memory). *Eysenck* (1993) points out that the distinction may not be all that clear cut, as experimental tests of amnesiacs typically involve testing memory of personal events *after* the onset of amnesia, whereas many amnesiacs still have good memories of pre-onset events, yet poor episodic and semantic memories post-onset.

Evidence for making this distinction

Declarative and procedural memory

Cohen and Squire (1980) drew a distinction between **declarative memory**, which is the equivalent of 'knowing that..' and **procedural memory**, which is the equivalent of 'knowing how..'. Evidence from amnesiacs suffering from Korsakoff's syndrome has established that typically, amnesiacs have no memory of events, yet still have the same unimpaired ability to form procedural long term memories, or in other words, how to *do* things.

Two further types of memory

LEVELS OF PROCESSING

Craik and Lockhart (1972) put forward the **levels of processing theory** in which they proposed that the processing at the time of learning determined the nature of the memory trace. The *deeper* the analysis of the information, the longer lasting, and more elaborate would be the memory trace. Craik and Lockhart criticised the multi-store model of Atkinson and Shiffrin for its over-simplified view of rehearsal. They drew a distinction between **maintenance rehearsal** which involves simple repetition of a stimulus without elaboration, and **elaborative rehearsal** which involves a deeper processing of the stimulus. Craik and Lockhart claimed that it was the latter which led to longer lasting traces in long-term memory.

Maintenance v elaborative rehearsal

Eysenck (1982) claims that both types of rehearsal appear to improve long-term memory, but elaborative more so than maintenance rehearsal.

The major assumptions of levels of processing theory are:

a) The level of processing received by a stimulus will have a significant effect on its memorability.

b) Deeper levels of processing tend to produce more elaborate and more long lasting memory traces than do shallow levels.

Memorability influenced by distinctiveness

Eysenck (1979) also makes the point that memory traces that are *distinct* in some way are more likely to be correctly retrieved from memory than memory traces that are like many other memory traces

Some empirical evidence

In support of the theory, evidence suggests that the nature of processing at the time of learning does have an effect on the subsequent long-term memory of the event (*Hyde and Jenkins*, 1973), but it is difficult to know what sort of processing has taken place, despite experimental manipulations, so the argument becomes somewhat circular. Although there is an intuitive logic to the ideas of the depth of processing theory, there are situations where deeper processing does *not* lead to better long-term memory of the event. Of crucial importance is the *relevance* of the processing that took place at the time of learning. If recall is more closely matched to processing normally carried out at a shallower level (e.g. analysis of the *sound* of words) then stimuli processed at that level will be better remembered.

A final criticism is the claim that the model merely *describes* what is happening rather than *explaining* it (*Eysenck and Keane*, 1990). Although Craik and Lockhart argued that deep processing would lead to longer lasting memory traces they failed to explain *why* deeper levels of processing would have such an effect.

ORGANISATION OF INFORMATION IN MEMORY

●● Organisation involving categories ●●

Category organisation

Experimental studies of the recall of word lists have established that if the lists contain **categories** of words, then even if the presentation of the words is random, recall tends to be in category clusters (*Eysenck*, 1972). Research by *Mandler* (1967) also demonstrated how subject imposed categories will also increase the number of words recalled. Mandler's subjects were instructed to sort words into a specified number of categories (between two and seven). The more categories that were used, the greater was the organisation imposed on the list, and the greater was the recall.

Organisation at storage and retrieval

At the start of this chapter, a distinction was made between issues relating to **storage** and issues relating to **retrieval**. Research by *Weist* (1972) has established the importance of organisational procedures at the time of learning for later recall. *Ausubel's* work on **advanced organisers** has also demonstrated this phenomenon in an applied educational setting. In this context, organisation is seen as aiding **storage**. *Tulving and Pearlstone* (1966) also showed the importance of organisational cues during **retrieval**. It appears that the presentation of category heading during retrieval acts as a cue which triggers the retrieval of information within those categories.

Semantic memory

Collins and Quillian (1969) proposed a model of **semantic memory** in which memory was organised in a hierarchical network. As can be seen from the diagram below, concepts such as animal and bird are represented on the network as nodes, and the features of those concepts (e.g. has skin, has wings) are associated with those concepts.

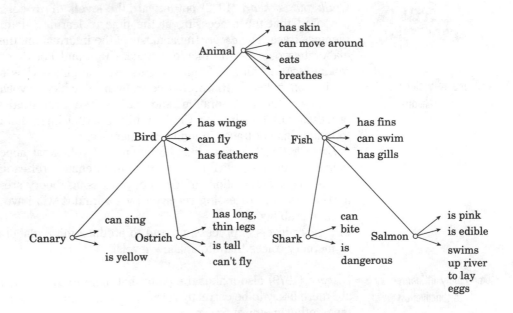

●● Hierarchical organisation ●●

The central idea of the **hierarchy** is that information is attached to its superordinate concept, rather than being attached to every example of its case, e.g. the fact that a shark eats is stored not with the shark concept, but with the animal concept which includes sharks among other animals.

Collins and Quillian provided support for their theory using a sentence verification task. Participants took longer to answer true or false to a statement where information was separated in the network (e.g. 'Does an ostrich breathe?') than where it was not ('Is an ostrich tall?').

However, the original theory could not explain why participants took longer to respond to connections that were not familiar. When familiarity was controlled within the sentences the distance on the network seemed to have no effect on the speed of

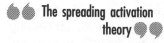 **The spreading activation theory**

response. A later theory by *Collins and Quillian* (1975), the **spreading activation theory** took this into account, arguing that semantic memory was organised *both* on the basis of semantic distance (on the network) and semantic relatedness (the degree to which the concept and the property are commonly associated).

Schemata

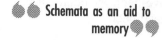 **Schemata as an aid to memory**

Bartlett (1932) originally proposed the idea that our memory comprises large chunks of organised knowledge (called **schemata**) which help to organise and *fill in* our representation of events. These schemata are mental representations of knowledge normally associated with a particular object or event. Bartlett's original work using the *War of the Ghosts* story showed how participants would tend to remember details from the story in a way that fitted their own cultural knowledge and expectations. Common errors included *rationalisation*, the tendency to change unfamiliar material to resemble more familiar representations of similar events; *flattening*, the tendency not to remember unfamiliar details in a story; and *sharpening*, elaboration of particular details to fit a theme.

However, Bartlett's work is not without its problems. Firstly, the experiment involved participants trying to remember highly unusual content, therefore not particularly well related to everyday events, and secondly, it appears that some of the distortions and inaccuracies were caused by deliberate attempts by the participants to produce an effective level of recall within the experimental situation. Bartlett believed that schemata distorted the way in which material was reconstructed during retrieval, whereas *Eysenck* (1993) suggests that it is more likely that if schemata do have an effect, it is on the way information is understood at the time of learning.

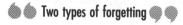 **FORGETTING**

 **Two types of forgetting**

Forgetting can be conveniently divided into two main types. **trace-dependent forgetting** means that the memory trace has actually been lost from the memory system, and **cue-dependent forgetting** which means that although the memory trace still exists in the long-term memory, it cannot be retrieved because of the lack of a suitable cue. Some of the explanations of forgetting are as follows.

Interference

 **Two types of interference**

The concept of **interference** means that an existing memory is distorted in some way by something learned in the past (**proactive interference**) or by something that might be learned in the future (**retroactive interference**). Interference is greatest when two different responses have been learned to the same stimulus. It is this fact that is one of the main criticisms of interference theory. The circumstances of having to learn two different responses to the same stimulus seem rather rare, and therefore would account only for forgetting in those kind of circumstances in real life.

Repression

Anxiety and repression!

Repression is generally taken to mean *motivated forgetting*, which is purposeful suppression of memories. Experimental psychologists have been unable to demonstrate this type of forgetting unambiguously in the laboratory. It does appear from such work, however, that participants are less able to remember information in anxiety laden situations. Whether or not this is an example of repression is debatable, as feedback of success (participants are normally given false feedback of failure to create the anxiety) also creates the same effect.

Eysenck (1993) suggests that such feedback merely serves to distract the participant from the task, which is why they do less well.

Retrieval failure

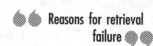 **Reasons for retrieval failure**

Retrieval failures may be more likely where there is a mismatch between the retrieval cue and the initial encoding of the stimulus. This was formalised by *Tulving and Thomson* (1973), with the **encoding specificity principle**. This principle states that the value of a retrieval cue depends on how well it corresponds to the memory code. Another explanation for retrieval failure is where the *fit* between the processing during encoding and retrieval is dissimilar. **Transfer – appropriate processing** occurs when the initial type of processing is similar to the type of processing required by the subsequent measure of retention (*Morris et al.*, 1977). Thus semantic processing during encoding is no use if the subsequent retrieval task requires acoustic processing.

Although there is real value in explanations which emphasise the importance of context both at the encoding and retrieval stages, there is a danger of circularity in explaining why they do or don't work. *Solso* (1974) points out the logical absurdity of stating that if a retrieval cue aids retrieval then it must have been encoded with the stimulus, and if it does not aid retrieval, then it must not have been.

Permanent memory

Research by *Penfield* (1969) on epileptic patients provided evidence that during electrical stimulation of the brain, these patients experienced vivid and detailed memories from their past. Penfield concluded that memory traces leave permanent neural imprints on the brain which can be activated many years later.

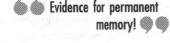
Evidence for permanent memory!

However, only a minority of Penfield's patients actually experienced these vivid memories, and of those who did, the memories were not independently verified for their accuracy. A related line of enquiry comes with the use of hypnosis. *Putman* (1979) showed participants a video tape of a traffic accident, and then asked them questions whilst under hypnosis. They made far more errors than a control group who answered the same questions in a non-hypnotic state. There seems no compelling evidence for the existence of permanent memories despite the popularity of the belief (*Eysenck*, 1993).

APPLICATIONS OF MEMORY RESEARCH

Eyewitness Testimony

Based on the idea of the **schema** in memory, *Loftus* (1979) has demonstrated how peoples recall of events in simulated **eyewitness testimony** tasks is subject to distortions and inaccuracies due to the memory schema for the event described. Experiments have also shown how information presented *after* an event can influence the recall of that event (*Loftus and Hoffman*, 1989).

Constructive and Reconstructive distortions

Unfortunately it is difficult in these experiments to distinguish between **constructive distortions** which occur when the person *encodes* the memory, and **reconstructive distortions**, which occur when the person *retrieves* it, and tries to fill in gaps in the schema.

Other research on eyewitness testimony using the ideas of **encoding specificity** has discovered that eyewitnesses are considerably more accurate in their memory of events when they were able to recreate the context in which the event had taken place (*Fisher*, 1987).

Mnemonic devices

Mnemonic devices are techniques for improving memory. The *method of loci* for example, allows people to enhance their memory ability by the use of mental imagery. Specific memories are remembered by means of relating them to imagined locations. Other methods involve the learning of names through the association of a feature of the person to a distortion of their name such that the two appear connected. Using this technique, *Morris et al.* (1978) produced an 80% improvement in people's ability to put names to faces.

Mnemonic techniques

Mnemonic devices have a number of limitations. They do appear to help us learn lists of unrelated items, and also assist in everyday skills like learning names and faces. They do not, however, assist in the learning of complex material, therefore must be seen as limited in their usefulness.

Memory for medical information

Many patients suffer from an inability to remember medical advice. *Ley* (1978) based his laboratory investigations on earlier research on forgetting. Typically, patients remembered; (i) information presented at the start of an interaction (**primacy effect**); (ii) information which was seen as more important by the patients; and (iii) information that was organised into categories rather than unorganised information.

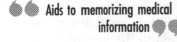
Aids to memorizing medical information

Another finding was that simple repetition of information had little impact on whether it was remembered. Using these various findings, Levy made suggestions to the medical profession about how medical information might be communicated for better retention. The retention rate of patients following the new ideas rose from 55% to 70%.

EXAMINATION QUESTIONS

1. Discuss psychological insights relating to the organisation of information in memory.   *(25)*
                                                                              (AEB 1993)
2. Discuss applications of psychological research on memory and describe the studies upon which these applications are based.   *(25)*
                                                                              (AEB 1992)
3. Use psychological evidence to discuss explanations of forgetting in humans. *(25)*
                                                                              (AEB 1991)

ANSWERS TO EXAMINATION QUESTIONS

OUTLINE ANSWER TO QUESTION 2

This is quite a tricky question, given that it turns the question around in the mind of the candidate. In these types of questions, it pays you to read the question very, very, carefully.

The question makes three quite different requests:

1. It invites you to show knowledge and understanding of applications of memory research. These might include educational applications (studying, for example), eyewitness testimony (particularly the work of Loftus et al.), memory for medical information and so on.
2. As the injunction was *discuss*, then you are required to offer evaluation of the material you have presented. This could take the form of the effectiveness and limitations of the techniques, the validity of the underlying research, the presence of other factors in performance etc.
3. The final part is to relate these applications back to their underlying research evidence. You may, for example, provide evidence for reconstructive memory (eyewitness testimony) by looking at research evidence on stress, the weapons effect and so on. Similarly, insights from research on the primacy and recency effect have been very useful in applications of memory for medical information.

TUTOR'S ANSWER

Question 3

Use psychological evidence to discuss explanations of forgetting in humans.

In an attempt to understand the process of forgetting, it is necessary to make a distinction between *availability* and *accessability*. The former is a question of storage and the latter a question of *retrieval*. Problems concerning storage are more to do with forgetting from the short-term memory and problems concerning accessibility or retrieval are more to do with the long term memory.

The trace decay theory (*Peterson and Peterson*, 1959) suggests that the memory trace is strengthened by rehearsal, and weakened by lack of use. *Hebb* (1949) originally believed that this 'neural decay' only applied to short-term memory forgetting, but more recently researchers have applied the same model to forgetting from the long term memory as well. Although the theory is plausible, and probably fits our subjective experiences quite well, there is considerable evidence which undermines it.

Some cases of brain damaged patients have shown that memories may not decay at all, they simply become inaccessible under normal situations. *Sachs* (1988) quotes evidence from patients who were able to 'unlock' seemingly decayed childhood memories following a mild stroke.

The belief that forgetting might be a consequence of brain damage or disease has produced some insights into the nature of forgetting, but is fraught with underlying methodological problems. Loss of memory following a head wound (*post-traumatic amnesia*) has led to the finding that a consolidation period is required after learning for the information to be fully absorbed into a person's memory (*Baddeley*, 1983). Forgetting may also be attributed to deterioration with age. In a study which controlled for levels of activity, *Harris and Sunderland* (1981) found no significant differences in memory failure between a group of young adults and a group of pre-retirement adults. Explanations of the reported deterioration with age may well centre around the fact that people notice memory failures more as they get older (in line with societal stereotypes), but not when they are still young. Similarly, the inability of older subjects to remember information may be caused by a motivational deficiency rather than a cognitive one.

A dominant explanation of forgetting for many years has been the *interference* theory. Interference may be *proactive* (existing material interferes with the retention of subsequent information) or *retroactive* (new material interferes with the retention of already learned material). The traditional view of interference has been that it mainly occurs with very similar material (*McGeoch*, 1942), but more recently, researchers (e.g. *Holmes*, 1974) have used the idea more broadly. Holmes suggested that one of the major causes of forgetting during examination preparation is that learning is often accompanied by anxiety about failing, and this interferes with the recall of more factual information. *Ekstrand* (1973) discovered a reduction in both proactive *and* retroactive interference following sleep. He suggested that sleep not only reduces interference, but also facilitates consolidation. Evaluation of interference theory presents the model with severe problems. Research by *Tulving* (1967) found that in three successive recall trials of a list of words, subjects recalled a variety of different words on each trial. Neither trace decay nor interference ('unlearned' words should not reappear) can deal with these findings. It appears that the different words were recalled due to different retrieval cues being used each time. A second major problem with interference theory is its inability to explain real life forgetting. Outside the lab, where the learning of potentially interfering material is spaced out over time, the demonstration of proactive interference is rare. It appears only when time is contracted and the interfering material greatly increased, a situation that rarely occurs in real life.

The idea that forgetting might be motivated was first suggested by *Freud* (1901). He argued that memories which might be considered disturbing are repressed into the unconscious mind. Research by *Bower* (1981) has suggested that negatively charged memories are more likely to be remembered when subjects are in a 'negative' mood. These memories do not appear to be as accessible under normal conditions. It appears that mood creates a mental 'set' which determines what is likely to be remembered. Such an explanation has been used to explain the rather selective memories of depressives who appear more likely to remember negative memories than positive ones, thus accentuating their depression. Freud's explanation of motivated forgetting is challenged by *Eysenck's* (1980) finding that emotionally charged memories, be they pleasant or unpleasant are more likely to be remembered, as they appear to stand out more in our memory.

More recent explanations of forgetting have tended to accentuate the role of *context* and *cues* in the retrieval or non-retrieval of information. *Tulving* (1974) claimed that the 'retrievability' of a memory was governed by the retrieval cues which were encoded at the same time as the material to be remembered. These cues may be internal (psychological or physiological states) or contextual (environmental variables). The former, *state-dependent forgetting* suggests that the internal state of our body affects our memory. *Goodwin et al.* (1969) showed how alcoholics, when they were sober, were unable to remember things that they had hidden when they were drunk. Once they were drunk again, however, they were able to remember. *Godden and Baddeley* (1975) demonstrated the importance of context on recall. Divers were less able to recall word lists if the context of recall (under water or on land) was different to the context of learning. This difference was not, however, apparent in recognition tasks.

A final explanation of forgetting might be inferred from the *depth of processing* model (*Craik and Lockhart*, 1972). Information which is accepted passively, or is processed at a fairly shallow pereceptual level is less likely to be remembered. *Bower and Karlin* (1974) showed how this might work for memory of faces. Subjects who were required to make more complex judgements about faces (e.g. 'Is it an honest face?'), rather than simple judgements ('Is it male or female?') were better able to later identify these faces. However, as with all research in this area, it is very difficult to know for certain the type of processing that has *actually* taken place, so the argument about processing and retention becomes somewhat circular.

The results of the preceding research models have highlighted the importance of context, physiological state, encoding cues and depth of processing for the retrieval of a memory. Forgetting occurs when these optimal conditions are not met. The earlier, more global explanations of forgetting as trace decay, unlearning through interference, or motivated forgetting, appear less able to explain the retrieval problems and enhancements demonstrated in such research.

STUDENT'S ANSWER WITH EXAMINER'S COMMENTS

Question 1

Over the years, there have been a number of theories relating to the organisation of information in memory. Experiments and theories by people such as Mandler, Weist, Tulving and Pearlstone, Collins and Quillian, Collins and Loftus, and Bartlett, have given a great deal of insight into organization of memory.

One of the main features of organization is categorical clustering, where pre-categorized word lists are to be be memorized. These words are often recalled by first placing them into the categories. As this is experimenter imposed organization, *Mandler* (1967) looked at subject imposed organization. Subjects were asked to rehearse their word lists out loud. Mandler found that, with words that had no obvious categorical structure, the subjects made categories themselves, and recalled words in this way. It was also found that of these subjects, those who used the most categories could recall more. There have been a number of arguments as to whether organization occurs at storage/learning or retrieval. *Weist* (1972) looked at organization during storage, while *Tulving and Pearlstone* (1966) looked at retrieval.

Candidate is starting to sacrifice critical discussion for less effective description of studies

Weist gave subjects word lists to memorize and asked them to recall the words using categories. On average, those who used seven categories recalled 20 more words than those who used just two. This was taken as evidence that the more categories there are, in general, the more information will be recalled. Tulving and Pearlstone also gave subjects word lists to memorize, who were then tested for free recall. They were then given retrieval cues (i.e. the actual category names), and managed to recall more words. This may have been due to too many categories to memorize. From this, it was decided that there is a two-tier hierarchy. Categories are in the top level, and members in each category are in the bottom level. As memory does have some limitations, Mandler suggested that people cannot recall more than five things from any single level. However, this is not realistic, as there are many people who have amazing memories, and most people can recall more than ten things.

More needs to be made of this point

Collins and Quillian (1969) drew up a hierarchical network, which was supposed to give an idea of the organization present in memory. Each level consists of several concepts and their properties, e.g. 'a canary can sing'. Collins and Quillian tested subjects by asking them to verify questions, e.g. 'can a canary sing?' followed by 'can a canary fly?' followed by 'does a canary have skin?' With each question that followed, the time taken to verify them got slower and slower. *Collins and Quillian* suggested this was because, with each question that followed, the number of hierarchical levels between concept and property was continually increasing. Where properties and concepts were on the same level, verification was immediate.

This theory has been criticised. First of all, the question 'does a canary have skin?' would cause anyone to pause. It does not really make sense, as most people would never have encountered this sentence before. It is not familiar.

Good point, and showing evidence guides reading

Collins and Loftus (1975) changed the main conclusion, and decided that speed of verification was really determined by semantic relatedness. Words which were closely related were recalled more easily than if they were not.

Bartlett (1932) claimed that schemata affected organization. Semantic memory is often used successfully because people infer the correct answer. Bartlett gave an example of inferring with his 'War of the ghosts' experiment. As it was from a different culture, it was difficult to infer, and so, subjects tended to fill in the gaps with conventional English, when told to re-write/re-tell the story.

All of the evidence shows that organization of information does actually aid/benefit the memory, whatever form of organization is used.

❝❝ Quite a good essay which is focussed on organisation, but is let down somewhat by its less well developed critical discussion, i.e. it is primarily descriptive. This is probably characteristic of a C grade. ❞❞

REVIEW SHEET

1. What is meant by the multi-store model of memory?

    _____

    _____

2. Give *three* evaluative points relating to the multi-store model.

    _____

    _____

    _____

3. What are the *three* parts of the working memory, and what do they do?

    _____

    _____

    _____

4. Give *two* criticisms of the working memory model.

    _____

    _____

5. Distinguish between episodic and semantic memory.

    _____

    _____

6. Distinguish between declarative and procedural knowledge.

    _____

    _____

7. What are the two major assumptions of the depth of processing theory?

    _____

    _____

    _____

8. What is meant by the *circular argument* applied to depth of processing explanations.

    _____

    _____

9. How did Collins and Quillian explain organisation of information in memory?

    _____

    _____

10. What was the major difference between Collins and Quillian's original theory and the *spreading activation theory*?

_____

_____

11. In relation to schemata in memory, explain each of the following.
    1. Rationalisation
    _____

    2. Flattening
    _____

    3. Sharpening
    _____

12. What does the *encoding specificity* principle state?

_____

_____

13. State *three* ways that research into memory has been used in an applied setting.

    1.
    _____

    2.
    _____

    3.
    _____

13. On which theoretical explanations of memory are each of these applications based?

    1.
    _____

    2.
    _____

    3.
    _____

INFORMATION PROCESSING AND SELECTIVE ATTENTION

GETTING STARTED

The information processing tradition became established in psychology some 25 years ago. In this chapter, the aims are two-fold, one is to look at this tradition in general terms, and the second is to look at a specific aspect of **information processing**, namely **selective attention**. Note also that in the AEB syllabus, the emphasis is on *selective* attention rather than *divided* attention. If a question asks for theories or evidence relating to selective attention, then material on divided attention will not be credited by the examiner. If a question appears which is a general question on attention (i.e. does not specify selective attention), then material on divided attention can be credited. Make sure you are aware of the distinctions between the two, and can provide *relevant* content. That way, you won't be wasting your time writing about material that isn't going to get any marks.

Common themes for questions in this area are:

■ Discussion of the assumptions and usefulness of the information processing approach to the explanation of cognitive processes. (*Note: This may be specifically applied to attention.*)
■ Discussion of theories and evidence on the nature of selective attention.

THE INFORMATION PROCESSING APPROACH

SELECTIVE ATTENTION

THEORIES OF SELECTIVE ATTENTION

THE INFORMATION PROCESSING APPROACH TO ATTENTION

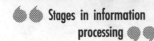

ESSENTIAL PRINCIPLES

For the period up to the end of the 1970s, cognitive psychologists generally accepted the views put forward by Broadbent, that **information processing** could be seen as a series of stages. Processing took place at each of these stages, during which different processes were activated, each of which transformed the stimulus in some way. This process was seen as largely stimulus driven, or **bottom-up processing**. This approach was exemplified by Atkinson and Shiffrin's multi-store model of memory, where information was thought to *flow* through the different processing stages in a sequential manner.

Bottom-up or top-down processing?

One of the problems with a model of information processing which relies exclusively on stimulus driven processing is that it takes no heed of the past experience or expectations of the individual doing the processing.

This latter set of influences constitutes **top-down** processing. Gibson's direct perception, for example, sees perceptual processing as a largely stimulus driven activity, whereas Gregory sees perception largely as a matter of inference, or top-down processing. Some theorists (e.g. *Neisser*, 1976) interpret perception as a far more active process, with an interaction of the two, the latter guiding the observer to sample certain aspects of the environment, and the former acting to monitor the accuracy of the guiding perceptual schema.

Serial and parallel processing

💧💧 Serial vs parallel processing 💧💧

Traditional information processing models see processing as **serial**, i.e. a *flow* of information from one stage to another. Processing tasks are thus completed one after the other. More contemporary views see the possibility of **parallel processing**, in which a number of tasks can be performed at the same time. *Eysenck* (1993) suggests that the predominance of the other type of processing depends largely on the processes necessary to solve a paricular task. Practice on a particular task seems to determine whether or not a person will engage in parallel processing. If someone is highly skilled at a task, they will display far more parallel processing than someone who is less practiced.

Models of parallel processing are still very new in cognitive psychology, and some critics (e.g. *Cowan*, 1988) regard them as too speculative to replace the serial processing of traditional models.

Computer models of processing

One way to try and make sense of the nature of information processing is to draw an analogy between human cognitive processing and **computer processing**. There are many similarities between the way in which computers process information, and human information processing. Both have some sort of central processing system (the attention system in humans) which has a limited capacity. Both receive new information, combine it with existing stored information, and produce an appropriate response. However, there are also important differences between the two. Until recently, few computers were able to process information in the parallel way possible in human cognition. Even then, as *Rumelhart* (1986) suggests such computer models are *inspired* by human cognition rather than being actual models of it. Neither do computers process material in a *meaningful* way. Both involve the processing of *symbols*, but only human cognition involves **semantic** processing, i.e. involves *understanding* of the symbols it manipulates. This is probably the main weakness of this approach, computer models are only *models* of processing, not accurate representations of human cognitive functioning.

💧💧 Only humans use semantic processing 💧💧

Neisser and ecological validity

💧💧 Artificial rather than real world processing 💧💧

One of the fiercest critics of traditional information processing models is *Neisser* (1976). He argues that most models have developed from highly artificial laboratory conditions, and therefore lack relevance to processing in the real world (i.e. they lack **ecological validity**). His proposal that cognitive psychologists should concern themselves far more with the conditions under which processing takes place in the real world presents problems of establishing sufficient experimental control to produce *reliable* data, yet sufficient real life relevance to make the results ecologically valid. However, experimental work has led to practical applications which seem to show the same benefits and deficits found in laboratory studies of cognitive processing (see for example *Practical applications of memory research* in Chapter 5).

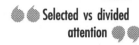

SELECTIVE ATTENTION

● ● Selected vs divided attention ● ●

It is important to make a distinction between *selective* attention and *divided* attention. **Selective attention** involves tasks where a person is required to respond to only one stimulus at a time, whilst perhaps being presented with other stimuli at the same time. **Divided attention** is characterised by tasks which require attention and processing of two or more stimuli at the same time. As the AEB syllabus only specifies *selective* attention, this is the only one which will be covered here.

Techniques of studying selective attention

● ● Binaural and dichotic listening ● ●

Early research used the **binaural** listening task, where two messages spoken by the same person were played to both ears at the same time. Typically, subjects found it very difficult to disentangle the messages when the only difference was one of meaning.

Later research has used the **dichotic listening** task, where different messages are fed into each ear. The subject then has to *shadow* (i.e. repeat aloud) one message. Typically, subjects are unable to extract more than the most basic physical characteristics from the non-attended message.

THEORIES OF SELECTIVE ATTENTION

1. BROADBENT (1958)

Broadbent proposed a single channel processor, in which stimuli first entered a sensory buffer. One stimulus is selected for further processing, by passing through a filter. This filter *selects* stimuli for further processing on the basis of their *physical* characteristics (e.g. novelty, loudness, intensity etc.). This is necessary to prevent the information processing system from becoming overloaded. Stimuli not selected for processing remain in the sensory buffer but decay rapidly.

Evidence for Broadbent's theory

● ● Evidence for single channel processing ● ●

The theory can explain *Cherry's* (1953) finding that subjects were unable to process characteristics of a second message such as the language or speech order, but were able to detect a physical tone inserted in the message (novelty).

Broadbent (1958) found that subjects were more likely to recall pairs of digits ear by ear rather than in pairs. Thus if 3,7,4 were presented to one ear, and at the same time 5,2,8 were presented to the other, the numbers 374528 would be recalled in that order. This suggests that the filter selected only one input at a time.

Evaluation of Broadbent's theory

1. *Eysenck and Keane* (1990) claim that the inability of naive subjects to shadow successfully was more due to their unfamiliarity with the shadowing task than an inability of the attentional system. They point out that experienced researchers on the shadowing task can often shadow both messages successfully.

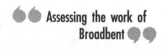
● ● Assessing the work of Broadbent ● ●

2. *Allport et al.* (1972) found that if the incoming stimuli were different, particularly in terms of their sensory modality, processing of both stimuli at the same time was possible. This is at odds with Broadbent's idea of a single channel processor.
3. Research by *von Wright et al.* (1975) established that stimuli might be processed without conscious awareness of processing. Pairing a word with an electric shock, they then presented the word (without shock) in the unattended message. Without them being aware of it, the GSR (a measure of emotional arousal) of the subject indicated that the word was actually being processed.

Most researchers did tend to agree with one aspect of Broadbent's theory – the existence of a bottle-neck in processing. What they disagreed on was the position of the bottle-neck. Two alternative theories are:

TREISMAN (1964)

Treisman (1964) suggested that the unattended message *was* processed, but in an *attenuated* or diminished form.

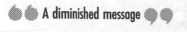

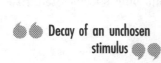
A diminished message

She proposed that a hierarchy of processing existed, with analysis of physical characteristics at one end of the hierarchy, and analysis of meaning at the other. If sufficient capacity for full stimulus analysis was *not* available, the higher levels would be omitted for the attenuated message.

Treisman's theory was thus able to account for the apparent processing of non-attended messages which appeared so problematic for Broadbent's theory.

DEUTSCH AND DEUTSCH (1963)

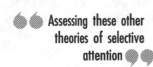
Decay of an unchosen stimulus

Deutsch and Deutsch (1963) proposed that all stimuli were fully analysed, with only one stimulus leading to a response on the basis of its relevance or importance in a specific situation. The unchosen stimulus then quickly decays. Thus, to Deutsch and Deutsch, the bottle-neck is much later in the process. This does seem a very uneconomical arrangement, but as *Eysenck and Keane* (1990) point out, lack of economy is not a valid reason for rejecting a theory.

Evidence and evaluation

Assessing these other theories of selective attention

1. *Treisman and Geffen* (1967) had subjects shadow one of two simultaneous messages, and at the same time monitor *both* messages in order to detect target words. Detection would then be indicated by tapping. According to Treisman's theory, detection on the attenuated message should be less than in the shadowed message, whereas Deutsch and Deutsch's model would predict no difference (due to both messages being fully analysed). In fact, the detection rate was much greater in the shadowed message.
2. Evidence from the von Wright study (*von Wright*, 1975), support the Deutsch and Deutsch proposal that *all* stimuli are analysed for meaning.

FLEXIBILITY AND SELECTIVE ATTENTION

Johnston and Heinz, (1978) suggested that the more stages of processing that a stimulus went through, the greater the demands on the processing capacity. Selection must therefore take place as early as possible, subject to the circumstances.

Research by *Johnston and Heinz* (1979) involved giving subjects a shadowing task in which target and non-target words were presented to both ears. In one condition, the non-target words were spoken in a female voice, and the target words in a male voice. In the other condition, both target and non-target words were spoken in the same male voice. According to the Deutsch and Deutsch model, there should be no difference in the number of non-target words recalled in the two conditions. There was, however, just such a difference with the numbers of non-target words recalled being much higher when subjects could not make an early discriminatory decision (i.e. male or female voice).

The conclusion from this and other similar studies is that selective attention is a more flexible process than previous theories had imagined. The amount of processing given to non-selected stimuli appears to be determined by the circumstances and task demands placed upon the processor.

Alternative perspectives on selective attention

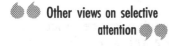
Other views on selective attention

1. *Neisser* (1976) criticised conventional explanations of attention. Laboratory studies typically involve situations where the subject has no active part to play in the selection of information. He considered that attention in real life involved an active need to build up information within a specific context, rather than a passive filtering out of unwanted information.
2. *Benjafield* (1992) concludes that contemporary research models no longer support the idea of a selective attentional filter. He suggests that people have a genuine ability to divide their attentional resources rather than switching rapidly back and forth between two tasks.

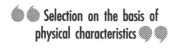

THE INFORMATION PROCESSING APPROACH TO ATTENTION

Early view of information processing

Although most attentional processes might be seen as a form of imformation processing, the debate on the *nature* of this processing is typified in the work of *Broadbent* (1958) and *Kahneman* (1973). Remember that mental activity is seen as the processing of information by the brain and that typically this processing is broken down into a number of stages.

The *information processing approach* to attention, therefore, is concerned with how information is transmitted and sees the attentional process as a way in which we select inputs for later processing. As the central processor cannot cope with all the information from the input stage, some information is discarded or attenuated (as in Treisman's theory) and thus fails to get beyond the early stage of processing.

Broadbent

This view of a *bottleneck* in processing, is demonstrated in Broadbent's single channel theory (*Broadbent*, 1958) Broadbent claimed that:
(a) The two ears acted like separate input channels of information.
(b) The system could only deal with one channel at a time.

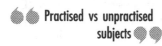

Selection on the basis of physical characteristics

Broadbent proposed the existence of a selective filter which selects one input channel for attentional processing. This filter would select on the basis of *physical* characteristics. It could not according to the model, select on the basis of *meaning*, as this is not a physical characteristic.

Evaluation of Broadbent's model

You might like to consider the accuracy of this model in the light of later models and research presented earlier in this chapter. It is possible when interpreting the results of Broadbent's study to view the difficulties faced by Broadbent's subjects as being the difficulty of responding to two conflicting stimuli. *Moray* (1969), suggested that selective attention experiments such as Broadbent's typically involve unpractised subjects. As they become more practised on a novel task, they become more effective processors, and the attentional deficit discovered by Broadbent largely disappears

Practised vs unpractised subjects

There is little doubt that such experimental work tells us little about attentional processes in real life. *Neisser* (1976) has suggested that attention should not be seen as a *process*, but as a *skill*. As tasks become more familiar, we become better able to allocate resources in an efficient manner.

Attention seen as a type of skill

Thus, modern attention theories talk in terms of *resource allocation* rather than of a single channel processor that can cope with only one channel at a time.

Kahneman

Kahneman's model of divided attention (*Kahneman*, 1973) proposes a model of attention which is based around the idea of *mental efforts*. This is a description of how demanding the processing of a particular input might be. Some tasks might be relatively *automatic* (in that they make few demands in terms of mental effort) despite the fact that they have a high information load. Kahneman thus proposes that:
(a) Some activities are more demanding (and therefore require more mental effort) than others.
(b) The total available processing capacities may be increased or decreased by other factors such as arousal.
(c) Several activities can be carried out at the same time, provided their total effort does not exceed the available capacity.
(d) Rules or strategies exist which determine allocation of resources to various activities and to various stages of processing. Attentional *capacity* will thus reflect the demands made at the perceptual level, the level at which the input is interpreted or committed to memory and the response selection stage.

Comment

Kahneman thus believes in the existence of a *central processor* which operates a *central allocation policy*, constantly evaluating the demands made by each task and adjusting attention accordingly.
Some critics of this model have suggested that such is our ability to develop skills that it becomes impossible to accurately judge the limits or capacity of the processing

system. *Allport* (1980) suggests that interference occurs when similar tasks compete for the same processing mechanisms, yet dissimilar tasks do not create the same level of mutual interference, therefore the individual can accomodate both.

EXAMINATION QUESTIONS

1. Discuss the assumptions and usefulness of the information processing approach in cognitive psychology.   *(25)*
2. Discuss the contribution that research on information processing has made to our understanding of attention.   *(25)*
                                                                                (AEB 1992)
3. Describe and evaluate experimental studies of selective attention.   *(25)*
                                                                                (AEB 1991)
4. (a) Describe techniques used in the experimental study of selective attention. *(5)*
   (b) Describe and evaluate *two* theories or models of selective attention.   *(20)*
                                                                                (AEB 1993)

ANSWERS TO EXAMINATION QUESTIONS

OUTLINE ANSWERS TO QUESTIONS 1 AND 2

Question 1

You are referred to the material at the start of this chapter (the information processing approach) which has largely been written in the form of an essay. Note that the material in this 'essay' is drawn from a variety of different areas of cognitive psychology (perception, computer models of thought, memory) therefore shows evidence of *eclecticism* (an AEB *Skill B*) i.e. selecting material from different areas in order to construct an argument.

Question 2

This is quite a tricky question, and it is easy to misread its requirements. The question is really asking for two things;

■ An account of research insights from the information processing approach (these may include the work of Broadbent, Shannon, Craik and Lockhart for example).
■ How these insights have helped psychologists understand the nature of attention.

The information processing approach has contributed to attention in a number of ways such as:

1. Broadbent's single channel processing system and his later work (e.g. the Maltese cross model, where a *central processor* allows us to rapidly switch our attention from one task to another – this is an example of *divided* attention).
2. Treisman's attenuator model and her later work on *feature detection theory* (i.e. in order to attend to objects in our world, we must extract the features of those objects in a process called pre-attentive processing).
3. Work on *automatic* processing (Kahneman) which sees attentional resources being allocated by a central processor which constantly monitors the level of demand of each task.
4. Baddely's idea of a central capacity processor (an aspect of his *working memory* model) which co-ordinates and controls behaviour.

TUTOR'S ANSWER

Question 3

Experimental investigations of selective attention usually involve a subject responding specifically to one stimulus from a presentation of more than one.

Early research by *Cherry* (1953) used the binaural task, where two messages spoken by the same person were played to both ears at the same time. Typically, subjects found it very difficult to disentangle the messages if the only difference between them was one of meaning. Later research has tended to use a dichotic listening task where different messages are fed into each ear. Subjects are then required to shadow one message. Typically, subjects are unable to extract more than the most basic physical characteristics from the non-attended message.

Studies of selective attention have been generated by the many models explaining attention. *Broadbent* (1958) dichotically presented pairs of numbers to subjects' ears (one of each pair to each ear). If pairs of numbers were presented 4-6, 5-9, 2-7, they were recalled in the order 452697, demonstrating that each ear acted as a processing channel, and one channel operated at a time.

Such research provided strong evidence for the existence of a single channel processor, but research by *Underwood* (1974) cast doubt on the validity of these conclusions. Underwood found that with subjects unused to the shadowing task, recall of material from the non-shadowed stimulus was extremely limited. However, when using subjects who were used to the shadowing task, recall of information from the non-shadowed stimulus was much higher.

Other research (*Allport et al.*, 1972) found that if the sensory modality of the incoming stimuli were different, then processing of both stimuli at the same time was much more likely.

Broadbent's central proposal was that unselected material would remain in a sensory buffer, where it would quickly decay. It would not, therefore, receive anything but the most rudimentary processing. Evidence from *von Wright et al.* (1975) challenged this assumption. They established that stimuli might be processed without conscious awareness. By pairing a word with an electric shock, and then presenting the word (without shock) in the unattended message, they produced GSR increases to the word without the subjects being aware of it.

Broadbent's theory clearly could not deal with the apparent processing of non-attended stimuli. Two alternative theories, those of Treisman, and Deutsch and Deutsch, provided explanations of how this might be possible. Treisman suggested that the unattended message was processed, but in an attenuated form. Deutsch and Deutsch proposed that a selective filter for processing did exist, but it was placed much further on in the processing sequence.

The implication of the Deutsch and Deutsch model is that all stimuli are processed, but only one stimulus leads to a response on the basis of its relevance or importance to a specific situation. Whilst the Deutsch and Deutsch explanation appears somewhat uneconomical, *Eysenck and Keane* (1992), point out that a model's lack of economy is insufficient cause for its rejection.

In an effort to resolve the problem of late versus early selection, *Treisman and Geffen* (1967) carried out research in which subjects shadowed one of two simultaneous messages, and at the same time monitored both messages in order to detect target words. Detection would be indicated by tapping. According to Treisman's theory, detection on the attenuated message would be less than on the shadowed message, whereas Deutsch and Deutsch's model would predict no difference in the detection rate. Treisman and Geffen found that the detection rate was much greater in the shadowed message than in the attenuated message, thus providing support for the early selection model rather than the late selection model.

Johnston and Heinz (1978) gave subjects a shadowing task in which target and non-target words were presented to both ears. In one condition, the non-target words were spoken in a female voice, and the target words in a male voice. In the other condition, both target and non-target words were spoken in the same male voice. Subjects were thus able to discriminate between target and non-target words early on in one condition (sex of voice) but not in the other. According to the Deutsch and Deutsch model, there should be no difference in the number of non-target words recalled in the two conditions (i.e. early selection would not take place). However, contrary to this position, the number of non-target words recalled was much lower in the condition where subjects were able to make an early discrimination about the target and non-target words.

The conclusion from this and other similar studies is that selective attention is a more flexible process than previous theories had imagined. The amount of processing given to non-selected stimuli appears to be determined by the circumstances and task demands placed upon the processor.

Filter theories have been criticised by *Neisser* (1976) who claims that the laboratory investigation of selective attention typically only deals with what is *done* to a person rather than what a person actively *selects* from the stimuli. Neisser proposed that perception was a process of selecting from the information available rather than simply filtering out unwanted information.

Benjafield (1992) concludes that contemporary research models no longer support the idea of a selective attentional filter. He suggests that people have a genuine ability to divide their attentional resources rather than switching rapidly back and forth between two tasks.

STUDENT'S ANSWER WITH EXAMINER'S COMMENTS

Question 4

(a) Selective attention is the response given when many messages are given at once. The message selected to attend to is the one with the most interesting informative content. Many techniques have been used to study selective attention. Split-span dichotic listening (Broadbent) is one. The subject is then asked to repeat the digits pair by pair, or ear by ear. Broadbent found that subjects gave a more accurate response when asked to give the ear by ear account.

Shadowing is another technique which was first introduced by *Cherry* (1953) to help him study the cocktail party phenomenon, where people can 'home in' on one particular conversation when there are many going on. Dual task techniques were used by Kahneman to show that when a subject is attending to one thing, they can also attend to another.

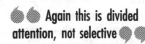 **This isn't *selective* attention therefore it isn't relevant**

(b) There are many theories and models of selective attention, as it is such a difficult thing to understand, as people are able to attend to whatever they like, even when there are many things going on.

Anne Treisman's 'attenuation' model of attention points out that the unattended message (the messages which aren't being listened to, or really seen) is still taken into the short term memory after being through an attenuator. A semantic analyser then analyses the information, which is eventually stored in the short-term memory until it is discarded.

Treisman used bilingual subjects to experiment with. She gave them messages over headphones, in English in one ear, and in French (or another language) in the other ear. Both messages meant the same thing. All subjects admitted knowing both messages, but the English one was the most prominent. Treisman's studies used the shadowing technique, but the subjects may have attended to the unattended message, as there was no way of knowing that this wasn't happening.

Kahneman's 'capacity theory' of attention saw attention as a skill, which depends on the type of state of the subject. If the subject is aroused and alert, the attention capacity is greater than when the subject is lethargic.

Again this is divided attention, not selective

Kahneman's model has a central allocation of attention, where each task the subject is performing is given a kind of capacity, as to whether the task is important or not, or whether a lot of skill is needed or not. Kahneman used skilled pianists (in dual tasks) to demonstrate this point. The pianists were told to sight read while listening to something else over headphones. They did this extremely well, but doesn't this demonstrate shadowing instead of a dual task technique, as the pianists weren't actually asked what had come over the headphones. Kahneman doesn't explain how his subjects could determine the most important task from the others.

Of the two theories, not one has given the whole idea of attention as a cognitive skill, which can be given to any stimulus. As in Cherry's cocktail party phenomenon, the attended message has usually got a content which interests the specified subject, so to get a more accurate idea of attention, subjects would have to have the same interests.

This is unfortunate because a lot of the material is irrelevant. Material on divided attention could have been made relevant (as evaluation of the concept of selective attention) but wasn't. Treisman's theory was never really developed either, so this answer is probably characteristic of an F.

REVIEW SHEET

1. What is the difference between *top-down* processing and *bottom-up* processing?

_____

_____

2. How does Neisser integrate the ideas of top-down and bottom-up processing?

_____

_____

3. What is the difference between *parallel* and *serial* processing?

_____

_____

4. Give *two* similarities and *two* differences between human thought and computer models of thought.

_____

_____

5. What is the difference between selective and divided attention?

_____

_____

6. What is involved in the dichotic listening task?

_____

_____

7. Whereabouts in the processing sequence, according to the following theorists, is the attentional filter?

Broadbent

_____

Treisman

_____

Deutsch and Deutsch

_____

8. Give two criticisms of Broadbent's theory.

_____

_____

9. What were the conclusions from the Treisman and Geffen study?

_____

_____

10. What does Benjafield feel is the problem with traditional models of selective attention?

_____

_____

11. Kahneman explains that some processing may be relatively automatic. What does he mean by this?

_____

_____

12. What did Neisser mean by 'attention as a skill'.

_____

_____

13. State Kahneman's four proposals relating to the information processing approach.

1.

_____

2.

_____

3.

_____

4.

_____

7

AFFILIATION, ATTRACTION AND PREJUDICE

GETTING STARTED

The grouping together of these areas is largely driven by the syllabuses. For example in the AEB syllabus these topics make up the whole of subsection (b) in the social psychology option.

These are areas which often tempt students into writing a whole range of subjective opinion which lacks psychological support. There is a surprising wealth of evidence available in the texts on these areas, you should familiarise yourself with a selection of studies for each area.

Information contained in this chapter should enable you to cover the following themes:

- **Psychological explanations of the processes of affiliation.**
- **Explanations for the formation, maintenance and breakdown of friendships.**
- **Psychological insights into the origins and reduction of prejudice.**

Useful definitions

Affiliation. This refers to the process by which people seek the company of others. It is also seen as a motivational variable, in that people differ in their *need to affiliate*.

Attraction. This may be explained in any number of ways. It refers to the characteristics and processes that draw certain people together. Discussion in this chapter will concentrate on friendships rather than sexual attraction or romantic love.

Prejudice. This refers to a particularly strong, usually negative attitude toward a person, group or issue. It often persists despite evidence to the contrary, and may also be characterised by *discriminative* behaviour such as *racism, sexism* or *ageism*.

AFFILIATION

THEORETICAL MODELS OF ATTRACTION

THE BREAKDOWN OF RELATIONSHIPS

ORIGINS OF PREJUDICE

THE REDUCTION OF PREJUDICE

AFFILIATION

ESSENTIAL PRINCIPLES

The term **affiliation** has already been defined in the previous section.

Reasons for affiliation

Avoidance of loneliness. Social loneliness occurs in the absence of a social network of friends and relatives. Reactions differ, in that some people may tend towards solitary lifestyles, whilst others actively seek to make social contacts to eliminate the negative feelings of loneliness.

 Some reasons for affiliation

Reduction of anxiety. Being around other people may reduce anxiety in a number of ways. Research by *Schachter* (1959) tested different explanations for why people sought the company of others in order to reduce anxiety:

Groups can reduce anxiety

a) Anxiety is reduced directly, simply because there is 'safety in numbers'.
b) Other people may act as a distraction, thereby indirectly reducing our anxiety.
c) Others may serve as a source of information, thus reducing our anxiety as we attain better 'cognitive clarity' about whatever it is which is causing the anxiety.
d) Others provide emotional support, and provide us with a way of evaluating and adjusting our own emotional responses through 'social comparison.'

Schachter's research showed most support for the 'social comparison theory', suggesting that comparison with the behaviour of others gives us cues as to appropriate behaviour and to verify our own responses.

Affiliation for attention. People crave the company of others so they can be the centre of attention. People high on this attentive need affiliate only if the people they affiliate to are likely to be appreciative. (*Hill*, 1987).

Critical discussion of Schachter's research

Schachter's main conclusion was that people respond to uncertainty and anxiety toward external events by seeking the company of others. This is to evaluate their own responses through a comparison with the responses of others in a similar situation. Critics of this point of view have argued that the circumstances and the characteristics of the affiliating individuals will determine why they affiliate. *Shaver and Klinnert* (1982) argued that Schacter's 'cognitive clarity' explanation could explain the tendency of people to often prefer the company of intelligent, competent others, whilst at other times, and in other circumstances, people will prefer the emotional support offered by friends and relations. Research by *Dakof and Taylor* (1990) supported this view. Cancer victims appear to expect informational support from the medical profession, as well as support from groups of people who had perhaps gone through, or were going through, the same process, and emotional support from friends and family. It is also clear, that the circumstances of Schachter's research, students waiting to receive electric shocks, may be questionable in how closely they relate to the reasons why people affiliate in the real world. As such they may lack **ecological validity**, i.e. not be relevant to real life behaviour. However, this need for reassurance which characterises the social comparison theory, is evident in the behaviour of many people who experience real life trauma (e.g. *Humphriss*, 1989, studying the behaviour of people after the earthquake in California in 1989)

Criticisms of groups as a means of reducing anxiety

THEORETICAL MODELS OF ATTRACTION

The term **attraction** is defined in the first section of this chapter.

THE REINFORCEMENT–AFFECT MODEL (BYRNE, 1971)

This model of **attraction** suggests that we are attracted to people who *reinforce* us in some way. One obvious example of reinforcement would be to be attracted to those people who hold similar attitudes to ourselves, in that it reinforces our belief in our own attitudes.

The model proposes:

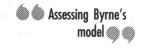

Reinforcement aids attraction

- The environment contains experiences which can be evaluated as either *good* or *bad*. Good experiences are potentially beneficial, whilst bad experiences are potentially harmful.
- Experiences which are seen as beneficial make us feel good, whilst harmful experiences make us feel bad.
- We like things that make us feel good, and dislike things that make us feel bad.
- Through the process of classical conditioning, we associate *people* with experiences that make us feel good or bad, are thus attracted to, or repelled by, them.

Evidence from *Byrne* (1971) and colleagues on these basic assumptions have made use of experiments where subjects see profiles of other 'people' and are asked to state how attracted or otherwise they are to that person. What Byrne found was that subjects based their decisions not only on the proportion of shared to not shared attitudes, but also on the importance of those attitudes to them.

Evaluation of the reinforcement–affect model

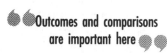

Assessing Byrne's model

- Despite the fact that research supporting the model can be criticised for its lack of *ecological validity* (in that it deals with people who never expect to meet the other person), it does enable researchers to establish the causal relationship between similarity and liking.
- The findings have been replicated in many different cultures and in different ages and occupational groups. The same findings are also apparent in both genders.
- The concept of reinforcement is somewhat loosely defined. It is difficult to predict what an individual will and will not find reinforcing, and therefore who will be attracted to who. It is easy, if not particularly informative to find examples of things that *could* be considered reinforcing in an existing relationship, but that does not guarantee that they are the factors which caused the liking in the first place.

THE INTERDEPENDENCE THEORY (THIBAULT AND KELLY, 1959)

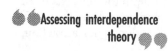

Outcomes and comparisons are important here

The **interdependence theory** differs from the reinforcement-affect theory in that it is more concerned with the development of relationships than with the initial attraction. According to this theory, individuals should try to maximise their *outcomes* in any situation. Outcomes are defined as rewards received minus costs incurred. Also important in this theory is the idea of *comparison*, a way of evaluating the relationship against some sort of standard of what they feel is appropriate to expect from the relationship. According to the theory, attraction may take place with only slightly positive outcomes, provided these are still greater than might be anticipated elsewhere.

Evaluation of interdependence theory

Assessing interdependence theory

- The theory proposes that individuals would be able to objectively calculate the projected rewards and costs of any relationship. This would be very difficult in practice.
- The theory supposes that the nature of interpersonal relationships is simpler than it actually is. Peoples opportunities for such relationships are more limited than the theory gives credit for.
- Despite the fact that all the positive outcomes might be present, attraction may still not take place, as individuals may interpret such consequences in a negative way (e.g. as intrusion, flirting, interference etc.).

INTERPERSONAL BALANCE THEORY (NEWCOMB 1961)

The **interpersonal balance theory** is a cognitive theory, and, as such predicts that people like to see the world in a balanced way. The theory proposes that we are attracted to people who share our attitudes as this makes for a balanced cognitive world. If these attitudes are not shared, or if one person behaves toward the other with a manner inconsistent with a friendship, this creates an inconsistency, or imbalance in the relationship, which must be removed either cognitively (reinterpreting the inconsistency) or behaviourally (changing or ending the friendship). Newcomb believed that the more attracted we were to someone, the more the pressure for our attitudes to become similar, in order to maintain this consistency.

Evaluation of interpersonal balance theory

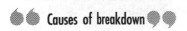

Assessing interpersonal balance theory

■ The original theory appeared to suggest that people needed cognitive consistency at all costs. This is now seen as a product of the time in which Newcomb was writing, as it is now known that people can put up with a great deal of inconsistency in their relationships.

■ Balance in a relationship can be achieved in many ways, which makes it difficult to predict what will happen in any one given situation.

■ Like the other theories discussed, the balance theory has a tendency to describe social relationships in an almost mathematical manner, which ignores other important factors such as the nature and content of any interaction, and the nature of the people themselves.

THE REPULSION HYPOTHESIS (ROSENBAUM, 1986)

Rosenbaum suggested in his **repulsion hypothesis** that rather than being attracted to people who hold similar attitudes to ourselves, we are initially attracted to all strangers, and only start to dislike them if we discover *dissimilarities* between them and us. Rosenbaum's research involved comparing 'liking ratings' given to photographs of other students in a 'no information condition' to those given to students with expressed similar attitudes to the raters. He found no differences between the two conditions.

Evaluation of the repulsion hypothesis

Assessing repulsion theory

■ It is difficult to create a true 'no information' condition. In the absence of information, people will often resort to the *false consensus effect*, i.e. they assume similarity, and given the nature of Rosenbaum's student raters, it is probable that they did just that.

■ Subsequent research (*Smeaton et al.*, 1989) found clear evidence to the contrary. As the perceived similarity of attitudes increased, so did the attraction, thus failing to support the repulsion hypothesis.

THE BREAKDOWN OF RELATIONSHIPS

Causes of breakdown

Interdependence theory

You may recall that in this theory, individuals are seen as trying to maximise their rewards and minimise their costs in a relationship. Under this theory, relationships might **breakdown** if the rewards from an existing relationship are less than we might expect, given previous rewards in the relationship. However, when compared with the alternatives (other people, isolation) the rewards of *staying* might be seen as greater than the rewards of going.

Dependency without attraction

In the above example, where the person stays because there are no better alternatives, there may be *dependency without attraction*. Here, our expectations are higher than our actual rewards, but the costs of going are too great. If the rewards of an existing relationship are both *less* than our expectations and *also* less than the anticipated rewards from alternatives, then there is neither dependency nor attraction, and the relationship may end.

Interpersonal balance theory

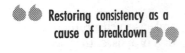

Restoring consistency as a cause of breakdown

The **interpersonal balance** theory proposes that perceived dissimilarities in important attitudes between two people cause a cognitive imbalance, and ending the relationship becomes a possible way to restore consistency in the individual's cognitive world. However, the theory fails to take into account the rather more human tendency to attempt to change attitudes through active measures such as nagging, discussion, argument and so on.

Transactional analysis (Byrne, 1964)

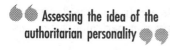
Three selves in interpersonal relationships

Complementary and crossed transactions

Transactional analysis has traditionally been associated with the resolution of the 'sick' aspects of relationships. According to Byrne, each of us has three distinct selves or needs in interpersonal relationships. Each of these selves, the *parent*, the *adult* and the *child* determine a particular pattern of behaviours which characterise that role. Within a relationship, if two adults operate at a level which is appropriate and desired (e.g. adult – adult or adult – child) then a **complementary transaction** exists. If, however, one partner operates at a level which is inappropriate or undesired by the other partner, then a **crossed transaction** exists. The needs of one, or both partners are not met, which puts a strain on the relationship.

Transactional analysis, as an explanation of the breakdown of relationships, however fails to meet the criteria necessary for a scientific theory. It is difficult to test the assumptions of the theory, as aspects of interactions may be given significance where none exists. Despite its limitations, however, transactional analysis provides a model for the active nature of human relationships, with its bargaining and negotiations, rather than the rather passive acceptance of events implied in the other theories discussed.

ORIGINS OF PREJUDICE

The term **prejudice** is defined in the first section of this chapter. There are a number of explanations as to the origins of prejudice.

PSYCHODYNAMIC EXPLANATIONS

Psychodynamic explanations of prejudice see it as the results of the individual's own personal conflicts. Prejudice is seen as a reaction to the insecurities of neurotic individuals.

The authoritarian personality (Adorno, 1950)

Main assumptions:

Authoritarian personalities

Authoritarian personalities have particular ways of viewing their social world. They are intolerant of ambiguity, overly respectful of authority, and appear hostile to any group which appears to challenge the status quo. Adorno's original subjects tended to idealise their parents, speaking of them as 'paragons of virtue'. Following interviews, it appeared that these subjects had experienced a very strict upbringing, and had repressed their hostility toward their parents.

This hostility becomes displaced onto other groups (i.e. minority groups) who are perceived as having the hostility toward authority that has been repressed in the subject and prejudice thus develops.

Thus authoritarian parents are seen as passing on their prejudices *indirectly*, with prejudice being a consequence of the authoritarian personality of their children.

Evaluation of the authoritarian personality

Assessing the idea of the authoritarian personality

■ More contemporary research by *Altemeyer* (1981) failed to replicate Adorno's central findings, particularly those relating to the type of child rearing experiences necessary to produce the authoritarian personality.

■ Adorno's measurement scale of authoritarian personality traits, the 'F' scale described someone who may well have been prejudiced at the time Adorno was writing. However, the centrality of authoritarianism within a particular culture has changed, with a great deal of evidence that it has diminished, particularly in Western culture. This seems to challenge the link between authoritarianism and prejudice, as the latter is still evident.

■ In Adorno's theory, the particular pattern of childrearing within a family is seen to determine prejudice. It seems more likely that such attitudes are now produced by social and cultural experiences rather than family ones. *Pettigrew* (1958) found evidence for *conformity* to racial prejudice, despite the fact that few of his subjects could be classified as 'authoritarian personalities'.

■ It is also clear that many prejudiced people are not only prejudiced but also contemptuous of traditional figures of authority. Motivational theories such as

Adorno's may lead to an underestimation of the extent of prejudice as it actually exists.

SOCIO-CULTURAL EXPLANATIONS

The emphasis of the **socio-cultural** explanations of prejudice is that stereotypes and prejudgements about others are embedded in a particular culture, and are therefore shared by its members.

Social identity theory (Tajfel, 1982)

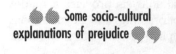

Some socio-cultural explanations of prejudice

Tajfel argued that the mere **identification** with a social group was sufficient to cause hostility towards 'outgroups'. In the original experiments by *Tajfel et al.* (1971), subjects were not aware that their division into groups had been arbitrary, but in later research by *Locksley et al.* (1982) even when subjects knew that they had been randomly assigned to groups, they still displayed strong 'in-group' preferences and 'outgroup' hostility.

Inter-group conflict (Sherif, 1966)

Sherif argues that if two groups have the same goal, and if one group is perceived as frustrating the other, then **inter-group** prejudice and hostility is inevitable. This idea was based on the famous 'Robbers Cave' study in which teams of boys at a summer camp were in competition with each other, and as a result of that competition, developed strong hostile stereotypes about the other group.

Sherif concluded that competition was sufficient cause for the development of prejudice and discrimination.

Scapegoating

The idea of **scapegoating** as a cause of prejudice is based on the Freudian idea of displacement, whereby substitute targets are used where hostility cannot be directed toward the original cause of the frustration. Frustration is also seen as inevitably leading to aggression. Scapegoats are usually socially legitimised groups, so it can be argued that culture prescribes who will be the targets of the prejudice even before it happens.

Evaluation of socio-cultural explanations

Assessing sociocultural explanations

Experimental studies of inter group hostility are, by virtue of the circumstances involved, artificial when compared to the real life situations in which prejudice develops and is expressed. *Tyerman and Spencer* (1983) suggested that Sherif's experiments produced only a transitory effect. The fact that such hostility was reduced when the groups worked together seemed to indicate that the members of the groups still saw themselves as belonging to the same superordinate group.

Reference to 'culture' seems to indicate that individuals are aware of what are the appropriate cultural reactions in any particular context. The idea of culture is being used in a rather abstract sense. Prejudiced reactions do actually create the culture so that people are constantly contributing to their *culture* rather than simply responding to it.

The value of the socio-cultural approach probably lies in its emphasis on wider issues in the determination of prejudice than are possible in the narrower personality theories previously discussed.

THE REDUCTION OF PREJUDICE

INTERGROUP CONTACT

Before increased contact can reduce prejudice, several conditions are necessary.

Conditions for reducing prejudice through intergroup contact

- People must have the opportunity to interact with each other and discover that some of their beliefs may be false.
- This interaction must be on equal status. Casual contact under existing roles may have little effect.
- Contact must provide evidence which disconfirms the negative traits perceived in the other group.

■ Increased intergroup contact must be supported by state or social agencies. School desegregation in the USA was seen as failing because it often lacked institutional support. People were not under psychological pressure to change their prejudiced attitudes because they were not convinced that what they were doing was seen as 'right'.

Research evidence

Minard (1952) studied miners in West Virginia, USA, and found that racial prejudice diminished underground, yet reappeared on the surface. It appeared that the miners found it socially permissible to be unprejudiced underground, but on the surface they were more influenced by social convention.

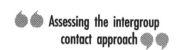 **Some empirical studies on common goals and the reduction of prejudice**

Jahoda (1961) found that white majority group members showed a dramatic decrease in preferred residential segregation after experience of black co-workers and neighbours.

Ramirez (1988) found that Hispanic high school students reported much less prejudice towards them where Hispanics occupied some of the authority positions in the school than when they did not.

Evaluation of the intergroup contact approach

Assessing the intergroup contact approach

■ In studies such as Jahoda's on residential desegregation, decreased prejudice is often found only where the housing is public (council), rather than when it is private. This suggests the existence of a whole range of different considerations in the minds of prejudiced individuals.

■ *Tajfel* (1982) suggests a *'loss of innocence'* compared to the optimism of the 50s and 60s. Intergroup contact also has the potential for *increased* prejudice as well as decreased prejudice. Situations that foster competition or which emphasise status differences between groups are likely to strengthen intergroup prejudice.

■ The procedures which bring about intergroup contact are likely to be evaluated by the group members. If such action is seen as fair, then its benefits in the reduction of prejudice are clear. *Nacoste* (1989) has demonstrated, however, that if the procedures which bring about such equal status contact are perceived as unfair by one group, then the beneficiaries of such action are likely to feel stigmatised, and prejudice toward them is strengthened.

PURSUIT OF COMMON GOALS

If competition for resources increases prejudice between groups, then it follows that if groups can be encouraged to co-operate towards the attainment of a **common** or **superordinate goal**, then hostility between the groups should diminish.

Research evidence

Sherif (1966) showed groups in conflict could work together if they were given a goal that could only be achieved through cooperation. Sherif arranged a series of joint projects for groups that had previously been at odds with each other. As a result of these projects, they became friendlier with each other and intergroup prejudice diminished.

Some empirical studies on common goals and the reduction of prejudice

Kramer and Brewer (1984) in laboratory studies of superordinate goals have established the importance of a change in group identity in reducing prejudice. Subjects were more co-operative when a superordinate group identity was emphasised than when intergroup identities were stressed.

Aronson (1978) studied the **jigsaw** method, in which each member of a group has responsibility for one part of a task, but is tested on the *whole* task. Each group member is therefore dependent on all the other members for their own success. Aronson believed that this method not only reduced the negative perceptions of members of other ethnic and gender groups, but also raised the self esteem of all group members, a necessary prerequisite for changing the hostile prejudices of group members.

Evaluation of the common goals approach

■ Although Sherif reported that cooperation over superordinate goals always proved successful in reducing aggression, this has not necessarily been the case in all

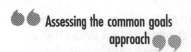

" Assessing the common goals approach "

similar research. *Worchel et al.* (1977) found that if cooperation over superordinate goals was not successful , and had been preceded by a competitive episode, then liking for the outgroup decreased rather than increased.

■ If groups do not have clear and complementary roles to play, and each groups contributions are not recognizable, liking for the other group actually decreases (*Brown and Wade*, 1987).

EXAMINATION QUESTIONS

1. Describe and evaluate the attempts of psychologists to explain the formation and breakdown of friendships.   *(25)*
                                                                          (AEB 1992)
2. (a) What do psychologists mean by the terms prejudice and discrimination?   *(4)*
   (b) Describe and evaluate *one* psychological study of prejudice reduction or discrimination reduction.   *(8)*
   (c) Critically consider why many attempts to reduce prejudice or discrimination have failed.   *(13)*
                                                                          (AEB 1992)
3. Describe and evaluate psychological insights into the origins of prejudice.   *(25)*
                                                                          (AEB 1993)

ANSWERS TO EXAMINATION QUESTIONS

OUTLINE ANSWER TO QUESTION 3

This is a fairly straightforward question. There are clearly two requirements, a *description* and an *evaluation* of appropriate material. It does ask for *psychological* insights, therefore personal opinion will tend to get very few if any marks.

A suggested outline is as follows:

1. A description of Adorno's 'authoritarian personality' theory, its psychodynamic origins, and an evaluation (in terms of methodology, history, and its underestimation of social factors such as conformity).
2. Discussion of sociocultural explanations such as the work of Tajfel (minimal groups) and Sherif (competition and prejudice).
3. The idea of scapegoating, its links with frustration-aggression theory and the importance of historical and economic factors in determining prejudice.

Note that the words *psychological insights* should be taken as meaning insights from theory *or* research. Note also that the question only asks for *origins*, therefore material on *reduction* will not be credited.

TUTOR'S ANSWER

Question 2

(a) The term *prejudice* refers to an attitude, usually negative, toward the members of a group based solely upon their membership of that group. It involves schemata for organizing, interpreting and recalling information towa rd that group of people and may predispose individuals to act in a way which is intolerant or unfair.

The term *discrimination* refers to a set of behaviours toward members of a categorized group which are unfair in comparison to members of other groups. They may occur at several levels, from simple avoidance to more active and hostile attacks upon the target. Discriminatory behaviours may be linked to underlying prejudiced attitudes or may be influenced more by social forces present at the time. They may also arise from a belief in the 'just world' in that discriminators may believe that their targets deserve such treatment.

(b) *Sherif* (1961) studied boys at a summer camp. Following their allocation to one of two groups, the boys demonstrated increased hostility toward the other group because of the competitive encounters between the two. Attempts to reduce the prejudices held by the two groups by the use of increased contact failed because the boys continued to view the encounters competitively. Sherif then set the boys to work on joint projects such as cooperating to fix a breakdown in the water supply. The key point about such cooperation was that it established superordinate goals, ie. goals which were desired by both groups but unattainable by one group alone. As a result of the two groups working together toward superordinate goals, many of the negative stereotypes each group held about the other disappeared. The boys became friendlier, seeing the good points in each other. Sherif found that for the duration of the camp, the majority of friendship choices were actually made with boys from the other group. This study lacked relevance to real life prejudice reduction on a number of counts. Firstly, the study took place over a relatively short period and was not dealing with prejudices which were more deep rooted. Secondly, the camp was a highly specific situation, the boys a specific and highly homogeneous group of individuals. It is possible, therefore, that the study may not have validity to wider issues in a wider social context. It is also evident, however, that the prejudiced attitudes that were developed during the study were not that easily eradicated. Many boys still went home with some hostile intergroup attitudes which raises ethical questions about the consequences of such research.

(c) Attempts to reduce prejudice have often failed because the circumstances of the attempt have failed to recreate the necessary conditions for reduction. *Worchel* (1977), commenting on studies such as Sherif's, noted that the imposition of superordinate goals may not always achieve their aims. In Sherif's studies, such cooperation always achieved it's aims, yet Worchel found that if cooperation did not achieve success, it might lead to less liking for the outgroup. It has also been established (eg. *Brown and Wade*, 1987) that in situations where the contributions of one group are not clearly recognisable by the other group, then such contributions might be undervalued, and liking for the other group might actually decrease. Other attempts to reduce prejudice in situations where the pursuit of common goals is inappropriate, have emphasised the importance of increased contact between prejudiced groups. *Jahoda* (1961) for example found that integrated housing projects involving white and black Americans produced a dramatic decrease in racial prejudice between the groups. However, such a decrease only seemed likely in public housing, attempts to control and reduce prejudice in integrated private housing projects have been less successful. Attempts to reduce prejudice are also likely to be evaluated by the majority group members. Procedures which offer to minority group members what are interpreted as undue advantage by the majority group members might strengthen prejudice toward them (*Nacoste*, 1989).

Aronson (1980) has reviewed the success and failure of integrated school projects in the USA in the 1960's. He suggests that prejudiced individuals who sent their children to schools in areas out of their own racial group experienced dissonance in that their behaviour was out of line with their attitude. They thus changed their prejudiced attitudes to regain consonance. Aronson suggested that when states did not give their full backing to integration procedures, then it gave prejudiced individuals justification for their attitudes which thus persisted. A final reason why attempts to reduce prejudice often fail comes from *Howitt et al.* (1992) who suggest that an individual's perception of their culture and it's norms (perhaps through exposure to stereotyped models in the media) causes them to react appropriately thus causing the perpetuation of a prejudiced culture through their participation in it.

STUDENT'S ANSWER WITH EXAMINER'S COMMENTS

Question 1

One of the main theoretical approaches to formation of friendship is the Exchange Theory first researched by *Thibault and Kelly* (1959). This theory recognizes the factors entailed in friendship ie. security, comfort, fun, etc, and sees them in terms of 'profit' and 'cost'. According to *Homan* (1974) the greater the 'profit' from a friendship, the greater the attraction to it. Contrasting with this is *Rubin* (1973) who dislikes this 'mercenary' concept in relationships and believes that in giving (cost) security, comfort, people receive internal joy and satisfaction. *Mills and Clark* (1980) recognize that such 'scorekept' friendships, in which each member demands more that the other, is doomed to failure. However, Rubin may not have as great a point as Homan, as the

❝❝ Lots of opening information which is also critical ❞❞

person is still gaining for him/herself by feeling internal satisfaction. Therefore, friendship may well occur from purely selfish motives.

Proximity and familiarity are key factors in formation of friendships. *Newcombe* (1961) offered male students free board and lodging in a Michigan boarding house if they took part in a study of aquaintancy. Students were given rooms randomly and after the first year, Newcombe found that friendships occurred where students shared values and beliefs. In the second year, Newcombe assigned students roomates either with those who shared their attitudes, or total opposites in this context. Predicting that friendships would occur only in 'matched' students resulted in a finding that familiarity was the key factor, as far more friendships formed than were predicted.

Zajonc et al. (1971) showed subjects photographs of strangers, and asked them to rate them in terms of likeability and dislikeability. Those that appeared most often were rated highest in likeability, least often rated highest in dislike ability. Therefore, it seems that people like what is familiar and dislike the unfamiliar.

Griffitch and Veitch (1974) paid thirteen men to spend ten days in a fall-out shelter. At the end of the study, men who shared interest, attitudes and values formed friendships. However, *Snyder and Franklin* (1980) believe that people like to think of themselves as unique individuals, therefore people of very similar characters may be disliked for this very reason. This also refers back to the 'selfish' facet to the individual in which choosing a friend may be purely beneficial to them, whether subconsciously or otherwise.

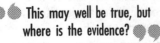 **Perhaps this is a point that warrants elaboration**

Aronson (1976) also believed this, according to his reward-cost principle, people like people who make entirely positive comments to them, and dislike negative comments. Therefore, forming a friendship is made up of many factors, charac ter, interest, values and expectations from the other person being entirely unique to the individual. However, many of the studies may be ecologically artificial, as they take place in the USA and are compiled of students – particularly men.

Many psychologists have found that lonely, introverted people are likely to have not practised social skills. They avoid eye-contact and smile less. Shy people are often perceived as 'snobbish' and 'aloof' resulting in people being 'put off'. In a sense, any relationships formed are already over as they are highly likely to be unsatisfying and short-lived.

A main factor of friendship breakdowns is when one member feels let-down and unsatisfied, and is putting unequal effort into the relationship. *Aronson* (1976) implies that if the cost is greater than the reward, the friendship will fail. *Argyle and Henderson* (1980) observe that there are 'rules of friendship' such as loyalty, support, comfort, etc. To break a major rule such as trust will invariably lead to breakdown: 'To disclose a friend or lover has been deceitful is devastating, more so, than deceit at the hand's of anyone else', *Duck* (1988).

Distance also plays a part, if it is increased between the members of a friendship (eg. one person moves 60 miles away) the cost of the friendship increases in the form of effort to maintain closeness and communication, *Aronson* (1976).

This may well be true, but where is the evidence?

Boredom and lack of stimulation also bring about failure, the feeling that the friendship was stagnant or 'wasn't going anywhere'.

Therefore, breakdown seems to refer mainly to Aronson's reward–cost principle and the exchange theory in that it is found unfulfilling and/or unequal. However, large studies on breakdown have not been done, most research on breakdown is to do with marriage and divorce, so perhaps the reason for breakdown has not been too difficult to pinpoint and expand on.

This is a difficult question to do well on, as there are four distinct parts to it. This candidate has handled the formation part of the question very well, but is less impressive on the breakdown part. Nevertheless the answer is probably characteristic of a grade B.

REVIEW SHEET

1. Define affiliation.

   _____

2. Give *three* reasons why the presence of others might reduce anxiety.

   _____
   _____
   _____

3. Research by Schachter (1959) found evidence for which explanation of affiliation?

   _____

4. Offer *two* evaluative points relating to Schachter's research.

   _____
   _____

5. What is the main proposal of the reinforcement-affect model?

   _____

6. Give *two* criticisms of this model.

   _____
   _____

7. What is proposed by interpersonal balance theory?

   _____
   _____

8. Give *two* criticisms of this theory.

   _____
   _____

9. What is proposed by interdependence theory?

   _____
   _____

10. Give *two* criticisms of this theory.

    _____
    _____

11. Briefly outline how interdependence theory explains the breakdown of relationships.

    _____
    _____
    _____

12. Under what conditions, according to transactional analysis, will relationships break down?

_____

_____

13. Give *two* characteristics of the authoritarian personality.

_____

_____

14. Give *two* criticisms of Adorno's theory.

_____

_____

15. How does the 'social identity theory' (Tajfel, 1982) explain prejudice?

_____

_____

16. What, according to Sherif, was sufficient cause for the development of prejudice?

_____

17. Give *two* criticisms of Sherif's conclusion.

_____

_____

18. What *three* conditions must be present if increased contact is to reduce prejudice?

_____

_____

_____

19. Summarise *two*, pieces of research which support the 'pursuit of common goals' approach to prejudice reduction.

1. _____

_____

2. _____

_____

20. Offer *two* criticisms of such an approach.

_____

_____

PRO- AND ANTI-SOCIAL BEHAVIOUR

GETTING STARTED

This chapter examines the issues behind the development of **pro-social** and **anti-social** behaviours. These terms are perhaps rather loose when describing behaviour as it is largely a matter of opinion as to what is pro- and what is anti-social behaviour. For the purposes of this chapter, altruism and helping will be described as pro-social behaviours, and aggression as an anti-social behaviour. It examines psychological explanations for the development of helping behaviour and bystander apathy. It will also examine psychological explanations for the origins of aggressive behaviour as well as recommendations for its reduction. It will also take a critical look at the media/aggression debate.

It is common to see aggression as being anti-social, and therefore bad, and cooperation as being good. In part this is a product of our belief that aggression is somehow a throwback to our animal ancestry. Quite apart from the role of aggression in bringing about social change, this biological view of aggression has been superceded by social psychological explanations. Thus, there has been a move away from the belief that aggressive behaviour somehow reflects the inner state of an individual.

The role of the psychologist is to avoid the simple scapegoating of television, alcohol and lack of discipline in order to gain a better understanding of a complex social phenomenon.

The social psychology of pro-social behaviour is not as well developed as the social psychology of aggression. As in some of the biological explanations of aggression, the process of natural selection may help to explain the transmission of socially beneficial behaviour through an individual's genes. Helping behaviour, alturism and pro-social behaviour are terms which are used interchangeably. Behaviourally they are identical, they may only differ in the underlying motives.

Common themes of questions in this area are:

- ■ **Discussion of psychological insights into altruism and helping behaviour.**
- ■ **Discussion of social psychological explanations of aggression and implications for its reduction.**
- ■ **Discussion of the relationship between the media and aggressive behaviour.**

BIOLOGICAL EXPLANATIONS OF ALTRUISM

PSYCHOLOGICAL EXPLANATIONS OF ALTRUISM

ORIGINS OF AGGRESSION

THE CONTROL OF AGGRESSIVE BEHAVIOUR

MEDIA INFLUENCES ON AGGRESSIVE BEHAVIOUR

ESSENTIAL PRINCIPLES

Defining altruism

Altruism is a term often used synonymously with *pro-social* behaviour and *helping* behaviour. It indicates some form of unselfish behaviour that benefits others yet involves some self-sacrifice from the altruist.

BIOLOGICAL EXPLANATIONS OF ALTRUISM

Reasons for altruism

Biological explanations of altruism stress the influence of natural selection in altruistic behaviour. Sociobiologists tend to explain altruistic behaviour in terms of either **kin selection** (we help those to whom we are genetically related) or **reciprocal altruism** (we help those whom we believe will help us in the future). According to sociobiologists, these *strategies* of behaviour ensure that each generation contains a proportion of altruists, as the gene for altruism has perpetuated itself through these strategies.

The *apparent* altruism explanation (apparent because altruistic behaviour is actually translated as genetic selfishness) runs into problems when applied to human beings for the following reasons:

Evaluation of biological altruism

Assessing biological altruism

1. This explanation suggests that genetically determined altruism is vital to the survival of a particular species. In human beings, this underestimates the effect that socialisation processes and general exposure to cultural norms mights have on the development of altruism.
2. Human altruism is far removed from the often simple behaviours (e.g. alarm calls, feeding behaviour) quoted as examples of animal altruism.

PSYCHOLOGICAL EXPLANATIONS OF ALTRUISM

Altruism clearly poses a problem for traditional theories of behaviour which tend to see people as basically selfish. In learning theory, for example, only behaviours that lead to positive consequences or *reinforcers* should become part of a persons behavioural repertoire. It is unlikely that many altruistic acts do this directly, although, it could be argued, that some do provide rewards *indirectly*, e.g. by raising the self-esteem of the altruist.

Some of the **psychological explanations** of altruism are as follows:

The empathy-altruism hypothesis

Empathy as a source of altruism

Batson (1987) suggests that many people help others because of the **empathy** they feel for them. (Empathy is defined as vicariously experiencing anothers emotions). Batson believes that these empathic feelings create an altruistic motivation to help which is based on 'feeling anothers pain' rather than on a selfish interest in satisfying ones own needs (i.e. reducing personal discomfort and distress). By experimentally manipulating the degree to which his subjects experienced empathy or personal distress in a potential helping situation. Batson was able to show that empathetically aroused subjects were more likely to help even when they could avoid their personal distress by escaping from the situation.

Critics of the empathy-altruism hypothesis suggest that empathic helpers might be motivated to help merely to avoid social disapproval or self-criticism from not helping. Further studies by *Batson et al.* (1988) indicated that this was not the case.

The negative-state relief model

According to the **negative-state relief** model, offered by *Cialdini et al.* (1987), people learn from their childhood that helping others is a desirable behaviour which can free them from negative psychological states such as sadness or guilt.

Using procedures similar to Batson's, Cialdini found that the likelihood of people helping another for empathic reasons could be manipulated by changing their negative psychological state by other means.

A challenge to the empathy-altruism theory

This finding does seem to challenge the empathy-altruism model, but has not always been supported in other research. Even the suggestion (*Smith et al.*, 1989) that empathic people help because they can share in the victims joy upon being helped, has not been supported in new studies in the area (*Batson*, 1993).

Batson does offer some notes of caution in the interpretation of altruism as being empathic concern for ones fellow man. He claimed that even highly empathic people will avoid helping if the costs of helping are high and escape from responsibility is easy.

Bystander effect (Latané and Darley, 1970)

One of the most influential studies in this area is the work by Latané and Darley on the **bystander effect**. This refers to the fact that people are less likely to help when they are in the company of others than when they are alone.

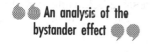 **An analysis of the bystander effect** Basing their experimental work on situations surrounding the murder of Kitty Genovese, they reproduced many of the key elements of this situation in the controlled conditions of the laboratory. They aimed to find out the conditions under which people chose to help someone in distress.

Contrary to common-sense theories of behaviour, Latané and Darley found that the prescence of others actually produced an *inhibiting* effect on helping behaviour. As a result of this and similar studies, they concluded:

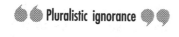 **Pluralistic ignorance**

(a) People evaluate situations for meaning, and look to others to determine the most appropriate course of action to take. They called this phenomenon **pluralistic ignorance** and the processes which produce it are an example of **social comparison theory**.

 **Diffusion of responsibility**

(b) People feel less of a personal responsibility to do something when other people are present. They referred to this as **diffusion of responsibility**.

Although Latané and Darley's research can be criticised for its lack of *ecological validity*, (it is possible that laboratory circumstances surround distress do not adequately reproduce distress conditions in real life), the study gains by its findings which contradict common sense explanations of the phenomenon. Using experimental methods they were able to establish the conditions under which people would and would not help, thus laying to rest the *fundamental attribution error* that people who do not assist someone in distress are personally deficient in some way.

THE ORIGINS OF AGGRESSION

The emphasis in this section is on **social psychological** explanations of aggressive behaviour rather than biological explanations, as all of the examining boards that include aggression on their syllabuses stress the former rather than the latter.

THE FRUSTRATION–AGGRESSION HYPOTHESIS

Dollard and Miller (1939) put forward the view that aggression was an inevitable consequence of **frustration**. If an individual is frustrated from achieving a particular goal, then the frustration would lead to aggression. The hypothesis has great intuitive appeal, but lacks the predictive ability to explain aggressive behaviour in all circumstances. There are many occasions when aggressive behaviour can be explained more appropriately by a breakdown in social norms such as the norm of reciprocity when one partner fails to return a favour. The weak point of the theory lies in the belief that frustration always underlies aggressive behaviour. A commonly quoted piece of evidence used to support the frustration-aggression hypothesis is the historical finding that in the Southern states of the USA in the years around the turn of the century, aggression against blacks was at its greatest in those years when there was a poor cotton crop.

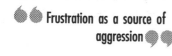 **Frustration as a source of aggression**

A parallel to this is that racial violence which exists both in the USA and the UK. It seems inappropriate to conclude that racial violence is a product of economic failing or personal threat, when many of those who are the most racially violent are those who are not economically threatened (i.e. frustrated). In this way, theories such as this have a tendency to marginalize violence, to see it as a natural human reaction rather than seeing it as shaped by social forces.

SOCIAL LEARNING THEORY

Bandura (1962) demonstrated in a series of experiments that children were capable of learning aggressive behaviour merely as a result of being exposed to it. The subsequent imitation of behaviour (or *modelling*) could also be manipulated by changing the consequences of the modelled behaviour.

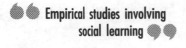

Empirical studies involving social learning

In experiments with the infamous *Bobo* doll, children saw an adult behaving aggressively toward the doll. They then tended to imitate those aggressive actions, but only if the adult was seen to be rewarded for doing so.

Bandura's experiments are often criticised for their artificiality. It is claimed that children's behaviour toward a doll which is obviously *designed* to be hit, tells us very little about aggression against another person (who may well hit back!). However, the theory does offer an explanation of how children acquire such behaviour from aggressive models. Parents seldom actively reinforce aggressive behaviour, yet in their own behaviour, perhaps even in the punishment of their own children's aggression, they are acting as aggressive models.

AGGRESSION AND THE ROLE OF CUES

Berkowitz (1982) concentrated on the importance of **cues** in the environment that might release aggressive behaviour. His basic experimental situation was to cause frustration in his subjects, and then manipulate the possible release of aggressive behaviour by presenting cues which could be seen as appropriate triggers to the behaviour. In one experiment, he provided a shotgun as a cue, and subjects behaved far more aggressively when it was present than when it was not.

Cues and aggression

Unfortunately, many of the effects discovered by Berkowitz could be more appropriately attributed to the effect of demand characteristics, with subjects unsure how to behave in the strangeness of the lab, using the 'aggressive' cues as a clue to appropriate behaviour.

Berkowitz's theory may also be criticised for its inability to explain exactly what cues would cause aggression. *Howitt et al.* (1992) suggest that almost anything could act as a cue for aggression.

They suggest that aggression is not inherent in the cue itself but in the psycho-social history of the individuals themselves. Aggressive behaviour may then be the outcome of the cognitive reasoning surrounding the cue in that particular context.

THE CONTROL OF AGGRESSIVE BEHAVIOUR

The possibility of reducing aggressive behaviour depends largely on the particular perspective taken. Several perspectives are presented here.

Psychoanalytic theory

Largely pessimistic about controlling aggression, Freud saw aggression as developing out of one of the basic human instincts – **thanatos**, the death instinct. Because this was so basic to our sense of being, it indicated little likelihood of freeing ourselves from our aggressive tendencies.

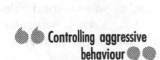

Controlling aggressive behaviour

Not all psychoanalysts share this pessimistic view, many Neo-Freudians believe that participation in socially acceptable aggressive activities releases aggressive energy.

Social learning theory

As children are seen as learning their aggressive behaviour through exposure to aggressive models, so exposure to non-aggressive models is likely to reduce aggression. *Baron* (1971) found that the presence of non-aggressive models can negate the effects of aggressive models.

Secondly, the non-reinforcement of aggressive responses would mean that the acquisition of aggressive responses is less likely, or that aggressive displays would become inhibited.

Frustration-aggression theory

A central belief of this point of view is that aggression is a natural consequence of frustration, and it follows therefore that to reduce aggression, first we must reduce frustration. Studies of black Americans living in Los Angeles in the 1960's showed that those with the most intense feeling of dissatisfaction and frustration were the ones most liable to be involved in crimes of violence. We should be cautious, however, about forming a causal relationship between the frustration of their social and economic position and the outbreak of violent action. As previously stated, there are many possible reasons for aggressive behaviour, and we may be guilty of an attributional bias if we attribute it solely to the frustration experienced by an individual.

Catharsis

Catharsis refers to the release of aggressive energy through expression of aggressive behaviour. It is based on the idea that aggression is a drive (rather than a learned response) and as such, could be purged by engaging in some type of aggressive behaviour.

There seems very little support for the catharsis explanation of reducing aggression. Indeed, research suggests that quite the opposite may occur, with expression of violent behaviour, either directly or vicariously, actually increasing aggression in a person. (*Ebbesen*, 1975).

Cognitive-neo-associationism (Berkowitz, 1989)

Berkowitz suggests three measures that would reduce aggressive behaviour.

1. Reduction of aversive stimuli (poor housing etc.).
2. Strengthening of social norms against aggression by reinforcement of non-aggressive actions and non-reinforcement of aggressive actions.
3. Reduction of exposure to aggressive models to minimise the acquisition of possible aggressive responses.

The Bandura studies (Bandura, Ross and Ross, 1961, 1963)

One of the earliest attempts to study the effects that *viewing* violence might have on the aggressive behaviour of observers came from the studies carried out by Bandura and his colleagues in the 1960's. You may recall that in these studies, children watched a film of an adult behaving aggressively, and were subsequently observed in the same situation. Although this study seemed to indicate that exposure to films of violent models *did* increase aggression in the observers, the conclusions can be criticised in terms of their ecological validity.

Firstly, the films used were not typical TV films, they did not portray 'typical acts' in typical situations. Secondly, the measured behaviour (remember that the Bobo dolls were designed to be abused) had little to do with realistic acts on other people.

Field studies of media violence

In an attempt to investigate this phenomenon in more natural settings, a number of investigators have studied how an individual's behaviour changes after exposure to violence on television. *Parke et al.* (1977) found that juvenile offenders in a hostel displayed more aggressive behaviour following 'exciting' violent films than a control group who watched 'exciting' non-violent films. Such field studies show a clear association between viewing violent television and displaying violent behaviour, but they do sacrifice an element of experimental control, so conclusions about the causal effects of viewing violent television tend to be somewhat speculative. It is also clear that artificial studies, which might isolate *individuals* in a viewing situation tell us very little about the *social* context of the viewing process. Field studies, which emphasise the natural context of television viewing (involving people interacting, talking about what they have watched etc.) do tend to capture this context more accurately than do laboratory studies.

The importance of the 'collective bravado' cannot be underestimated. An alarming report by *Barlow et al.* (1985) revealed that one-third of British school children had seen videos containing extreme violence (many of which were designated as illegal by the Director of Public Prosecutions). This research was criticised by *Cumberbatch* (1990) who repeated the research design, but this time made up titles that sounded like the real thing. Approximately the same percentage of children claimed to have seen these videos.

Longitudinal studies

As mentioned, one of the problems with field studies is that they often present us with difficulties concerning the determination of causality. **Longitudinal studies** (e.g. *Eron*

Margin notes:
- 66 Catharsis and aggression 99
- 66 Ways of reducing aggression 99
- MEDIA INFLUENCES ON AGGRESSIVE BEHAVIOUR
- 66 Viewing and aggression 99
- 66 The social context can be important 99

et al. 1972) have observed viewing habits and aggressive behaviour over a more longer time span than would be possible in an experimental study.

Results have consistently shown that the incidence of aggressive behaviour in late adolescence is significantly related to the amount of violent television watched in earlier childhood. Although the data yielded by these studies is only correlational, it does suggest that early viewing habits are one of the main determinants of aggressive behaviour later in life.

Evidence on viewing and violence

EXPLANATIONS OF THE TV VIOLENCE/VIOLENT BEHAVIOUR RELATIONSHIP

1. Children may learn through observation, and may imitate behaviour if they:
   (a) Identify with the aggressive model.
   (b) Believe that violent TV is an accurate representation of real life.
2. The high impact of violent acts on TV may make such behaviours more conspicuous and therefore more accessible in memory. By contrast, helpful, non-violent characterisations are often more subtle and therefore less easily remembered.
3. TV violence may have a *desensitising* effect in that frequent viewing produces less arousal in viewers who then become more accepting of violence in everyday life.
4. Normally, aggressive behaviour is *inhibited* by social norms, but frequent exposure to violent TV may cause viewers to see violence as more socially acceptable, therefore their own aggressive behaviour becomes *disinhibited.*
5. Studies in this area are often criticised because it is claimed that aggressive people *choose* to watch aggressive TV because it justifies their own aggressive behaviour. *Berkowitz* (1965) carried out a study where subjects watched either justified aggression or unjustified aggression.

Reasons for a correlation between viewing and violence

Those who watched justified aggression in a film were subsequently far more aggressive in giving electric shocks to a stooge.

Appealing as this explanation is, it remains somewhat debatable that the short term effects in such an artificial situation have any bearing on aggressive behaviour in real life.

EXAMINATION QUESTIONS

1. Discuss explanations of altruism and helping behaviour in humans. *(25)*
2. (a) Discuss one or more of the social-psychological theories of aggression. *(12)*
   (b) Consider the implications that social-psychological theories of aggression might have for the reduction of aggressive behaviour. *(13)*
   (AEB 1993)
3. Describe and evaluate the evidence of the influence of the media on either aggressive behaviour or pro-social behaviour. *(25)*
   (AEB 1992)

ANSWERS TO EXAMINATION QUESTIONS

OUTLINE ANSWER TO QUESTION 2

You are given a choice here, either to write about one theory or *more than one* theory. As a rule, the more theories you present in this kind of question, the more superficial their coverage tends to be, and inevitably it is the evaluative/discursive content which suffers. However, you may not have sufficient knowledge of any *one* particular theory, thus finding it more advantageous to write about more than one.

(a) Requires *'discussion'* i.e. description and evaluation of the chosen theory(ies). Note that the question asks for discussion of *social-psychological* theories, therefore theories rooted more in *biology* (e.g. the work of Lorenz) would not be relevant.

(b) Note that this second part of the question is not tied to the theories you have presented in the first. It too asks you to *discuss* material, therefore evaluation of the ideas you prose should also be offered. Points that could be made might include:

i)   The presence of non-aggressive models and the non-reinforcement of aggressive models (social learning theory).
ii) Release of aggressive energy through cathartic experiences.

iii) Reduction of aggressive behaviour through social policy (frustration-aggression theory).

TUTOR'S ANSWER

Question 1

The term altruism refers to any behaviour which is seen as unselfish in that it benefits others with some degree of self-sacrifice to the altruist.

Sociobiologists tend to explain altruism in terms of either kin selection (helping those to whom we are genetically related) or reciprocal altruism (helping those who will help us in the future). Because of the need to pass on our genes, and the adoption of the most effective strategies that ensure this, the gene for altruistic behaviour (so they argue) is thus perpetuated through the gene line.

Explanations of altruism have tended to move between these biological and social psychological origins, with most social scientists downplaying the role of natural selection of favoured genotypes in determining human behaviour. Such biological explanations are at best provocative yet some anthropologists and biologists are continuing to test these basic ideas against the available anthropological evidence. *Chagnon and Bugos* (1979) for example, in an analysis of fighting in southern Venezuela, found that the likelihood of a person helping another in such inter-group fights was determined almost entirely by the degree of genetic relatedness between the two. *Wilson*, (1978) argues that reciprocity too is a vital determinant of altruistic behaviour between unrelated individuals.

Psychological explanations of altruism have tended to emphasise more the personal and situational determinants of altruism. The empathy-altruism hypothesis for example sees helping behaviour arising out of the empathy one person feels for another. In experimental studies of this idea, *Batson* (1987) found that empathetically aroused individuals were more likely to help even when they were under no pressure to do so. Critics of this explanation suggest that *pressure* can be felt in quite subtle ways, with empathic helpers being motivated to help to avoid disapproval (an impression management explanation).

Cialdini's negative-state relief model (*Cialdini*, 1987) built on this idea. People, it claims, learn from early childhood that helping others is socially desirable and can free them from feelings of guilt. Research support for this model has been rather thin, and at times contradictory.

Research into bystander behaviour by *Latané and Darley* (1970) has provided a number of insights into the determinants of helping behaviour. Latané and Darley found that the presence of others actually produces an *inhibiting* effect on helping behaviour. They suggested that people use others to judge the most appropriate course of action in a situation. If others are not responding, then through *pluralistic ignorance*, the observing individual fails to respond either. Latané and Darley also suggested that people are more likely to help when they are on their own, the presence of others, they argue, tends to lessen the sense of personal responsibility they feel.

Latané and Darley concluded that a bystander effect occurs when bystanders judge from each others inactivity that nothing is wrong, that inaction is the norm in that situation (action may produce group disapproval) and when they feel no personal responsibility to act. Latané and Darley's work may be criticised, however, for its lack of ecological relevance (it was mainly carried out in laboratory conditions). *Real* emergencies may well be interpreted differently by bystanders, who may feel a greater sense of responsibility, and because of socialisation experiences, judge action rather than inaction as socially desirable.

Whether or not someone helps may also be determined by a range of situational factors. Potential helpers tend to be influenced by the clarity of a person's need, i.e. they are more likely to help when a person is *clearly* in distress than when the signals are ambiguous. However, excessive clarity of need may sometimes *prevent* a person from helping, as it imposes extra costs for the helper (through interacting with 'stigmatized' individuals) (*Harris*, 1976).

Piliavin et al. (1981) proposed an arousal/cost–reward model, which claims that the likelihood of a person helping another is determined by a sequence of decisions made by the potential helper. They must first be aware of the need for help, experience arousal as a result of that awareness, interpret the arousal as being caused by the perceived need, judge the potential costs and benefits of helping and not helping, and acting accordingly. Despite the intuitive appeal of this explanation of helping behaviour, it has a number of flaws. For one thing, arousal often clouds a person's ability to reason with clarity, nor can the model explain the impulsive helper who pitches in 'without thinking'. It is also evident that many patterns of helping (mother/ child, teacher/student etc.) are established patterns of behaviour that have more to do with expectations and obligations than the social decision making implied in the Piliavin model.

STUDENT'S ANSWER WITH EXAMINER'S COMMENTS

Question 3

> **Good opening, shows awareness of the contradictory research findings**

The claim that TV violence produces violent children has a divided opinion. Published in 1972, the Surgeon General's report claimed that no discernable patterns could be found. This in itself did not satisfy the American National Institute of Mental Health (NIMH) who then published the findings of a 10 year longitudinal study in 1982. It concluded that children and teenagers who watch violent television are more likely to behave aggressively. Possible explanations as to how TV violence is connected to aggressive behaviour includes the view that it provides learning opportunities. Children learn their personalities from experiences and interactions with others around them. They will also learn how to act through observing what they see on the television.

Research by *Belson* (1978) showed that long term exposure to violent television increases the degree to which boys engage in serious violence, also the effect is greater if the violence is portrayed in close emotional relationships, good guys, within law and order, if it is realistic, gratuitous or in violent westerns. However, 50% of Belson's participants did not report any violent acts at all.

> **This needs to be treated critically**

Stemming from Freud's theory, the prediction is that watching or partaking in aggressive behaviour releases built up energy. Supporting this view, *Feshbach and Singer* (1971) suggested that watching aggression reduces the arousal via fantasy thus the threat of reprisal in real life is averted. What is being said here is that a person gets into the habit of using television to release tension because it's safer.

> **Hasn't really defined these terms**

TV violence increases emotional arousal especially if the watcher is already angry or frustrated. In those who watched a lot of TV violence the effect was weaker, suggesting desensitisation. It is argued that each person has an optimum level of arousal. Too much or too little is unpleasant. Both sensitive and desensitised people can use TV violence to achieve arousal but the latter needs more to reach the desired level, which explains the relatively greater level of tolerance for TV violence, the tendency to seek it out and the tendency to reproduce it. An alternative explanation to this is that by watching aggression, it lowers inhibitions to aggress.

> **Good evaluative point**

Studies on television and aggression are often criticised because it is thought that people who chose to watch it are more aggressive in the first place. In 1982 The NIMH presented a report based on 2,500 studies to the US government. It stated 'We have come to the unanimous conclusion that there is a causal relationship between television violence and real life violence.' But also taken into account was the increase in family breakdown, unemployment, family violence and child sex abuse within those 10 years. These as well as TV violence could have a part to play in real violence. The focus of research has shifted from 'Does TV violence cause real violence?' to ask exactly who is affected. After all, not everybody acts in the same way.

The Chicago Circle consists of a group of researchers including Eron and Huesmann. They are conducting ongoing, large scale research . In a summary of recent findings, published in 1982, it was found that violent television affects aggression in both boys and girls, but boys are still more aggressive, and aggressive children tend to be disliked by other children. They have active aggressive fantasies and prefer masculine activities, they enjoy violent television and identify more strongly with it.

> **What do these studies involve?**

Studies with more carefully controlled methods and sophisticated statistical techniques have shown that there is now a great deal of evidence to suggest a causal link between aggressive media and aggression in the consumer.

> **An enjoyable essay to read in that it shows awareness of a lot of relevant research and ideas into the TV violence debate. Several of the more important ones did tend to be passed over without elaboration, however, so this essay would probably be characteristic of a grade B.**

REVIEW SHEET

1. What is altruism?

   _____

2. What *two* reasons do sociobiologists give for biological altruism?

   _____

   _____

3. Give *two* reasons why these explanations might not apply to humans.

   _____

   _____

4. What is meant by the empathy-altruism hypothesis?

   _____

   _____

5. Give *one* criticism of the empathy-altruism hypothesis.

   _____

   _____

6. What is the difference between the empathy-altruism hypothesis and the negative-state relief model?

   _____

7. What is meant by the bystander effect?

   _____

   _____

8. Give *two* conclusions from Latané and Darley's research.

   _____

   _____

9. Offer *two* evaluative points about this research.

   _____

   _____

10. How does the frustration-aggression theory explain aggressive behaviour?

    _____

    _____

11. Offer *one* criticism of this explanation.

_____

_____

12. What would be the implications of this theory for the reduction of aggressive behaviour?

_____

_____

13. What were Bandura's main conclusions from the Bobo doll studies?

_____

_____

14. What *two* factors are suggested by social learning theorist as contributing to the reduction of aggressive behaviour?

_____

15. What according to the cognitive neo-associationism model are the *three* measures that would reduce aggressive behaviour?

_____

_____

_____

16. Does violent television make violent children? Summarise the argument in 50 words.

_____

_____

_____

_____

_____

_____

GETTING STARTED

This chapter explores the nature and functions of **attitudes**, how they develop and how they might be changed. It also examines the relationship between attitudes and behaviour.

The idea of attitudes allows us to account for regularity and predictability in our social world. The importance of this concept of attitude will be evident only in a cultural context where there is a substantial element of choice in individual behaviour.

Thus in cultures where there exists an individuated notion of the person, the concept of attitude thrives.

In Western cultures, an individual's decisions are seen as a product of individual rather than group choice, thus reinforcing a belief in an inner state or attitude which influences these decisions. However, in some other cultures, this view of unique human beings is less prevalent and behaviour is viewed not as a result of individual intention and emotion, but rather as a communal product. Attempts to change attitudes, and indeed to link them to behaviour depends, therefore, on the former view of human behaviour.

The main themes of questions in this area are:

1. **Discussion of explanations of the development and function of attitudes.**
2. **Discussion of theories of attitude change and their practical applications.**
3. **Discussion of the effectiveness of persuasion techniques.**
4. **Explanations of the relationship between attitudes and behaviour.**

Of the above question areas, 1, 2 and 4 are common to the AEB 'A' level; 1, 2, 3, and 4 to the AEB 'AS' level, and 2 and 3 to the Oxford and Cambridge 'A' and 'AS' levels.

THE FORMATION OF ATTITUDES

THE FUNCTIONS OF ATTITUDES

ATTITUDE CHANGE

PERSUASION AND ATTITUDE CHANGE

ATTITUDES AND BEHAVIOUR

ESSENTIAL PRINCIPLES

Attitudes are hypothetical constructs (i.e. they cannot be measured directly, but must be inferred from behaviour). They are seen as states of readiness, based on past experiences, which guide, bias, or otherwise influence our behaviour.

Attitudes may also be seen as **responses that locate objects of thought on dimensions of judgement** (*McGuire*, 1985).

Attitudes may be seen as having three components, the *cognitive* (belief about an object), *affective* (feelings about it) and the *behavioural* (how a person might actually behave toward the attitude object).

THE FORMATION OF ATTITUDES

 Types of learning

LEARNING THEORY EXPLANATIONS

Attitudes may be acquired from other people by procedures which form part of **learning theory**. The *affective* (emotional) component can be acquired through **classical conditioning**, in the same way as other emotional responses can. The agreement expressed by other people may reinforce an attitude through **operant conditioning**. The attitudes of other people may also be acquired through **observational learning**. If an individual sees another expressing an attitude and sees that attitude being reinforced, that attitude may then be acquired.

Evaluation of Learning theory explanations

Assessing learning theory

- The simplicity of the learning theory explanation is probably its greatest criticism. *Emler and Hogan* (1981) stress that attitudes have an extremely complex developmental history and reflects the interaction between the person, their social experiences and their **social cognition** (their knowledge and reasoning of their social world.)
- The theory also offers a restricted explanation of how people acquire attitudes, since at least in part it deals with how attitudes are (or are not) reinforced by others. It is clear that many attitudes are formed by *direct experience* of the attitude object.

DIRECT EXPERIENCE

Impact of direct experience

Research evidence (e.g. *Fazio and Zanna*, 1981) has demonstrated that attitudes which are formed as a result of **direct experience** with an object (as opposed to attitudes which are acquired from someone else) tend to be stronger, more long lasting, and more resistant to change. Other research (*Schlegal*, 1975) has shown that attitudes which are *not* acquired through direct experience of an attitude object are simpler and more able to be expressed in terms of a single affective response. Attitudes which are acquired through direct experience are more complex in their organisation and are less likely to be successfully expressed in a single affective response.

Evaluation of the direct experience explanation

 Assessing direct experience theory

- Both intuitive reasoning and research evidence support the idea that directly acquired attitudes are stronger and more resistant to change. As direct experience is more potent than 'borrowed' attitudes or anticipated experience, it is possible to *change* a negative attitude by exposing a person to positive direct experiences of the attitude object (see chapter on *prejudice*).
- There are a number of contradictions in the research literature over the assessment of directly acquired attitudes. *Schlegel and DiTecco* (1982) argue that as directly acquired attitudes are more complex, their expression is likewise more complex and therefore more difficult to measure. *Fazio and Zanna* (1981) on the other hand, argue that such attitudes have greater *clarity* (i.e. are more available to the individual) therefore will be more stable over time, and more positively linked to the individual's behaviour.

THE FUNCTIONS OF ATTITUDES

THE MOTIVATIONAL FUNCTIONS OF ATTITUDES (KATZ, 1967)

Ego-defensive functions.

Attitudes may protect individuals from experiencing negative feelings about themselves by allowing the individual to project negative feelings onto others. This might explain prejudice toward minority groups.

Value-expressive functions

Attitudes are ways of expressing things that are important to us. Attitudes are thus seen as reflecting central values, particularly when these values are important in the process of *impression management*.

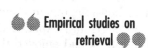 **What attitudes do (i.e. functions)**

Instrumental functions

Attitudes may be used and expressed in order to gain social acceptance or to avoid undesirable consequences. As the attitudes may be adopted not because they reflect some central belief, but rather because they match the attitudes of a particular desired person or group, they are therefore referred to as *instrumental*.

Knowledge functions

Attitudes enable us to organise and structure our social world along evaluative dimensions. They help to simplify our social world and lead to a greater sense of understanding and prediction about events in it.

ATTITUDES AND INFORMATION PROCESSING

The final one of Katz's functions suggests that attitudes enable us to **process information** about our social world in a more efficient and useful way. This function has been elaborated in a number of theoretical positions.

Dissonance theory (Festinger, 1957)

Cognitive consonance and dissonance

This proposes that people are motivated to seek out information which is *consonant* with their attitudes and to avoid information which is *dissonant*. This is necessary to maintain **cognitive consonance** and to avoid **cognitive dissonance**.

Research by *Frey and Rosch* (1984) established that subjects who showed a strong commitment to an attitude were more likely to show selective exposure to consonant information as predicted by the theory.

Assimilation-contrast theory (Sherif and Hovland, 1961)

This proposes that our own attitudes serve as a 'judgemental anchor' against which other attitudes can be judged.

Attitudes which are relatively close to our own are judged as being closer than they actually are (assimilation) and are therefore seen as being fairer and more objective. Attitudes which are seen as discrepant to our own are perceived as being in contrast and are judged as unfair and propagandist.

Attitudinal guidance of the retrieval process

Empirical studies on retrieval

Although research findings in this area have been quite contradictory, sufficient evidence exists to support the proposition that attitudes actually exert directive influences on the **retrieval** of memories about past behaviour. *Ross et al.* (1981) found that subjects who had their attitudes toward a particular behaviour manipulated (so that they were either positive or negative toward that behaviour) remembered more similar instances of their own behaviour under the positive attitude condition than in the negative attitude condition. However, it is possible that their responses were influenced not so much by selective memory, but more by the need to engage in **impression management**.

ATTITUDE CHANGE

ATTITUDE CHANGE AND COUNTER-ATTUDINAL BEHAVIOUR

If a person is forced to act in a way which is contrary to his/her attitude, then this may exert an influence on the changing of that attitude. Why and how this happens is described in terms of the following perspectives.

Dissonance theory (Festinger, 1957)

According to this theory, an individual who acts in a manner contrary to their attitude experiences an unpleasant emotional state called **dissonance**.

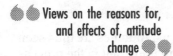

Views on the reasons for, and effects of, attitude change

As the behaviour may not be changed, the individual may change his/her attitude in order to rid themselves of the dissonance by making their attitudes consistent with their behaviour.

Research by Festinger and Carlsmith established the basic accuracy of this statement, but added several qualifications. *Firstly*, attitude change was more likely if they had freedom of choice when deciding to behave in the way they did. *Secondly*, attitude change was more likely if their behaviour led to negative consequences for another person. *Thirdly*, if the incentives to behave as they did were low rather than high, i.e. were inadequate to justify the inconsistent behaviour, then attitude change was more likely.

Critics of dissonance theory points to its existence only as a **hypothetical construct**, claiming that it may be no more than a realisation that one has chosen a course of action that has had unpleasant consequences (*Cooper and Fazio*, 1984) or might simply be an expression of good old fashioned guilt.

Self-perception theory (Bem,1972).

Bem has been one of the main critics of dissonance theory. He suggests that people are not particularly accurate in identifying their own attitudes. Expressing an attitude, he argues, is an *inference* drawn from the observation of our own actions.

Bem's re-interpretation of the Festinger and Carlsmith experiment using self-perception theory

Bem (1972) re-interpreted the Festinger and Carlsmith experiment using the **self-perception theory**. In the original experiment, subjects were paid either $1 or $20 to tell another subject that a (boring) task was interesting. Festinger and Carlsmith found that when asked how interesting they had found the task, those paid $1 reported it as being more interesting than those who had been paid $20. (Note: this is a **counter-intuitive** finding, therefore reinforcing the value of social-psychological research). Under dissonance theory, this was interpreted as being evidence of the $1 subjects having *insufficient cause* for their behaviour. Thus, to avoid the dissonance, they changed their attitude to the task. Bem, however, suggested that the $1 subjects used the fact that they told another subject that the task was interesting to convince themselves that it actually was. Those paid $20 attributed their behaviour to the money, and therefore had no need to search for another reason for their behaviour.

However, rather like Festinger's theory, Bem's self-perception theory relies on inference, i.e. the fact that subjects *could* have identified their attitudes from their behaviour is no proof that they actually did.

Impression management

Impression management and attitude change

More recently, psychologists have attempted to explain the phenomenon of attitude change following counter-attitudinal behaviour by using an **impression management** perspective. Impression management refers to the strategies that people use to create the images that they desire. *Tedeschi et al.* (1981) suggested that people are motivated to appear consistent with their attitudes (perceived as a desirable thing to be) and therefore *report* consistency to an experimenter, when it is possible that no such consistency exists. In a re-interpretation of the Festinger and Carlsmith experiment, Tedeschi suggested that the $1 subjects simply pretended that they had enjoyed the task (to *appear* consistent) whereas in the $20 subjects, it was quite easy to attribute their behaviour to external factors (the $20). Therefore they could be honest, and reported the task as boring.

A major problem with this theory is that we have no way of knowing whether subjects are being honest or merely feigning change. Using the *bogus pipeline* (subjects are told it monitors *real* attitudes) Tedeschi hypothesised that in a low incentive condition, reported attitude change would not now take place. This was the case and can be seen as evidence for the impression management theory.

PERSUASION AND ATTITUDE CHANGE

Research in this area has concentrated on trying to establish the processes by which communications might **change attitudes**. The different models of **persuasion** presented here are not necessarily seen as competing with each other but rather should be seen as complementary explanations of different parts of the persuasive process.

PERSUASION AND THE TRADITIONAL APPROACH (THE YALE STUDIES)

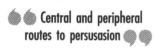

Persuasion and attitude change

Traditional approaches to the study of persuasion have stressed the study of *who* says *what* to *whom*. Studies in this area, most notably the work of *Hovland et al.* (1953), have attempted to identify the characteristics of *source, content* and *audience*, which are most likely to bring about attitude change.

Research showed that:

Factors in changing attitudes

a) People who are *attractive, popular* and are perceived by the audience to be *experts* are more likely to bring about attitude change than those who are not.
b) Messages that present *two sides* of an argument are more successful than those which only present one. Fear evoking messages are more effective if they are accompanied by recommendations about how the negative situation could be avoided.
c) Persons *low in self-esteem* are more susceptible to persuasion, as are those who are 'distracted' whilst listening to a persuasive communication.

Evaluation of the traditional approach

■ More recent research (e.g. *Baumeister and Covington*, 1985) has failed to provide support for some of the original findings, which are now interpreted as *generalisations* about the process of persuasion.
■ Although such an approach provides answers to the *when* and *how* of persuasion, it fails to provide answers to *why* people change their attitudes. More recent approaches have stressed the *cognitive* processes involved in attitude change.

THE ELABORATION LIKELIHOOD MODEL (PETTY AND CACIOPPO, 1986)

Central and peripheral routes to persuasion

This model distinguishes *between* the *central route to persuasion*, and the *peripheral route to persuasion*. In the central route, the recipients of a communication engage in critical evaluation of the message. However, if they are unwilling or unable to do this, they may base their decision to accept the content of the message on other factors such as the credibility of the communicator (the peripheral route).

The model proposes that if a communication is well structured and convincing, persuasive impact is greater the more recipients are both motivated and able to think about (elaborate) the arguments presented in it. On the other hand, if arguments are vague and weak, the persuasive impact of a communication will be greater if recipients are unable (perhaps through distraction) or unmotivated to think about the arguments.

Evaluation of the elaboration likelihood model

Assessing the elaboration likelihood theory

■ Research evidence on the claims of the model have been a little contradictory. The model's proposal that distraction increases the persuasive impact of a communication has been confirmed in some studies (*Osterhouse and Brock*, 1970) but not in others (*Haaland and Venkatesan*, 1968).
■ Although the model identifies that convincing arguments increase persuasive impact, it does not identify what makes a communication convincing.
■ Despite this limitation, the model is useful, in that it explains, in cognitive terms, the impact of many of the variables that have been found to affect persuasion.

THE PROTECTION MOTIVATION THEORY (ROGERS, 1975)

This theory has mainly been used to investigate the impact of **fear appeals** on attitude change.

In order to persuade recipients to change a health related attitude (e.g. to HIV or smoking) the following cognitions must be stressed.

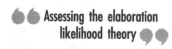

Fear appeals

a) The negative consequences of their present behaviour.
b) The probability of these negative consequences being higher than thought.
c) That avoidance of these negative consequences is possible if attitude change is achieved.

Later revisions to the theory proposed that the appeal should also stress the costs to the individual and the realistic assessment that a change in the behaviour discussed might be possible.

The theory stresses that individuals *combine* these cognitions in order to make a decision about attitude change. If fear alone is elicited (cognitions a and b), then the individual is motivated to protect or rationalise their behaviour as they are not given any suggestions how they might avoid these negative consequences.

Evaluation of the protection motivation theory

■ Evidence (*Rogers*, 1983, 1985) provides strong support that all these factors do, in fact, influence health related behaviour. However, the claim that people combine these cognitions, and if one was missing then persuasion would not take place, has consistently been found to be false.

ATTITUDES AND BEHAVIOUR

There is an implicit assumption that people will act in accordance with their attitudes. A number of studies have demonstrated inconsistencies between **attitudes** and **behaviour** such that as a predictor of behaviour, the concept of an attitude may be useless (*Eagly and Himmelfarb*, 1978).

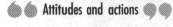 Attitudes and actions

The LaPiere study (1934)

LaPiere (1934), together with a Chinese couple, visited 250 hotels and restaurants over a three month period, and only once were they refused service. Later, LaPiere wrote to the establishments to enquire if they would serve them. Most said they would refuse service.

The Yarrow Study (1952)

In a similar study by *Yarrow* (1952), a black woman joined two white women seated in a restaurant. In all the restaurants sampled, she was never refused service, but later attempts to book a reservation, received six refusals, and five acceptances.

However, there are several problems with these studies:

1. Both studies measured **behavioural intention** rather than *attitude*. There could be many reasons why the *intention* was not to serve them.
2. There was no way of knowing whether the person who refused the reservation was the same person who later showed acceptance in the restaurant.

REASONS FOR THE WEAK RELATION BETWEEN ATTITUDES AND BEHAVIOUR

The level of specificity

Most investigators have used a very general measure of attitude, yet a very *specific* measurement of behaviour. However, studies which have used specific attitudes *and* specific measurements of behaviour have found a link. *Weigel et al.* (1974) found no relation between attitude to a general issue (e.g. health) and behaviour toward a related specific object (e.g. brushing teeth regularly), but there was a strong relation between the attitude toward the specific issue (e.g. dental hygiene) and the behaviour toward it.

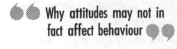 Why attitudes may not in fact affect behaviour

Single acts versus multiple acts

Generally, investigators have selected a *single* behaviour to test the prediction. It does make more sense to look at a *range of behaviours* rather that just one. Behaviour is multidetermined, and any specific behaviour may not provide the most accurate test of a specific attitude.

Multiple actions should be examined

Role of situational factors

When **situational** pressures are strong, people of different attitudes may act in a similar way. The stronger the situational pressures toward some behaviour, then individual differences in attitudes are less likely to affect behaviour.

More than one attitude involved

One attitude may override another. Attitudes toward charity may be overridden by attitudes toward maintaining ones own personal finances!

REASONS FOR ATTITUDE-BEHAVIOUR CONSISTENCY

Direct Experience

Attitudes formed through *direct experience* with an object show more consistent relations to behaviour than do attitudes formed less directly.

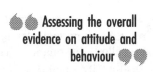 **Why attitudes may affect behaviour**

Personal relevance

If a person has a *vested interest* in an issue, behaviour is more likely to reflect the stated attitude (*Sivacek and Crano*, 1982).

THE ATTITUDE-BEHAVIOUR ISSUE – A RESOLUTION

Fishbein and Ajzen (1975) conclude

■ Attitudes toward specific behaviours will provide the best predictor of a single act.
■ Attitudes toward general behaviours will provide the best predictor of multiple acts.

Fishbein's model (1975)

Behaviour is determined primarily by a person's intention to behave, which is influenced by:

 Assessing the overall evidence on attitude and behaviour

■ Their attitudes.
■ Their perception of normative beliefs (i.e. what they think is the *agreed* way to behave).
■ Their motivation to comply (i.e. pressure from others).

Evaluation of the model

■ It has been tested successfully to predict women's use of contraceptives (*Werner*, 1979) and church attendance (*Brinberg*, 1979).
■ Its major advantage is that investigators can consider the role of *other people* in determining whether or not a persons behaviour may be consistent with their attitude.

EXAMINATION QUESTIONS

1. (a) What is meant by an attitude?   *(5)*
   (b) Critically consider the view that attitudes are an accurate predictor of behaviour.
                                                                                     (20)
                                                                                  (AEB 1993)
2. Discuss psychological explanations of attitude change.   *(25)*
3. Describe and evaluate psychological insights into the processes of persuasion. *(25)*

ANSWERS TO EXAMINATION QUESTIONS

OUTLINE ANSWER TO QUESTION 3

There are two skill requirements in this question, a *description* of psychological insights (research and/or theoretical accounts) and an evaluation of the same material. Appropriate content for this question would be:

1. **Traditional approaches** (e.g. the work of *Hovland et al.*).
   These studies investigated the characteristics of the source, message and recipient necessary for persuasive communication. The findings are now interpreted more as generalisations about the process of persuasion.
2. **Cognitive models**, e.g. the elaboration likelihood model which distinguishes between the central route and the peripheral route to persuasion. Enduring attitude change is more likely with the central route in which listeners consider the content and logic of a message. In the peripheral route they are more affected by factors outside the message (e.g. the credibility of the source).
3. **Protection Motivation theory**. This theory proposes that fear appeals can change an attitude toward health issues provided the message also contains information about how the negative consequences hinted at in the message can be avoided.

TUTOR'S ANSWER

.Question 2

One of the first significant theoretical attempts to explain attitude change was the **Balance theory** of *Fritz Heider* (1958). Heider proposed that people try to maintain a consistency between various cognitions that they have of themselves, other people and objects or events. If, he claimed, an imbalance exists in that two people like each other yet disagree over some other matter, then this is an imbalanced relationship which causes tension in the people concerned. They are then motivated to restore that balance by one person changing their attitude either to the object or to the other person.

However, this theory was developed at a time when it was believed that people could not tolerate imbalance in their cognitions, a belief that is not shared by contemporary social psychologists. The theory is altogether too simple, being restricted to such triadic relationships, and discounting degrees of liking and the relative values attached to events by the participants.

A related theory, cognitive dissonance theory (*Festinger*, 1957) suggests that if people have inconsistent cognitions (e.g. doing something that they feel strongly against doing) then they experience an unpleasant state called dissonance. The individual is then motivated to reduce the dissonance, possibly by changing their attitude. Festinger proposed two major types of dissonance, counter-attitudinal dissonance, which is produced when we act in a way which is contrary to our attitudes, and post-decisional dissonance which is produced after we make a choice between attractive alternatives. People tend to increase the perceived attractiveness of the chosen event, and decrease the perceived attractiveness of the unchosen event, thus reducing the dissonance. However, although research (e.g. *Erlich*, 1957) has demonstrated that people *do* seek consonant information, there is less evidence that they avoid dissonant information.

Festinger and Carlsmith (1959) persuaded subjects to act in a way which was inconsistent with their attitudes. Those subjects who had insufficient cause to explain their behaviour in terms of other factors, displayed more attitude chan ge toward the previously disliked action than did those who were given sufficient cause.

This basic explanation of counter-attitudinal dissonance has been criticised widely. *Elms* (1967) found that discrepant behaviour had a totally different effects if it was engaged in privately rather than publicly, leading to the idea that the attitude change observed in such experiments is merely a function of impression management as subjects strive to *appear* consistent with their attitudes (seen as socially desirable). *Tedeschi* (1981) believes that subjects only *report* consistency to the experimenter when no such consistency really exists. The difficulty with this interpretation, however, is the difficulty of knowing when the subject is being honest and when they are not. In an experiment using the *bogus pipeline* under which condition subjects believed that their real attitudes were being monitored, no attitude change was evident.

Bem (1972) criticised the cognitive dissonance theory in that he claimed that people were not particularly accurate in identifying their own attitudes. They merely *infer* their attitudes from observing their behaviour. A major weakness with Bem's alternative interpretation of the Festinger and Carlsmith findings is that we have no way of knowing if the subject *had* inferred their attitudes from their behaviour. The fact that they could have is no proof that they did. Also self-perception seems to work primarily when people do not have clearly defined attitudes about the object in question (*Chaiken and Baldwin*, 1981).

Later developments of cognitive dissonance theory established some qualifications to the original theory. *Collins and Hoyt* (1972) found that dissonance was greater if a person was *committed* to an attitude yet engaged in counter-attitudinal behaviour. Dissonance was also greater if a person engaged in counter-attitudinal behaviour of their own volition, and if the consequences of their behaviour was serious and negative for s ome other person.

There is clearly some support for this theory, and it has been used as an explanation for various social phenomena. *Aronson* (1980) explained the success of integrated racial schooling in the USA in the 1960s and 1970s as a product of cognitive dissonance. If prejudiced individuals engaged in counter-attitudinal behaviour by sending their children to racially mixed schools they experienced dissonance and this led to a reduction in their prejudice. Where the arrangements lacked support from the local state authority, dissonance was removed and prejudice remained largely unchanged.

However, it is difficult to test the theory outside the artificiality of the lab with any degree of control, and there are other reasons (self-perception, impression management) for the results obtained within it. A major problem for the theory is the nature of dissonance as a hypothetical construct, difficult to measure and often leading to circular thinking in trying to prove its existence, i.e. attitude change has occurred, therefore dissonance was present.

Cooper and Fazio claim that dissonance may be no more than a realization that one has chosen a course of action that has unpleasant consequences (supported by Collins and Hoyt's finding that dissonance is greater where the consequences are serious and negative).

An alternative view of attitude change is to examine the effects of direct persuasion. *Petty and Cacioppo's* (1986) elaboration likelihood model proposes a *central route* to persuasion is taken when people carefully ponder the content and logic of persuasive messages, and a *peripheral route* is where attitude change is more likely to be determined by non-message factors such as the credibility of the source. Studies suggest that more enduring attitude change is possible with the central route than the peripheral one.

Although this conclusion is appealing, the model fails to predict what makes a communication convincing and what, therefore, will ensure that people will take this central route in the first place.

STUDENT'S ANSWER WITH EXAMINER'S COMMENTS

Question 1

(a) There are many definitions of an attitude. The basic concept of an attitude is that it is the internal orientation that would explain the actions of a person. *Secord and Backman* (1964) said that every attitude is comprised of three components;

A sensible idea to elaborate the definition

i)   cognitive – the things in which we believe
ii) affective – how people feel about things
iii) behavioural – how people act in response to the cognitive and the affective.

(b) *Eagly and Himmelfarb* (1978) said that as a predictor of behaviour, the concept of attitude is useless. There have been numerous studies into the link between attitudes and behaviour, such as LaPiere's study in 1934. LaPiere travelled all over the United States with a Chinese couple. They visited many hotels, motels and restaurants to see if people were prepared to serve them. Out of 250 establishments, only one refused service. Later, LaPiere wrote to the same establishments to book reservations, and half wrote back with a massive 90% refusals. *Yarrow* (1952) conducted a similar study where one black woman joined two white women in a restuarant. There were no refusals. However, when later the restaurant was contacted over the telephone to reserve a table, there were six refusals and five acceptances.

The main criticisms of studies such as these are:

i)   Both measured *behavioural intention* as opposed to attitude.
ii) They tested the establishment rather than the individual.
iii) It may not have been the same person who took the booking.

66 Perhaps too much is made
of the La Piere study 99

66 Such as? 99

Another criticism of the LaPiere study is that the quality of the clothes and the fact that LaPiere was with them could have had a big influence on how they were treated. So these studies, taking all the criticisms into account do not give a good overall view that attitudes accurately predict behaviour. The restauranteurs etc. in the LaPiere study did not refuse service when confronted face to face with the Chinese couple. This could be because they felt embarrassed to say anything even though they may have a negative attitude to ethnic minority groups. However, they felt at ease about refusing service when they were written to. More recent studies have shown that despite a lack of such methodological difficulties (that were shown in the LaPiere and Yarrow studies) there still is no definite link between peoples attitudes and behaviour. There are some reasons for such weak relations between attitude and behaviour. Research has shown a very specific measure of behaviour relates accurately to a specific attitude (level of specificity).

Many of the studies have used only one measure of an attitude, whereas more accurate assessments can be made from multiple acts.

There are also two factors which can affect attitude/behaviour consistency. If an attitude has been formed through direct experience, there is generally more consistency in the way the person behaves. If a person has a vested interest (i.e. when something has a direct affect on their life) their behaviour is more likely to coincide with their attitude.

One major criticism of the majority of research on attitudes and behaviour is that it tests general attitudes such as religion, politics etc. rather than an individual's specific attitudes. This may be the reason for such a weak link between attitude and behaviour. It has been shown that strong attitudes are an easier predictor of behaviour than weaker attitudes. From the studies conducted so far, it is difficult to say whether attitudes really are a good predictor of behaviour. More studies will need to be carried out with clearer aims to test this concept.

66 A little limited in its scope of discussion, but very little irrelevant material. Candidate used material effectively and this is probably characteristic of a B grade. 99

REVIEW SHEET

1. Define an attitude.

   _____

   _____

2. What are the *three* components of an attitude?

   _____

3. How, according to learning theory, do attitudes develop?

   _____

   _____

4. Give *two* criticisms of this explanation.

   _____

   _____

5. How do attitudes formed through direct experience with an attitude object differ from those which are not?

   _____

   _____

   _____

6. Summarise the research position on this relationship.

   _____

   _____

   _____

7. Give *three* functions of attitudes.

   _____

   _____

   _____

8. What is 'counter-attitudinal dissonance'?

   _____

   _____

9. How is it reduced?

   _____

   _____

10. What were the main findings of the Festinger & Carlsmith research?

_____

_____

11. How did Bem interpret these?

_____

_____

_____

12. How might the Festinger and Carlsmith result be explained within an impression management perspective?

_____

_____

_____

13. Give *one* criticism of this explanation.

_____

_____

14. Distinguish between the central and peripheral routes to persuasion.

_____

_____

15. Give *three* cognitions that must be stressed for a fear appeal to bring about attitude change.

_____

_____

_____

16. What were the main findings of the LaPiere study of the attitude–behaviour relationship?

_____

_____

17. Under what conditions might attitudes predict behaviour?

Give two conditions.

_____

_____

18. What, according to Fishbein, determines a person's intention to behave?

_____

_____

_____

SOCIAL INFLUENCE

GETTING STARTED

This chapter deals with issues central to the idea of **social influence**. It covers a wide range of topics, all of which have the same essential focus, i.e. the psychological pressure which is put on us by others, and the influences that pressure has on our behaviour.

The main themes of question in this area are as follows:

■ **Discussion of theories and research into audience and co-action effects.**

■ **Description and evaluation of procedures and results of studies of conformity.**

■ **Description and evaluation of procedures and results of studies of obedience.**

■ **Discussion of research into the emergence and effectiveness of leaders.**

■ **Description and evaluation of studies of group decision making.**

The influence of the *presence* of others on our performance on some tasks has been a topic of interest for a long time, since *Triplett* (1898) developed his theory of **dynamogenesis** – the generation of action by the presence of others.

More recently, *Latané* (1981) suggested the **social impact theory**, which proposed that the influence of others is determined by three main factors.

1. The *number* of people. As the number of people present increases, so does their influence, although the impact of others over a certain number gradually diminishes until further increases have no effect at all.
2. The *immediacy* of people. The more physically close the others are, the greater the impact they will have.
3. The *strength* of people. Defined as the perceived status or power of the others. This factor was particularly important in Milgram's study of obedience.

These basic ideas about social influence underlie all of the areas to follow, and might be appropriately incorporated into discussion of these areas.

AUDIENCE AND CO-ACTION EFFECTS

CONFORMITY

OBEDIENCE

LEADERSHIP

EFFECTIVENESS OF LEADERS

GROUP DECISION MAKING

ESSENTIAL PRINCIPLES

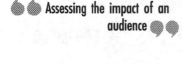
AUDIENCE AND CO-ACTION EFFECTS

AUDIENCE EFFECTS

 Impacts of an audience

Audience effects are defined as the influence on our behaviour by virtue of the fact that we are being *watched* by others as we perform some task. This influence may be beneficial, in that it increases the quality of our performance (**social facilitation**), or may be decremental, in that it decreases the quality of our performance (**social inhibition**). *Zajonc* (1965) provided one of the first systematic explanations of audience effects. He proposed that the presence of others was arousing and that this arousal affected performance in different ways. Zajonc reasoned that if a behaviour was well learned, the increased arousal would result in better performance. If the behaviour was not well learned, however, the increased arousal would inhibit performance as it would produce other responses (e.g. feeling of uncertainty, embarrassment etc) that would interfere with the behaviour being observed. Drawing on animal models, Zajonc believed that this audience/arousal relationship was innate. This was not, however, a view shared by all. Alternative explanations are:

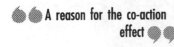 Alternatives to viewing the audience/arousal relationship as innate

1. Audiences are arousing because we anticipate that they will **evaluate** our performance. Research studies (e.g. *Guerin*, 1986) have supported this view, showing a clear distinction between the effects of an audience with and without anticipation of evaluation.
2. Audiences are both arousing and distracting, (**distraction – conflict theory**, *Baron*, 1986). According to this theory, the nature of the influence will be determined by how people react to the distraction. Attentional conflict may produce increased performance if it causes clear focus on a well learned task, but decreased performance if it causes frustration, anxiety or embarrassment on a complex task.

Evaluation of explanations of audience effects

Assessing the impact of an audience

- There is little support for Zajonc's view of audiences being *innately* arousing. Whilst it is a fairly unprovocative and understandable statement to make regarding animal social behaviour, it appears less valid to apply this reasoning to humans who might justifiably expect *evaluation* of their performance.
- Given the contemporary interest in *impression management* as a determinant of much of our social behaviour, research into audience effects has established that people's performance on a task will often suffer simply because they experience *evaluation apprehension*.

CO-ACTION EFFECTS

Co-action effects occur when individuals work *alongside* others. Early research (*Dashiell*, 1930) found that when people worked alongside each other, they worked faster if less accurately.

A reason for the co-action effect

The main explanation of co-action influence has been through **social comparison theory**. This theory proposes that we use other people to evaluate our own performance. This evaluative process may lead to increased attention to performance in order to compete, thus producing a social facilitation effect.

Social loafing and its causes

Latané et al. (1979) have carried out research into the phenomenon of **social loafing**. Social loafing occurs when the presence of others co-operating on a task leads to a performance deficit compared to the sum total of what each person could accomplish individually. Various explanations for social loafing have been proposed, including the idea of **deindividuation** where individuals working in groups may become less self aware, thus reducing the attentional focus which occurs in competitive tasks.

Evaluation of explanations of co-action effects

- The phenomenon of **social loafing** has been supported in a variety of settings, showing it's practical relevance to be immense. However, recent research (*Harkins and Jackson*, 1985) has demonstrated that it may be avoided if group members feel that their contributions will be evaluated, but increased if group members believe that others are going to loaf.

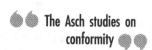

CONFORMITY

66 Informational and
normative conformity 99

Conformity occurs when people go along with the behaviour which they believe to be the acceptable behaviour within a group. If people conform because they believe others to be better informed about a situation, they are demonstrating **informational conformity**, if they conform in order to gain approval or avoid disapproval, they are demonstrating **normative conformity**.

RESEARCH ON CONFORMITY

The Asch studies

66 The Asch studies on
conformity 99

Asch (1952) carried out research where seven students were asked to participate in an experiment on visual discrimination. Unknown to the one *real* subject, all the other subjects were confederates of the experimenter. On six 'neutral' trials, the confederates gave correct answers, on the other twelve trials they unanimously agreed on the same incorrect answer. At the end of the research, Asch discovered that, overall, his 'real' subjects had made 37% errors (note: this does not mean that 37 subjects made errors – actually 75% made at least one error, compared with only 5% in a control condition).

Asch found that in approximately one-third of cases, subjects went along with the judgements of others because they wanted the approval of the group (normative conformity). Other subjects had genuine doubts concerning their own judgements and thus went along because of information conformity.

Normative and informational conformity have been studied as separate phenomena by a number of researchers.

Normative conformity

Deutsch and Gerard (1955) promised rewards for the groups that made the fewest errors of judgement. This had the effect of increasing the interdependence of the group and resulted in twice as much conformity than a control (Asch type) condition.

Informational conformity

Di Vesta (1959) found much greater conformity in later trials if the early trials had mainly been neutral (i.e. the majority gave correct judgements). This meant that the subject attributed much greater competence to the other group members and was therefore more likely to trust their judgement in later trials.

OTHER VARIATIONS ON THE 'ASCH EFFECT'

Size of the majority

66 Conformity and size of
majority 99

Asch found that the influence of the majority increased up to three people. No further increase in conformity was evident once the majority size went beyond three. Other studies (e.g. *Latané and Wolf* (1981) have suggested that increased majority sizes beyond three *will* increase conformity, but by smaller and smaller increments.

Presence of another deviant from the majority position

66 Impact of a 'deviant'
opinion 99

Asch replaced one of the confederates by another person (also a confederate) who made his judgement *before* the real subject. This 'deviant' was effective in reducing conformity to very low levels (5.5%). In later research by *Allen and Levine* (1969), they found that if the deviants position was the same as the real subject (i.e. he gave the correct answer) then this was effective in both unambiguous stimulus situations such as Asch's, and also in statements of *opinion*. However, if he deviated not only from the majority, but also from the correct answer, then his effect on the latter condition was weakened and the real subject was still likely to conform to the views of the majority.

Evaluation of Conformity research

66 Assessing research on
conformity 99

- *Harris* (1985) argues that as the majority of trials in the Asch studies (63%) yielded *non-conforming* responses, then these were largely studies of *unconformity*.
- *Perrin and Spencer* (1981) claim that the Asch studies reflect a particular *historical and cultural* perspective and point out that such conformity effects are no longer evident in similar experimental studies.

■ However, cross cultural studies in Belguim (*Doms and Van Avermaet*, 1982) and in the Netherlands (*Vlaander and Van Rooijen*, 1985) have obtained roughly the same results as did Asch in the 1950s.

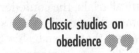

OBEDIENCE

Obedience occurs when an individual performs actions when instructed to do so by some other person. It is also assumed that the individual would not have performed these actions independently.

THE MILGRAM EXPERIMENTS (1963)

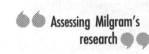

Classic studies on obedience

Milgram's classic studies investigated the impact of authority on behaviour. He carried out a series of experiments in which subjects, ostensibly taking part in an experimental investigation of the effects of punishment on learning, delivered (or thought they delivered) electric shocks to a 'victim' who was really a confederate of the experimenter.

Milgram found that over three-fifths of the subjects gave shocks right up to the maximum shock level. In subsequent experiments, Milgram found that obedience was reduced from having the victim in another room (**remote victim condition**) to having the victim in the same room (**proximity condition**). He also established that obedience was less if other subjects were present who also defied the experimenter, or if the experiment was carried out away from the prestiguous settings of Yale University.

Evaluation of Milgram's research

The validity of the research

Assessing Milgram's research

Orne and Holland (1968) criticised Milgram's research on two major counts. They claimed that the study lacked *internal validity*, in that Milgram's subjects had not been deceived at all and therefore the conclusions drawn from the experiments were inappropriate. Milgram defended his original claim through evidence from debriefing sessions (during which subjects admitted they had believed they were giving the shocks) and also from film of the subjects who appeared to be in considerable distress during their role as 'teacher'. Orne and Holland's second claim was that the study lacked *ecological validity*, i.e. the findings could not be extended outside of the laboratory. This is a more difficult claim to discuss. *Epstein et al.* (1973) from a survey of 300 students discovered that their perception of the experiment was that subjects were 'contractually' obliged to be cooperative. Epstein also found that the students put great trust in the experimenter, trusting in their *professional integrity* and therefore showing willingness to hand over personal responsibility for their actions to them. An attempt to reproduce the spirit of Milgram's research in a natural setting was made by *Hofling* (1966) where nurses in a hospital ward were given instructions over a telephone to act in a way which clearly contradicted hospital rules and procedures. A very high proportion obeyed, thus tending to offer some degree of ecological validity to · this type of research.

Ethical issues in Milgram's research

Baumrind (1964) criticised Milgram's research on the ground that it was not ethically justified. She claimed that:

a) Subjects suffered considerable distress that was not justified given the aims of the research.

b) Subjects would suffer permanent psychological harm from the experiment, including a loss of self esteem and distrust of authority.

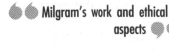

Milgram's work and ethical aspects

c) Migram failed to obtain *informed consent* from subjects. She claimed that subjects would probably not have volunteered if they had known what they were to do. He also made it difficult for them to withdraw through the use of *experimental prods* (e.g. 'You must go on, you have no choice').

Milgram's responses:

a) In a follow-up survey, 84% of his subjects were 'glad to have taken part', and felt they had learned something extremely valuable about themselves.

b) Psychiatric examinations one year after the experiment showed no sign of psychological damage which could be attributed to the experiment.

c) Milgram claimed that at no point were subjects forced to do anything, and the fact that some subjects had withdrawn indicated that all were free to do so.

OTHER RESEARCH ON OBEDIENCE

Gender differences

Sheridan and King (1972) replicated Milgram's research using a puppy instead of a human subject. No deception was required, and female subjects showed greater obedience in continuing giving shocks up to the end of the scale. However, other investigations have failed to show gender differences.

National differences

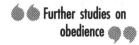
Further studies on obedience

Most investigations have yielded more or less the same levels of obedience as in the US research, although *Mantell* (1971) found that 85% of German subjects (compared to Milgram's 67%) obeyed, whilst *Kilham and Mann* (1974) found lower rates than the US figures in Australian subjects.

Familiarity with the subject

Despite the intuitive reasoning that familiarity would lessen likelihood to shock, research by *Farina et al.* (1966) found that if subjects were introduced to their 'victims' beforehand, a higher level of shock was given to those who appeared to have had a previous life history full of negative events (i.e. troubled childhood, divorce, etc). This tends to support the *'just world'* hypothesis that such 'losers' are often seen as legitimate targets of aggression.

LEADERSHIP

Leadership may be defined as existing in any group interaction where one member acts and the rest of the group agree to be led. *Rauch and Behling* (1984) explain leadership as 'the process of influencing the activities of an organised group towards goal achievement'.

Research has tended to emphasise two approaches. The first is the personality characteristics of the leader, and the second is the situational factors that effect the leadership role.

THE NATURE OF THE LEADER

Traits of the leader

Early theories stressed the **traits** of leaders. *Stogdill* (1948) found that most leaders have higher levels of *intelligence* than their followers, are more active and involved, and tend to have higher *socio-economic status*. *Borgatta* (1954) in studies of leadership carried out in the US Air Force found that people who consistently attained leadership positions tended to score highly on leadership traits than did others who did not attain leadership positions.

Most research on the nature of the leader has made use of questionnaires, (e.g. *Halpin and Winer*, 1952) with correlations then drawn between trait scores and leadership behaviour.

Evaluation of the trait approach

■ Questionnaire based studies have largely been contradicted by observational studies (e.g. *Lord*, 1977). *Ilgen and Fujji* (1976) suggest that questionnaires are inappropriate measures of leadership qualities as respondents frequently present desirable characteristics rather that realistic ones.

■ Most research nowadays has confirmed that the characteristics of a leader are more determined by the demands of the situation itself (*Bass*, 1981).

SITUATIONAL DEMANDS ON LEADERSHIP

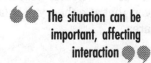
The situation can be important, affecting interaction

The importance of this perspective is that it emphasises the importance of the **situation** and therefore of *interaction* in leadership. Leaders interact both with the situation and with their followers. Both exert important influences on the leadership role.

Early studies (e.g. *Lippitt and White*, 1943) established that different leadership styles were appropriate to different group aims. Looking at the effect of different leadership styles (authoritarian, democratic and laissez-faire) they established that authoritarian leaders were more effective where task completion was the most important factor.

Democratic leaders tended to produce the greatest motivation to work, and such groups were generally more happy and self-reliant.

There are a number of problems with this research:

■ Leaders were adults imposed on groups of children therefore would not represent natural groups.
■ Leader behaviour was rigidly prescribed by the experimenter so that they could not act in accordance with the nature of the groups needs and skills.

EFFECTIVENESS OF LEADERS

💬💬 Ideas involving the least preferred co-worker (LPC) 💬💬

FIEDLER'S CONTINGENCY THEORY (FIEDLER, 1969)

Fiedler used measures of leadership based on leaders' feeling toward their **least preferred co-worker** (LPC). Those with a low opinion of the LPC tended to be more task motivated, controlling and structuring in their leadership role. Those with a high opinion of their LPC tended to be more relationship-motivated, relaxed and less directive. Fiedler found that the low LPC leader was more effective under conditions of either high or low control structure in a task, whereas high LPC leaders were more effective where the amount of control structure was only moderate. Control structure is defined here as:

a) The degree to which the leader-member relations are supportive and reliable.
b) The structure of the task, in terms of clear goals and operations.
c) The power of the leader to reward or punish subordinates.

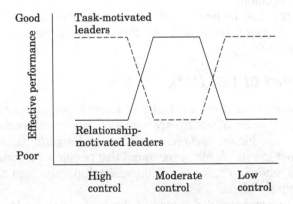

Fig. 10.1 Situational control and performance of leaders (Fiedler and Potter, 1983)

Thus, to Fiedler, leadership effectiveness in any group situation is determined as much by the demands imposed by the situation as by the leadership styles adopted by the leaders themselves.

Evaluation of Fiedler's theory

■ Interpretation of the LPC score is rather vague. *Hosking* (1981) has suggested that not knowing, in more precise terms, the meaning of the LPC score has made it difficult to correlate it precisely with group effectiveness. LPC scores were obtained from people who were not in leadership positions at the time they worked with the LPC.
■ There is considerable disagreement among researchers as to whether research *supports* or *refutes* Fiedler's theory. All are agreed however, that as a theory, it is far from providing complete answers to questions in this area.

GROUP POLARIZATION

Research by *Stoner* (1961) identified the phenomenon of **risky shift**. This referred to the tendency of individuals to reach decisions as a group which were riskier than they would reach as individuals. A number of other studies also found evidence of this **group polarization**, yet in the opposite *cautious* direction. *Moscovici and Zavalloni* (1969) demonstrated that groups would shift (polarize) in the direction of the attitudes that they had, on average, prior to the discussion.

Myers (1982) thus refers to group polarization as an enhancement of an initially dominant position due to group discussion.

Explanations of group polarization

■ **Normative influences.** Such explanations propose that individuals are motivated to be **perceived positively by others.** This is represented by subjects' desire to be both viewed as *correct* and also more *extreme* than the others. If subjects perceive the *direction* of the group decision, the extreme judgements in that direction become more correct and desirable.

■ **Informational influences.** These explanations suggest that during group discussion, individuals are exposed to **new arguments and information from group members.** The group polarization then becomes a process of persuasion, where the shift toward one direction or the other is determined by the quality of the argument presented. If the majority of the group members hold a particular point of view, then the combination of their arguments will result in an increased shift in the direction of that position.

Evaluation of normative and informational influence explanations

■ A study by *Burnstein and Vinokur* (1973) manipulated the availability of both knowledge of other group members' positions and the availability of their arguments. Results showed that the informational influences were more important.

■ *Meertens* (1980) suggests that research in this area has overlooked the importance of other group processes which could also explain the phenomenon of group polarization.

GROUPTHINK

Groupthink is the name given to an extreme form of group polarization. According to *Janis* (1972), groups which are a highly cohesive collection of like minded individuals often reach *extreme* consensual decisions which tend to be unwise or unrealistic. Janis proposed that a number of conditions are necessary for this process to occur – a highly cohesive group, cut off from alternative opinion, and with a leader who clearly favours the option under discussion. If such conditions are present, the group ignores or discounts information which is inconsistent with the option chosen, and the overwhelming expression of support exerts strong normative influences on potential dissidents. The resulting decision appears, then, to be endorsed by all. Janis suggests that the social and political consequences of groupthink may be extremely far reaching.

EXAMINATION QUESTIONS

1. Critically consider research into the nature of conformity.   *(25)*
2. (a) Describe research findings in the study of obedience in humans.   *(10)*
   (b) Describe and evaluate research procedures used in the investigation of this area.
                                                                                 (15)
                                                                          (AEB 1993)
3. Discuss psychological theories and research into the emergence and effectiveness of leaders.   *(25)*
                                                                       (AEB 'AS' 1992)
4. What has psychological research told us about the processes of decision making in groups?   *(25)*

ANSWERS TO EXAMINATION QUESTIONS

OUTLINE ANSWERS TO QUESTIONS 3 AND 4

Question 3

This is another involved question that would benefit from careful reading. It asks you to *discuss* (i.e. describe and evaluate) *theories* (note: in the plural) and *research* into the *emergence* and *effectiveness* of leaders. There are lots of things to do, and failure to address them all will lose you valuable marks. A typical answer would:

1. Describe trait and situational theories on the emergence of leaders.
2. Evaluate these theories, or maybe even compare and contrast them.
3. Look at research into the emergence of leaders.
4. Evaluate this research, perhaps by looking at the problems of questionnaires vs observation.
5. Describe contingency theory(ies) on the effectiveness of leaders.
6. Look at research in this area.
7. Offer evaluation of contingency theory(ies).

Question 4

Most of the accessible research evidence is on *group polarization*, in particular the risky shift. An answer to this question might mention:

1. Research into risky shift and explanations of the phenomenon (e.g. polarization toward existing attitudes).
2. Normative and informational influences, and the former's link with concerns about impression management.
3. Research into 'groupthink' and explanations for the phenomenon.

Recent research (e.g. *Stasser*, 1989) has found that groups will often use a system of *social decision schemes* such as the *majority wins rule*, which seems to be most successful in judgemental tasks, or the *truth rule* (i.e. a belief that the correct decision will eventually emerge) which predicts group decisions most successfully on tasks where there is a correct answer.

TUTOR'S ANSWER

Question 1

Research on conformity has attempted to discover when and why people conform. The classic study in this area was carried out by *Asch* (1952) who, although providing insights into the conditions that promote conformity, failed to provide a convincing account of *why* people conform in the first place. It is probably the case that many people conform because they doubt their own knowledge and ability within a situation, and so are influenced by the behaviour of others (informational conformity). Others may conform to escape social disapproval through not conforming. This latter form of conformity (normative conformity) tends to involve a conflict between what the individual believes to be the right decision or course of action, and what appears to be the dominant norms displayed by the rest of the group. Thus the individual, in conforming, is yielding to the social influence imposed by the group members.

Asch's research involved subjects ostensibly taking part in an experiment on visual discrimination. Naive subjects were placed singly in groups of confederates who were primed to give unanimous wrong answers on some of the trials. Asch found that his real subjects made 'errors' on 37% of the trials, compared with 5% errors in a non-conformity control condition. This fact led *Harris* (1985) to conclude that although 37% of the trials contained errors, the vast majority did not, thus suggesting that what Asch had discovered was not the circumstances of conformity, but rather the circumstances of non-conformity. However, Asch found that most subjects conformed on at least one occasion.

It has been suggested (*Perrin and Spencer*, 1981) that the 'Asch Effect' is rooted in a particular cultural and historical tradition and that the effect is difficult to replicate in contemporary research. This does not appear to be the case in all investigations, however, as more recent studies (e.g. *Vlaander and Van Rooijen,* 1985) have obtained much the same results as Asch. *Nicholson et al.* (1985) found evidence of the Asch effect among British and American undergraduates but considerably less than in 1952. In an interesting variation, *Perrin and Spencer* (1981) found that the composition of the group was an important influence on the naive subject, and that conformity was most likely when the perceived costs of not conforming to the majority decision were high.

These findings suggested that a number of critical factors will influence the likelihood of people yielding to group pressure. *Crandall* (1988) studying conformity to 'binge eating' in a sorority house, found that as cliques became established, the cohesiveness of the group exerted a stronger conforming force on its members toward binge eating.

Several studies have attempted to study the effect of group size on conformity behaviour. Most studies (e.g. *Gerard et al.,* 1968) seem to indicate that as the group size increases, so does the conformity, but beyond a certain point, the effect levels out. *Wilder* (1977) suggests that this may be due to a suspicion of collusion among group members, as it is rare to find such unanimous agreement in large groups.

In an extension to his original study, *Asch* (1952) introduced another 'deviant' in that this confederate also disagreed with the majority. Having an ally proved very effective in reducing conformity to very low levels. However, later research by Allen and Levine has suggested that this conclusion was misplaced. They suggested that if the deviant not only disagreed with the majority, but also offered a position different from that of the real subject, then the effectiveness of the support was diminished. Allen and Levine found that in such situations, the deviant's position *could* help the real subject to break the need to conform, but this was only the case in unambiguous stimulus situations such as those in the original Asch research. In situations concerning opinion statements, the deviant's support was only effective in reducing conformity if it was a position consistent with that of the real subject.

Most investigations of conformity, like other areas of social influence, involve the subject as a *receiver* of social influence rather than a participant in the process. *Howitt et al.* (1992) suggest that the artificiality of the lab situation places the subject in an unfamiliar situation which prevents them from playing anything other than a passive recipient role. This, they argue, is not the same as the normal social world, in which individuals play a more active, initiating role, and their motivation to conform is influenced by a range of factors outside the scope of the laboratory situation.

STUDENT'S ANSWER WITH EXAMINER'S COMMENTS

Question 2

(a) A number of experiments have been carried out on obedience, these include those by Milgram, Zimbardo and Hofling. These studies have had numerous findings. Milgram's experiment involved subjects who believed they were administering shocks to another person in a training situation. The shocks ranged from 15 volts to 450 volts. He wanted to see how many would continue to the end. His first experiment involved 40 males between 20 and 50 and of these all continued to 300 volts, when only five dropped out. Between 315–375 volts, only nine dropped out. Thus 65% of the subjects continued giving shocks until the maximum 450 volts. In further experiments, it was found that a number of factors influenced how many people continued to the maximum shock. These factors included where the experiment took place, the presence of an experimenter, the distance between the experimenter and the subject and if they had a model or someone to blame.

Zimbardo had 25 male students in his prison simulation experiment. They were split into two groups of prisoners and guards. After being unexpectedly taken from the streets, they were taken to the prison, within the university. Within a few hours the prisoners had taken on a submissive role, while the guards had taken on their authoritative roles. Zimbardo found that the more submissive the prisoners became the more aggressive the guards became toward them.

In Hofling's experiment, nurses were rung and told they should give a patient a particular drug, which, for many reasons, was odd. In a prior questionnaire, the 22 nurses were asked, if placed in this situation, would they do it. Most of them replied that they wouldn't. But in the actual experiment, 21 of the 22 nurses did as they were

🌑🌑 Good, awareness of variations of Milgram's research 🌑🌑

🌑🌑 What, exactly, happened to the level of obedience in these situations? 🌑🌑

🌑🌑 Some confusion here – suggests that the same 22 nurses were used 🌑🌑

told. This seems to show that when people are placed in certain situations, they will obey what they are being told to do.

(b) Milgram's obedience experiment involved respondents to a newspaper advertisement. They were to be the teacher and a confederate the learner. With the experimenter in the room, the subject read out pairs of words to the learner who had to report back the pairs. Each time they got it wrong, the teacher had to supply an electric shock which increased. From about 300 volts, the learner began to complain and groan progressively until 450 volts when all was silent. Subjects did protest, but the experimenter used prods to make them continue. A number of people have criticised this experiment. Baumrind criticised it for being unethical, because the subjects suffered unnecessary stress and may have suffered from long term effects of the experiment. Milgram basically replied that the subjects could have stopped if they really wanted to, and he found that they suffered no long term effects. In fact, he said that most were glad they did. Orne and Holland said that some of the subjects probably guessed nothing was really happening, or else the experimenter wouldn't have sat passively by. They also said it was similar to the magicians trick with the guillotine, where s/he first shows it works with a cabbage and then asks a volunteer to take part. The volunteer trusts the magician and knows his head won't be cut off, but still obeys. Another criticism they made was that you couldn't apply it outside the experimental situation. In a real world setting, this probably wouldn't occur. Milgram uses Hofling's experiment as a reply to this, when a man pretending to be a physician rings up the nurse and asks her to give medicine to a patient. This is strange because the medicine isn't on the stocklist, they are told to give double the maximum dose and its against hospital policy. But when the experiment was carried out, 21 out of the 22 nurses did it anyway.

Zimbardo's experiment involved 25 healthy male students when unexpectedly picked up by a police car off the streets and taken to the university prison simulation. All their personal possessions were taken away and a process of deindividuation began. The guards became quite aggressive and the prisoners began to act like prisoners. Again, this experiment can be criticised for being unethical. Many of the subjects were suprised at the way they acted. In fact, one subject had to be withdrawn from the experiment, because he reacted by crying and was very distressed.

As we can see, these experiments show that people will obey orders to do things that we wouldn't normally expect them to do. However, there are faults in these experiments.

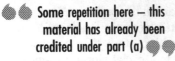 **Appropriate discussion on the validity of the experimental conclusions**

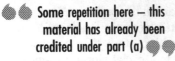 **Some repetition here – this material has already been credited under part (a)**

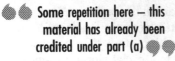 A good essay which did manage to disentangle the quite different requirements of parts (a) and (b). Discussion was a little underdeveloped at times but the candidate did show an awareness of problems relating to both ethics *and* validity in this type of research. This answer is probably equivalent to a grade B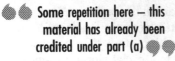

REVIEW SHEET

1. Latané's social impact theory proposes that the influence of others is determined by which *three* factors?

   _____

   _____

   _____

2. Distinguish between an audience effect and a coaction effect.

   _____

   _____

3. Give *two* explanations for the audience effect.

   _____

   _____

4. What is social loafing?

   _____

   _____

5. Distinguish between informational and normative conformity.

   _____

   _____

6. What percentage of errors were made among naive subjects in the original Asch research?

   _____

   _____

7. What happens to conformity if the majority size increases?

   _____

   _____

8. What might Perrin and Spencer have meant by 'The Asch effect, a child of its time.'?

   _____

   _____

9. What proportion of Milgram's subjects gave the maximum shock?

   _____

   _____

10. Offer *two* criticisms of the validity of Milgram's research, and two criticisms of the ethics of the research.

Validity

_____

_____

_____

_____

Ethics

_____

_____

_____

_____

11. Give *two* characteristics of leaders that have been supported by research evidence.

_____

_____

12. Give *two* criticisms of this trait approach to leadership.

_____

13. What did Fiedler mean by the LPC?

_____

_____

14. Off *two* criticisms of Fiedler's theory.

_____

_____

15. What is risky shift and what causes it?

_____

_____

EVOLUTIONARY DETERMINANTS OF BEHAVIOUR

GETTING STARTED

This chapter explores the major evolutionary concepts in the explanation of the social behaviour of non-human animals. Central to this issue is an understanding of **Natural selection**, and its related concept of **Sexual selection**. Although natural selection is a familiar concept to most people when applied to the evolution of physical characteristics, it is less familiar when applied to the evolution of behaviour. **Sociobiology** is the name given to the branch of evolutionary biology that deals with such explanations.

Also of considerable importance in this area is the phenomenon of biological **altruism**, which has been described as the greatest challenge to evolutionary theories of behaviour.

Material in this chapter will enable you to answer questions on subsection 1 of the AEB comparative psychology option.

The following are typical of questions in this subsection.

- Discussion of the interaction of genetic and environmental factors in development of behaviour.
- Discussion of the role of evolutionary concepts to an understanding of the behaviour of non-human animals.
- The role of apparently altruistic behaviour in non-human animals.

INTERACTION OF GENETIC AND ENVIRONMENTAL FACTORS

EVOLUTIONARY CONCEPTS IN ANIMAL BEHAVIOUR

SOCIOBIOLOGY

EVOLUTION OF SOCIAL BEHAVIOUR – AN EXAMPLE

CRITICISMS OF EVOLUTIONARY EXPLANATIONS OF ANIMAL BEHAVIOUR

ALTRUISM

ESSENTIAL PRINCIPLES

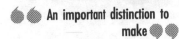

Animals may either be born with a set of responses already 'pre-wired' into the nervous system (crudely referred to as **instinctive** behaviours which are **inherited**), or may have the ability to modify their behaviour over time in the light of experience in their environment (**learning**).

INSTINCTIVE BEHAVIOUR

An important distinction to make

Instinctive behaviour evolves gradually and is modified by natural selection in order to adapt animals to fit a fixed and unchanging environment. This gives an evolutionary advantage to the animals that possess them, in that they are better adapted to their environment than animals that do not possess such characteristics. However, such traits can only become widespread in a species if the environmental demands remain constant over time.

Genetically determined behaviour changes through natural selection

Instinctive behaviours are advantageous for animals that have short life spans and have little or no parental care, and therefore little opportunity or need for learning. Such behaviours ensure that animals are optimally adapted to their environments. This is brought about by the forces of natural selection which change behaviour to bring about adaptation over evolutionary time.

LEARNED BEHAVIOUR

Learning enables animals to experiment with their environment, to learn which responses give the best results in given circumstances, and to modify their behaviour accordingly.

Higher animals have a greater opportunity to learn, and although they may have instinctive tendencies, they need to learn how to direct them as a result of their exposure to environmental experience.

An important point

The ability to learn gives animals an adaptive advantage in that it gives them a greater potential for changing their behaviour to meet changing circumstances. The mechanisms of learning enable animals to change their behaviour within their own lifetime. Thus if the environment changes, it makes a great deal of evolutionary sense if animals can adapt their behaviour to the different circumstances which are thus created. Learning thus becomes a survival trait.

AN INTERACTION

Learning cannot be fully understood without reference to the adaptive significance of the kinds of behaviour involved. *Seligman* (1970) proposes that animals are **biologically prepared** to learn some things more readily than others. According to Seligman, some associations are more biologically useful than others (e.g. taste avoidance and predator avoidance) and are therefore learned more quickly and are more resistant to extinction.

Research on *bird song* has demonstrated the importance of both instinct and learning ability. Although most male birds inherit the rudiments of their song, they need to experience singing and listening to the songs of other birds before their song takes its final form. However, the production of, and reaction to, alarm calls appears perfect without previous experience. Thus, natural selection favours an inherited response in those situations where a delay in the development of a behaviour due to learning would be fatal.

Even the ability to learn is seen as affected by genetic factors

However, few behaviours can be said to be entirely dominated by *either* inheritance *or* learning. *Grier and Burk* (1992) suggest that nearly all animal behaviour is affected by heredity to some degree. If there is any heritability in a particular behaviour, then it follows that it is subject to the forces of evolution.

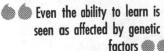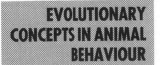

Natural selection

Evolution through **natural selection** can be defined as a change in the frequencies of genes within a population, thereby altering the gene pool from one generation to the next. The existence of processes of natural selection can be inferred from the following basic propositions.

a) All species are capable of over-reproducing.
b) Populations of species remain stable over time.
c) Resources are limited.

Important to understand natural selection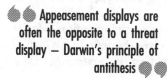

Thus a struggle exists among individuals, and over many generations the nature of the gene pool changes as some animals adapt more successfully than others.

Adaptedness

Adaptedness is the property of being well suited to an environment in which an animal lives. Evolutionary adaptation takes place as species adjust genetically to changes in their environments. This should not be confused with *phenotypic* adaptation in which animals adjust during the course of their lifetimes through processes such as *maturation* and *learning*.

Ecological niche

The precise environment to which an animal is adapted is referred to as its **ecological niche**. The ecological niche exerts a 'selective pressure' on each species such that the genes of the species changes in response to the pressures imposed by that environment.

Sexual selection

In some species, it is male choice not female choice

Thus, many males develop 'handicaps' such as bright plumage, purely for sexual selection

What, therefore, does the survival of the fittest actually mean?

Whereas natural selection results in animals being better adapted to their environment, **sexual selection** refers to the advantages that individuals have over others of the same sex solely in terms of reproduction. Sexual selection, according to Darwin depended on (usually) female choice. Once evolved, female choice leads to the development of characteristics in males that have nothing to do with survival. They continue to exist because any female that bucked the trend and picked a mate without these characteristics would immediately disadvantage her offspring in that they would not possess the characteristics which would lead to *their* choice as mates.

Fitness

An animals individual **fitness** is a measure of its ability to leave behind offspring. The characteristics which determine an animals fitness are determined by the processes of natural and sexual selection. The term **inclusive fitness** refers to the total number of an animal's genes present in subsequent generations. These may not be direct offspring but may be relatives who profit from the *altruistic* behaviour of the animal concerned.

SOCIOBIOLOGY

Sociobiology refers to the use of evolutionary ideas to explain the **social** behaviour of animals. Originally associated with *Wilson* (1975), its more contemporary writers include *Dawkins* (Selfish Gene theory, 1976). Ideas central to sociobiology include the following:

Strategies

A **strategy** is one of a number of possible courses of action that might be taken by an animal. Strategies that are subject to genetic control (e.g. parental care, altruistic behaviour etc.) are thus subject to the laws of natural selection. Those which contribute to increased inclusive fitness are thus more likely to become established in the behavioural repertoire of a species.

Evolutionarily stable strategies (EES)

Appeasement displays are often the opposite to a threat display – Darwin's principle of antithesis

A strategy may be described as an **Evolutionarily Stable Strategy** (ESS) if it becomes widespread in a population and resists invasion by other alternative strategies. It is an optimum strategy dependent on the circumstances in which it is used. For example, the use of and response to appeasement displays may become widespread in that it confers advantages on both parties in a dispute. A victorious animal that does not respond to an appeasement display by breaking off from a fight risks further injury and hence less reproductive fitness. However, response to the appeasement posture may not always be in the best interests of the victorious animal, so the ESS may be *conditional* upon circumstances (*Dawkins*, 1980).

Arms races

●● Based on ideas of human weapon escalation ●●

These refer to the evolutionary 'race' which exists between predators and prey. *Dawkins and Krebs* (1979) point out that evolutionary 'improvements' in predator behaviour does not mean that they catch more prey, because the 'selective pressure' this exerts on the prey means that they too improve in order to evade capture.

Levels of selection

There has been a good deal of controversy over the actual mechanisms of natural selection that determine a particular behaviour pattern. The need for such an analysis came about largely as a result of the need to explain the **altruism paradox**. According to Darwin's theory, behaviours would only become established in a species (note that Darwin did not have an understanding of the mechanisms of genetic transmission) if they conferred some advantage (mainly in terms of increased fitness) to the animals concerned. Therefore altruistic behaviour (helping another at some cost to the altruist) should not be present in the gene pool, but it is. Early explanations stressed the importance of **group selection** (*Wynne-Edwards*, 1962) whereby individuals low in social status may sacrifice their reproductive potential in order to ensure that the group did not exceed the resources available. Later explanations focussed on individual selection where the evolutionary interests of a particular gene are seen as most important.

●● Why is this explanation implausible? ●●

Adaptations in an individual which are geared toward helping close relatives are said to evolve through *kin selection* (*Hamilton*, 1964; *Dawkins*, 1979).

EVOLUTION OF SOCIAL BEHAVIOUR, AN EXAMPLE

COMMUNICATION

The central belief in modern ethology is that behaviour, like every other aspect of animal nature, has evolved because it benefits the *genes* of the behaving animal. However, communication involves at least two participants, one to send and one to receive. The question is, do both participants benefit or just the sender (or in fact just the receiver)?

Conventional wisdom in ethology is that both parties benefit and the whole signalling system has evolved through mutual benefit. Natural selection favours e.g. males who signal to influence the behaviour of females, but at the same time it favours females who respond to those signals. This joint selection pressure leads to the evolution of more and more effective signals interacting with more and more receptive sensory apparatuses.

Krebs and Davies (1978) argue that communication is not simply to benefit the sender, but that the reason it does so is because it allows the sender to manipulate the receiver's behaviour. They argue that the reason why communication has evolved is because, by allowing such manipulation it confers an evolutionary advantage on the sender. This view of evolution, that behaviours evolve because of the fact that they benefit animals in a basically selfish way, is an example of the *Sociobiological* perspective. An example of a manipulative signal which clearly only benefits one part can be found in the lure of the angler fish. The angler fish exploits an aspect of the sensory–response system of its prey species which usually benefits the prey because it leads them to worms.

Natural selection will also favour changes in the discriminatory powers of the prey species such that they do not respond to the lure, but this in turn places selective pressure on the predatory angler fish such that over generations, the lures become more convincing. This escalation of lure and counter-lure is an example of a *biological arms race*.

However, not everybody accepts this rather cynical view of communication. *Marler* (1984) argued that to some extent, both sender and receiver benefit in an act of communication, and that the key element of communication is *mutuality*. Even

Dawkins, a leading sociobiologist, acknowledges that despite the quite common occurrence of these 'deceptive' examples of communication, it is probably true that, on the whole, both parties benefit from communication. It appears to be the case that the balance of selective forces acting on both sender and receiver is pushing in the same evolutionary direction, i.e. towards the evolution of an efficient mutual signalling system. Such basic 'honesty' in communication would be vital in courtship, parent-offspring interaction, and in the signals exchanged between animals in the variety of different forms of social organisation.

<table>
<tr><td>

CRITICISMS OF EVOLUTIONARY EXPLANATIONS OF ANIMAL BEHAVIOUR

</td><td>

1. Many evolutionary explanations of behaviour cannot be falsified. Unlike explanations of the evolution of physical characteristics, the evolution of behaviour does not leave fossils for examination. Explanations tend, therefore, to be a matter of inference based on theoretical consideration rather than empirical evidence.
2. Traditional interpretations of Darwinism tend to see evolution occuring in a gradual manner rather than through sudden or random changes. It is evident that species do, from time to time, develop in such a way. Such changes appear to cast doubt on Darwinian theory. However, these processes (saltation and genetic drift) appear to offer a more flexible interpretation of Darwinian theory rather than undermining it.
3. The existence of altruism in the behaviour of non-human animals is seen as the greatest challenge to Darwinian theory. The theory of natural selection proposes that animals should behave selfishly and that altruists would be less likely to reproduce. Altruism then, should not exist within a gene pool, but it does. However, sufficient explanations of altruism exist (kin selection theory, reciprocal altruism) to allow for such apparent altruism within a Darwinian framework.

</td></tr>
</table>

 The altruism paradox

4. Because natural selection is a slow process, it does not enable species to adapt quickly to changes in their environment. Animals which are born into unchanging environments are able to respond with purely inherited characteristics, but in a more rapidly changing environment, inflexible inherited characteristics would place animals at a disadvantage. It is thus beneficial for an animal to be able to *learn* during the course of its lifetime. Whilst it is possible, if not probable, that such a strategy has evolved in higher animals, it is nevertheless the case that evolutionary explanations of behaviour tend to underestimate the importance of learning in the development of behaviour.

Not to be confused with psychological altruism in humans, which implies a kindly intent

ALTRUISM

Definition

An **altruistic** act refers to any act of behaviour which increases the chances of survival of one organism whilst decreasing the chances of survival of the altruist.

EXAMPLES OF ALTRUISM

a) Belding's ground squirrels

Research by *Sherman* (1985) has demonstrated that these squirrels have different alarm calls for different predators. A whistle call is given when they see a goshawk, and a trill call when they see a coyote. In the former case, the 'altruist' benefits from the confusion effect, increasing its own chances of escape, but in the latter case calling increases the likelihood of being caught. However, those who do escape in this situation are likely to be close genetic relatives of the caller.

b) Florida scrub jays

These birds are communal breeders. Breeding birds are regularly assisted by nonbreeding helpers at the nest. Research by *Woolfenden and Fitzpatrick,* (1984) found that helpers normally assist their own parents, and that nests with helpers produce more fledglings than nests without. The benefits for female helpers are partly direct (staying increases the chances of their survival) and partly indirect (by increasing the survival rates of close genetic relatives). Male helpers gain in the long run, as helping their parents in territorial disputes enables them to increase the size of the territory so that eventually they take over one section of it for their own breeding purposes.

EXPLANATIONS OF ALTRUISTIC BEHAVIOUR

1. Group selection (Wynne-Edwards, 1962)

This explanation emphasised the importance of altruistic self-restraint in breeding. This would allow some *groups* to survive whereas other groups consisting of more selfishly reproducing individuals would become overpopulated relative to the resources available and die out.

The trouble with this explanation is that within any group, selfish individuals (who do reproduce) would flourish, whereas altruistic individuals (who do not reproduce) would fail to pass on their genes. The genes for altruism would therefore soon die out within a population.

2. Kin selection (Hamilton, 1964).

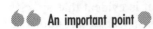 **An important point**

Hamilton proposed that to understand how the gene for altruism might evolve within a population, one had to look not only at the consequences of the gene for the altruist, but also for the relatives of the altruist. This **inclusive fitness** thus refers to both the individual's reproductive success plus the extra reproductive success enjoyed by its relatives as a result of its altruistic behaviour. Thus, one of the commonest forms of apparent altruism, parental care, can be explained simply in terms of **kin selection**. As in many examples of altruism through kin selection, the benefits to the recipient are often greater than the costs to the altruist.

Of key importance in kin selection theory is the recognition of relatives. Four mechanisms for kin recognition are proposed (*Grier & Burk*, 1992).

Mechanisms for kin recognition

a) **Spatial distribution**: Kin tend to be found in a certain place.
b) **Association mechanisms**: Kin tend to be recognized as individuals that the altruist has associated with at a specific time.
c) **Phenotype matching**: Characteristics are compared with some 'relative related' referent.
d) **'Green beard effect'** (*Dawkins*, 1976): The altruism gene is seen as having a simultaneous effect on some other physical characteristic such that relatives can recognise animals who possess it. (The 'green beard' is such a hypothetical characteristic).

Hamilton's kin selection theory was able to explain what had first appeared to be an 'insuperable' problem – the behaviour of social insects. Many social insects, it appears, have a rather peculiar form of genetic transmission whereby they are closer genetically to their siblings than to their offspring. It thus benefits the *selfish gene* to assist siblings to reproduce than to bear their own offspring.

Reciprocal altruism (Trivers, 1971)

This form of altruism can explain altruistic behaviour among non-relatives. Trivers suggested that animals might exhibit altruistic behaviour toward others provided that the other animal reciprocated in the future. *Packer's* (1977) study of mating alliances in olive baboons provided support for this. The conditions necessary for the development of **reciprocal altruism** are:

Conditions necessary for reciprocal altruism

a) Low dispersal rate (so that animals have the opportunity for future meetings and thus reciprocity).
b) Long life span (as above).
c) Ability to recognise altruists (for reciprocity) and cheats (to apply sanctions for defection).

Note that tit for tat is still theoretical

Axelrod and Hamilton (1981) proposed a 'tit for tat' strategy (each animal would simply respond to the other animal's last response. Cooperation would be followed by co-operation, defection by mutual defection). Tit for tat is effective because it is 'retaliatory' (punishes cheats) and also conciliatory (in that future cooperation would be responded to mutually). Axelrod and Hamilton suggested that tit for tat would eventually become an evolutionarily stable strategy (see previous section on sociobiology).

Manipulated altruism.

Although not a particular challenge to Darwinian theory, examples of **manipulated altruism** do conform to the definition of altruism given at the start of this section. Manipulated altruism (e.g. a 'foster parent' feeding a young cuckoo) occurs when a set of responses e.g. putting food into a gaping chick's bill, are subverted to the advantage of selfish individuals. The strategy here is to burden the cost of parental care onto another.

Conclusion

The explanations detailed above do tend to explain most examples of apparent altruism within a Darwinian framework although some examples (e.g. in Artic plunder fish, males may 'babysit' the young of a removed female non-relative) still seem to defy explanation in such terms.

EXAMINATION QUESTIONS

1. Discuss the interaction of genetic and environmental factors in the development of the behaviour of non-human species. *(25)*
2. Discuss the role of apparently altruistic behaviour in non-human species. *(25)*
   (AEB 1989)
3. Describe and critically assess the role of evolutionary concepts in understanding the behaviour of non-human animals. *(25)*
   (AEB 1993)

ANSWERS TO EXAMINATION QUESTIONS

OUTLINE ANSWER TO QUESTION 1

This question asks for a *discussion*, therefore needs both description and analysis/ evaluation of the material presented. It might include the following:

- Outline of what is meant by instinctive (genetic) behaviour and what is meant by learned behaviour.
- Advantages of each, e.g. genetically controlled behaviour is useful in an unchanging environment. Learning is advantageous in that it allows an animal to modify its behaviour within its lifetime to meet changing circumstances.
- Consideration of the interaction between the two, e.g. discussion of the concept of biological preparedness. Also relevant is Grier and Burk's point that heredity lurks behind most behaviours, and the ability to learn may be seen as an adaptive strategy.

TUTORS ANSWER

Question 2

Biological altruism might be defined as any act of an organism which increases the survival or the reproductive fitness of another animal whilst decreasing its own. Biological altruism should be distinguished from psychological altruism in humans, which implies some kindly intent on the part of the altruist. Its use in biology is quite specific, an altruistic act is one that has the effect of benefitting another organism at the altruist's expense.

Examples of supposedly altruistic behaviour might include parental care, whereby the parent decreases its own chances of survival, but at the same time increases the survival chances of its offspring. Similarly, the altruistic acts of the Florida Scrub Jay, where the offspring of earlier broods often remain at the nest in order to help with the rearing of later broods.

Another common and potentially more dramatic example of altruistic behaviour can be found in the behaviour of social insects. In many species, workers devote all their energies to helping rear the offspring of another, the queen, and forego their own reproductive chances. Some insects engage in defensive behaviour that results in their own death. This often has the benefit of protecting other members of the colony, and has led some commentators on this phenomenon to suggest that such behaviour must be occuring *for the good of the species.*

Such widespread demonstrations of apparently altruistic behaviour creates a problem for students of natural selection. The principle of natural selection means that it only favours adaptations that cause animals to bear more offspring. To engage in behaviour that directly contradicts such a principle creates what has been termed the *altruism paradox,* (*Wilson,* 1975). Altruists, by definition, leave fewer offspring than non-altruists, so by the forces of natural selection, non-altruists should be at an advantage over altruists. Altruism, therefore, should not exist, but it does, and that is the paradox.

There are four major explanations for why altruism exists, although only three of them remain valid, given our present understanding of biology.

The one of the four which appears invalid is the 'group selection theory' (*Wynne-Edwards,* 1962). This theory supposes that natural selection works at the level of whole groups, and if individual and group interests come into conflict, the group interest will prevail. Such an explanation fits the behaviour of the social insects quite nicely, but can be rejected on two main grounds. First of all, natural selection works at the individual level, and groups only benefit when the interests of the group are identical with those of the individual. Secondly, there are other more plausible explanations of altruistic behaviour that do seem to fit the Darwinian theory of natural selection, and its more recent developments (Selfish Gene theory, *Dawkins,* 1976). The examples of parental altruism given earlier can be explained using the 'kin selection theory' (*Hamilton,* 1964). In a sense, this is the easiest type of altruism to explain. A parent is likely to leave behind more offspring by caring for them, than by not caring for them, so genes for parental behaviour would rapidly become widespread in a population. The same principle of kin selection can also be used to explain the phenomenon of 'helpers at the nest'. Natural selection would favour the evolution of helping at the nest behaviour if, by helping, an animal increases the number of its siblings by more than the number of offspring it would, on average leave if it bred alone. Evidence for this claim in the Florida Scrub Jay (*Woolfenden,* 1976) showed that not only did more siblings survive in nests where there were helpers, but when the helpers eventually had their own broods, more survived when the parent had previously been a helper in another brood. Thus, not only was the helper helping close genetic relatives (the degree of genetic relatedness is the same between siblings as it is between parents and offspring) but was also benefitting its own genetic fitness by leaving behind more birds with the gene for helping at the nest.

The altruism shown in insect societies can likewise be explained in terms of Hamilton's theory of kin selection. The social insects have a peculiar genetic system, which results in females having very similar genetic makeups to their sisters in the colony. It therefore benefits the gene-line of an individual to produce more sisters than offspring, because of the closer genetic relatedness with their sisters. The development of this argument has led some writers (e.g. *Dawkins,* 1982), to conclude that it is the gene rather than the individual which is the unit of natural selection. This is not a point of view shared by all biologists, many of whom continue to see the individual as an entity on which natural selection acts, objecting to the reductionism inherent in Dawkins' claim. For the kin selection theory to be a valid explanation of altruism requires animals to be able to recognise close genetic relatives. It is probable that the young animal forms social attachments to those in proximity. In a natural group, proximate individuals will probably be close relatives, thus altruism develops.

A critical feature of Hamilton's theory is that it is testable. While the theory cannot be proved by simply finding examples of altruism which can be explained by the kin selection model, it can be discounted in cases of cooperation among non-relatives in a natural population. For example, *Massey* (1977) discovered that rhesus monkeys were more likely to help each other in fights in proportion to their degree of relatedness. *McCracken and Bradbury* (1977) on the other hand demonstrated that the degree of relatedness in colonial bats is too low to explain their cooperative coloniality on the basis of kin selection. It is obvious that a further explanation is necessary to accomodate this latter example.

The third theory is referred to as 'reciprocal altruism' (*Trivers*, 1971). This theory predicts that altruism will often be found between animals that are not genetically related, or even of the same species. *Packer*, (1977) found that olive baboons often form pairs in order to mate successfully with females. Pairs of baboons are better able to defend the female from competing males than are single males. Only one member of the pair mates with the female, therefore the other appears to be behaving altruistically. Packer found that such apparent altruism was favoured because when the next female came into season, the pair of baboons would reform, although this time the position would be reversed, with the former altruist now having the opportunity to mate. As with many other examples of mutual cooperation, such an arrangement only works when animals can recognise each other such that acts of altruism can be reciprocated. This also means that 'cheats' (who do not reciprocate) can be recognised and discriminated against.

According to Trivers, natural selection acting at the level of the individual could produce altruistic behaviours if, in the long run they benefit the individual performing them. Trivers believed that the preconditions for the development of reciprocal altruism are; long life of the animals concerned, low dispersal rate and mutual dependence, in that the clumping of individuals, for example in the avoidance of predators, increases the chances for reciprocation. *Wilkinson* (1984) tested the model with reference to the cooperative blood sharing behaviour of vampire bats. He found that although most blood sharing exchanges were between mother and offspring, those that were not could be predicted on the basis of how often the pair had shared in the past.

Through the use of game theory, *Axelrod and Hamilton* (1981) developed a model for the evolution of cooperation among non-relatives. The 'tit for tat' model, in which an animal simply mirrors the last behaviour of another animal enables cooperation to become widespread, and thus evolutionarily stable.

Lin and Michener (1972) have attempted to explain the cooperative behaviour of social insects by using the principle of reciprocity. They argue that mutualism in social insects gradually led to division of labour, leading some individuals to give up reproducing altogether. Each individual gambles that the benefits it gives will be returned at a later time in some way that increases its own fitness.

The final explanation concerns manipulated altruism. Animals carry a set of responses which are normally appropriate, but which may be subverted. A cuckoo, for example, exploits the normal response of a parent bird to a gaping chick's bill. Natural selection may well favour the development of such manipulated altruism in both intra- and interspecies interactions.

These, then, are the major explanations of altruism. It is clear that no one explanation is, by itself, sufficient to explain the incidence of supposedly 'altruistic' behaviour. Most can be fitted to natural selection theory, but sufficient examples remain (e.g. 'babysitting' among non-related male Artic plunder fish) that the evolutionary significance of altruism is still a source of considerable controversy.

STUDENT'S ANSWER WITH EXAMINER'S COMMENTS

Question 3

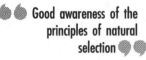 Good awareness of the principles of natural selection

The theory that presently holds sway is that of Darwin. This theory of natural selection suggests that all species are capable of overproducing but the population must remain relatively stable over time due to a limitation of available resources. Therefore, there must be a differential rate of survival. Some traits that occur in a particular species, by chance or mutation, may make certain individuals more likely to survive and reproduce. Because these chance traits occur only to unique individuals, and because this uniqueness is inherited, the offspring will also be at an advantage. Eventually, after many years, the trait will saturate the gene pool as those without the trait cannot survive or reproduce and do not have access to the available resources.

In terms of non-human animals, in which only the fittest or most able to reproduce, will survive, most if not all behaviour must be favoured by natural selection. For instance, song in songbirds has been attributed to many variables from pleasure to language, but most feasibly it has been attributed to sexual selection. For instance,

Appropriate example which illustrates the nature of sexual selection

Again, relevant and accurate

A bit of circularity here. If it has saturated a gene pool it must have been favoured

Tails off here, which is a pity

monogamous song birds have evolved long, spontaneous, varying songs because females pick the mates with the most complex song. Meanwhile, polygamous song birds sing in order to mark out territory and the females pick the males with the largest and best territory.

However, even behaviour which appears to not be favoured by natural selection, such as altruism (or performing an act for another with some cost to the self), if it is fully investigated will reveal its inherent advantages. For example, Woolfenden has documented an example of helpers at the nest in Florida Scrub Jays that apparently foregoes its breeding for a time in order to help its parents with the next brood of young. This is obviously not favoured by natural selection, however, when one looks at the helper in later life it is easy to see the advantages because the helper has larger broods, gains parental experience producing a higher survival rate amongst young and it has a high chance of inheriting its parent's territory. So it can be argued that natural selection produces evolution so whenever a new behaviour saturates the gene pool it must be favoured. Therefore considering that many thousands of chance behaviour patterns have occurred in many thousands of generations, the animals that we see today must be the product of a massive amount of natural selection meaning that most, if not all behaviour is favoured by that natural selection process.

Overall comment: This essay is a sensible and well argued attempt to answer the question. It shows a clear understanding of the nature of natural selection and uses appropriate examples. It is a little limited in its discussion of evolutionary concepts, however, and despite dealing competently with the altruism paradox, doe not really treat the material presented in a critical manner. The answer is characteristic of a grade 'C'.

REVIEW SHEETS

1. Distinguish between instinctive behaviour and learned behaviour.

    _____

    _____

2. When is instinctive behaviour particularly advantageous?

    _____

    _____

3. Under what conditions does natural selection favour an inherited response?

    _____

    _____

4. What are the *three* basic propositions which underlie the principles of natural selection?

    _____

    _____

5. What is the difference between evolutionary adaptation and phenotypic adaptation?

    _____

    _____

6. What is an ecological niche?

    _____

    _____

7. What would happen if a female animal chose a more viable (from a survival point of view) male who lacked the 'attractive' features of sexually successful males of that species?

    _____

    _____

    _____

8. What does *survival of the fittest* actually mean?

    _____

    _____

9. When does a strategy become an ESS?

    _____

    _____

10. What is the major flaw in the group selection model?

_____

_____

11. Give *three* criticisms of evolutionary explanations of animal behaviour.

_____

_____

_____

12. What is *inclusive* fitness?

_____

_____

13. Give *three* ways that animals may recognise their own kin.

_____

_____

14. Give three conditions necessary for the development of reciprocal altruism.

_____

_____

_____

15. What happens in a *tit for tat* strategy?

_____

_____

_____

12

LEARNING

GETTING STARTED

This chapter deals with many of the issues contained in subsections 2 and 3 of the AEB comparative psychology option. There are three strands to the material presented. The first is to examine the role of learning in the natural environment of non-human animals. As discussed in the previous chapter, learning plays an important part in the adaptation process for animals. Through learning (defined as a change in behaviour as a result of experience), an animal may acquire behaviours appropriate to, for example, optimal foraging strategies, avoidance of predators, avoidance of sickness and so on.

A special form of learning is *imprinting* (defined as a process by which an animal learns to make a particular response only to one type of animal or object). This chapter looks at the main characteristics of imprinting, and examines the claims for its special status as a unique type of learning.

Finally the chapter will focus on conditioning and its applications to education and clinical psychology. Because of the nature of this material, reference will frequently be made to material elsewhere in this book.

Material in this chapter will prepare you for questions in the following topic areas.

- ■ **The nature and role of learning in the behaviour of non-human animals.**
- ■ **The nature and functions of imprinting and a comparison of imprinting with other forms of learning.**
- ■ **Discussion of theories of learning and their application to education and clinical psychology.**

LEARNING IN THE NATURAL ENVIRONMENT

TYPES OF LEARNING

BIOLOGY OF LEARNING

IMPRINTING

CONDITIONING AND ITS APPLICATIONS

OPERANT CONDITIONING

THE ROLE OF COGNITION IN LEARNING

APPLICATIONS OF CONDITIONING

ESSENTIAL PRINCIPLES

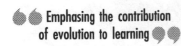

Adaptation through
learning

WHY IS LEARNING IMPORTANT?

As previously discussed, instinctual patterns of behaviour are appropriate only if most aspects of the environment remain stable. However, if the environment changes in some crucial way, such instinctive behaviours may become maladaptive. If an animal's behaviour changes in response to these environmental changes, then such changes can be attributed to **learning**. This ability to modify behaviour as a result of environmental stimulation might be seen as an effective strategy in the adaptive process.

Habituation

Habituation involves a change in response to a stimulus that proves to be safe or irrelevant to the animal. Animals normally respond defensively to novel stimuli. If, after repeated presentations of the novel stimulus, there is no significant threat or interest to the animal, the stimulus is ignored i.e. it no longer produces a response.

Habituation is of considerable biological significance in that it allows an animal to discriminate between novel (and hence potentially significant) and familiar events and to respond appropriately.

Sensitisation

Sensitisation refers to an animal's *increased* response to a stimulus or group of stimuli because of their significance to the animal. An example of sensitisation would be the increased alertness of flocking birds to attacks by predators as a result of previous experience with those predators. Although habituation and sensitisation appear to involve different responses to the same stimuli (repeated presentations of stimuli), they are thought to involve different neural processes.

The study of, and applications of **conditioning** will be discussed in more detail in the final section of this chapter, but for now the relevance of these paradigms of learning for the natural behaviour of animals will be considered.

Classical conditioning

Classical conditioning is of great biological significance to animals. Through this type of conditioning, animals may learn to associate significant events (food, sickness etc) with other naturally occurring phenomena. An example is the phenomenon of *sign tracking* where predators may learn to associate the signs (auditory, olfactory etc.) with the prescence of prey. Animals thus learn to track the signs because of their association with a potential meal.

It is sometimes difficult to distinguish between the outcomes of *sensitisation* and *classical conditioning*. Classical conditioning has occurred when the behaviour observed has been produced by the contingency between stimulus and reinforcer.

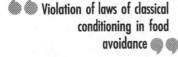

Emphasing the contribution
of evolution to learning

Recent research on **biological preparedness** (see previous chapter) has also challenged the traditional view of classical conditioning. Research on food-avoidance (thought to be a special kind of classical conditioning) violates the laws of classical conditioning on a number of counts (*Garcia and Koelling*, 1966).

a) The interval between stimulus and response can be many hours, whereas laboratory investigations of classical conditioning tend only to produce learning when the interval is less than 30 seconds.

b) Such aversion may take place after just one 'trial' whereas in classical conditioning, many such pairings are normally necessary before conditioning takes place.

Violation of laws of classical
conditioning in food
avoidance

c) Contemporary research on classical conditioning has stressed the importance of cognition, or expectation, in learning, but in food avoidance such cognition appears irrelevant.

d) This type of learning seems resistant to the extinction normally found in classical conditioning when the reinforcer is no longer present.

Operant conditioning

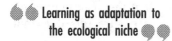
66 Difference between classical
and operant conditioning 99

Operant (or instrumental) conditioning differs from classical in that instead of focussing on the connections that develop between the unconditional and conditional stimuli, it focuses on the association that develops between the response of an animal and the consequences of that behaviour.

The process of operant conditioning serves to maximise the efficiency with which an animal obtains an appropriate reinforcer. Research by *Krebs et al.*, for example, has demonstrated the importance of operant conditioning processes in developing **optimal foraging strategies** in birds. Birds learn which aspects of their environment are most likely to produce the greatest gain (food), but will also switch between 'patches' in order to constantly check the possible greater rewards of an alternative patch.

THE BIOLOGY OF LEARNING

66 Learning as adaptation to
the ecological niche 99

Some ethologists believe that experiments carried out in laboratories cannot tell us very much about the way that animals learn in their natural environment (*Rozin and Kalat,* 1972). They believe that an animal's learning capacity if influenced by its ecological niche. The types of learning that might take place are, therefore, tailored to the life of the animal. As well as being able to learn some things more easily than others (the influence of biological preparedness) it is also claimed that animals may be pre-programmed to learn certain things at certain ages. This idea of 'sensitive or critical periods' of development has been applied to the development of bird song and the imprinting of young animals. This will be discussed in depth in the next section, but it is important to realise that imprinting is a type of learning, and is, therefore relevant to questions in this area.

Animals become imprinted upon different aspects of their environment at different stages of their development. Imprinting may, therefore, influence habitat selection (which enables animals to choose habitats similar to those of their kin, and hence enhance the development of inclusive fitness), courtship and mate choice. *Bateson* (1976) suggests that sexual imprinting enables birds to choose a mate who is slightly different, thus balancing the need for a balance between inbreeding and outbreeding.

IMPRINTING

Definition

A type of learning in which an animal learns to make a particular social response to only one type of animal or object.

BASIC PRINCIPLES OF IMPRINTING

1. It is long lasting.
2. It is irreversible.
3. It occurs during a 'critical period' in the development of an animal.

TYPES OF IMPRINTING

1. Filial imprinting

Filial imprinting typically involves a following response to an adult. It is established in the neonatal period and is important to the survival of the animal.

2. Sexual imprinting

66 The plumage of the female
has been fashioned by natural
selection, the male by sexual
selection 99

Exposure to conspecifics results in **sexual imprinting**, and affects future mate choice. In sexually *dimorphic* ducks, (sexes different), the male must normally imprint upon the female to learn the subtle differences between the female of his species and the females of other species. In *monomorphic* species (sexes similar) both males and females tend to imprint.

3. Habitat imprinting

It is often important for animals to return to 'home ground' either for mating (thus increasing the inclusive fitness of the animal) or for migration. The migratory response may, for example, be imprinted in salmon, as they tend to migrate back to their 'home stream' when fully grown.

IMPRINTING CLAIMS EXAMINED

1. It is long lasting

As a result of filial imprinting animals which *do* imprint form an attachment with an adult, but this ceases to be important when the animal reaches adulthood.

Claims have been made, however, for the importance of this imprinting in the long term social behaviour of mammals. It is a matter of some debate, however, whether this is the same process.

The sexual preferences of many birds is influenced by sexual imprinting. Experiments on **cross-fostering** carried out by *Warriner et al.* (1963) demonstrated that birds will show a sexual preference for their foster species over their own. This sexual preference can be extremely long lasting. Ducks raised with geese foster parents can continue to court geese (despite the lack of cooperation) for a number of years. Research on hand reared species has also discovered that they can imprint on people, leading to the development of special procedures to ensure this does not happen (see Chapter 3).

e.g. feeding by 'parent' glove puppets

2. It is irreversible

According to Lorenz, the ending of the critical period effectively closes the imprinting opportunity. Evidence does not necessarily support this. *Boakes and Panter* (1985) suggested that filial imprinting can be reversed if the young bird was confined with a novel stimulus and was unable to flee from it. Sexual imprinting appears to be less easily reversed. Animals have a natural bias to imprint upon members of the same species, but experience with a different species will lead to a sexual preference for that species. Such cross-fostered species *will* court and mate with their own species, but not if they are given the choice of their foster species.

3. It occurs during a critical period

Research by *Hess* (1959) has demonstrated that imprinting takes place more readily at certain times rather than others. Imprinting may be difficult if not impossible outside this sensitive (rather than critical) period. The decline of sensitivity that occurs toward the end of the sensitive period has been explained by the development of fear and avoidance toward novel objects.

Why might this be the case?

Evidence suggests the existence of different sensitive periods for different types of imprinting. *Gallagher* (1977) suggests that the sensitive period for sexual imprinting is later than that for filial imprinting.

IMPRINTING AND LEARNING

Claims for imprinting being a unique type of learning have tended to stress the following:

Imprinting as a unique type of learning

1. No reward is necessary for learning to take place (in contrast to conditioning).
2. Performance of a response is not necessary for the animal to learn to discriminate.
3. There exists a bias to imprint upon certain things rather than others.
4. In sexual imprinting, delay between learning and eventual performance of the discriminatory reponse may be considerable.
5. Imprinting is seen as an extreme form of prepared learning in that it is established quickly and is resistant to change.

Claims for similarities between imprinting and other forms of learning

Comment: This view of imprinting as distinct from other forms of learning is not widely held today. Imprinting bears many similarities with perceptual learning (*Bateson*, 1964) and operant conditioning (*Bateson and Reese*, 1969). It appears that an animal may learn the characteristics of it's mother through perceptual learning, and through operant conditioning may learn responses that bring her into close proximity.

BIOLOGICAL SIGNIFICANCE OF IMPRINTING

Imprinting is significant for the following reasons:

●● Biological importance of
imprinting ●●

1. It ensures that parents only care for their own young, and that young animals attach to the animals that will care for them (and avoid those that would attack them).
2. The sexual imprinting period normally corresponds to the period of parental care, and ends *before* animals begin to mix with others that are not their own kin.
3. *Bateson* (1979) suggests that in birds, the timing of sexual imprinting coincides with the development of adult plumage (thus facilitating later species recognition).
4. Bateson also suggests the importance of imprinting in kin recognition. Bewick swans imprint on the bill markings of their kin, and choose mates that differ *slightly* (thus optimising the balance between the advantages of inbreeding and outbreeding).

●● What are the advantages of
achieving a balance? ●●

CONDITIONING AND
ITS APPLICATIONS

CLASSICAL CONDITIONING

By pairing a (neutral) stimulus with another that already produces a response, the former also comes to produce the response. It is then described as the **conditioned stimulus** and the response that it produces as the **conditioned response**.

 A Pavlovian view ●●

In Pavlovian terms:

$$NS + UCS \rightarrow UCR$$

eventually

$$CS \rightarrow CR$$

Generalization and discrimination

In generalization, the conditioned response also occurs to stimuli which are similar to the original conditional response. Animals may also show **discrimination** in that they may respond (**generalization**) to stimuli which are similar to the CS, but if the similarity of other stimuli becomes less evident, the animal can discriminate between them and the original CS.

Extinction

Continued presentation of the CS *without* the UCS will eventually weaken the CS → CR link such that the CR is no longer produced. This process is called **extinction**. However, later trials tend to elicit the CR much more easily than in the original trials, demonstrating that it is not lost completely (a process referred to as **spontaneous recovery**).

Recent developments in classical conditioning

●● Cognitive factors ●●

Original work on classical conditioning stressed the autonomic nature of the process – i.e. no cognitive factors were involved. More recent models of classical conditioning have emphasised the importance of **predicatability** (*Pearce*, 1987). In other words, presentation of a CS enables an animal to retrieve a mental representation of the UCS from memory with subsequent behaviour being influenced by that representation.

Pavlov's original theory stressed the importance of **temporal contiguity** (the NS, or CS as it becomes, must be presented at the same time as, or shortly before, the UCS). However, *Rescorla* (1972) argues that the importance of the CS is that it allows the animal to predict what will happen next (i.e. the UCS). In experimental work, Rescorla showed that this was more important than temporal contiguity.

Seligman (1971), found that if rats had no reliable predictor (CS) of an electric shock (UCS) then they were continuously fearful. Seligman's work on **biological preparedness** in classical conditioning is also important, demonstrating that, in survival terms, important associations might be learned in just one trial rather than the multi-trial learning of normal classical conditioning. This claim is supported by experiments by *Garcia and Koelling* (1966) where rats were more likely to learn an association between taste (followed by an injection of a mild poison) and food avoidance, than an equivalent association between electric shock (followed by a similar injection) and food avoidance.

<table>
<tr><td>

OPERANT CONDITIONING

</td><td>

Animals are seen as *operating* on their environment. The consequences of these behaviours determine the future probability of that behaviour reoccurring. Traditionally **operant conditioning** is seen as different from classical conditioning in that behaviour in operant conditioning is largely voluntary whereas in classical conditioning it is seen as an autonomic response (i.e. it is reflexive).

</td></tr>
</table>

REINFORCEMENT AND PUNISHMENT

Reinforcement can either be *positive* (e.g. a reward such as food to a hungry animal) or *negative* (the termination of an unpleasant stimulus).

66 Important to distinguish between negative reinforcement and punishment 99

Punishment is the presentation of an aversive (unpleasant) state following the behaviour.

Both types of reinforcement will *strengthen* a behaviour, punishment will generally *weaken* it.

Reinforcement may be **primary** in that it satisfies a direct need of the animal, or **secondary** in that it has acquired its reinforcing ability through a learned (through classical conditioning) association with a primary reinforcer.

Schedules of reinforcement

The way that reinforcement might be used in learning may vary. **Continuous reinforcement** (cvcry appropriate example of the behaviour reinforced) may give way to **partial reinforcement** (reinforcement given either at fixed or random intervals, or for fixed or random ratios e.g. once every twenty trials). Partial reinforcement thus *maintains* the behaviour over a longer period of time, and makes it less likely that extinction will set in. Such a finding is counterintuitive, thus adding to the appeal of the theory.

Shaping

Operant conditioning can be used to create desired behaviours by reinforcing successive approximations to the behaviour. The 'trainer' gradually moves the animal toward the desired behaviour by only reinforcing those behaviours that at each stage approximate more closely to the desired behaviour.

Superstitious learning

Brown and Jenkins (1968) found that animals would often learn to perform a particular behaviour because it was *associated* with reward, even though it did not directly cause it. Such findings suggest that traditional views of conditioning based on **Thorndike's law of effect** underestimate the importance of cognitive factors in learning. Superstituous learning does lend some credibility to the claim that expectation does play an important part in learning.

<table>
<tr><td>

THE ROLE OF COGNITION IN CONDITIONING

</td><td>

Gross (1992) puts forward five points which emphasise the importance of **cognitive processes** in conditioning:

</td></tr>
</table>

1. Conditioning might be seen not just as *associations* between events, but as evidence of an animal's learning of the *relationships* between those events (see the earlier point about *predictability* in conditioning).

66 Importance of cognitive processes in conditioning 99

2. As well as conditioning developing causal relations between events, it also enables an animal to predict that an event will *not occur*. Previously learned associations can be *inhibited* if the animal now predicts that a particular reinforcer is no longer being presented.
3. Animals may be presented with spurious extra stimuli during classical conditioning. If another CS already produces a CR, then an extra NS introduced at the same time fails to produce the same response. This is because it is *blocked* by the first CS. As the second stimulus adds no extra information which enables the animal to predict e.g. a shock, it becomes irrelevant.
4. Animals which are prevented from escaping from an aversive situation, later show evidence of **learned helplessness** (*Seligman*, 1974), in that they later seem incapable of learning avoidance behaviour when given the opportunity to do so.

This, it appears, is because they have learned that no behaviour on their part is effective in escaping form the unpleasant situation, so they give up trying.

5. Skinner's original claim was that the use of reinforcement and punishment led to an automatic strengthening and weakening of behaviour. *Bandura* (1977) claims that they provide the learner with information about the *likelihood* of future reward or punishment by giving us *feedback* about our behaviours. Thus, the way an animal behaves is largely determined by the *expectations* of future outcomes.

APPLICATIONS OF CONDITIONING

CLINICAL APPLICATIONS (SEE CHAPTER 18)

EDUCATIONAL APPLICATIONS

1. Programmed learning

 Linear or branching

These techniques break down the learning tasks into a sequence of predetermined steps. The programmes may be **linear** in which the sequence of steps is the same for all, or **branching** where alternative routes through the information are determined by the nature of the errors made.

■ **Advantages of programmed learning**
(i) Students are more likely to *succeed* on each task (because it is small) than they are to fail, therefore motivation tends to be greater.

Advantages of programmed learning

(ii) Feedback on the task is virtually immediate, therefore learning is more *efficient*.
(iii) Learners work *at their own pace*, therefore individual differences between students are catered for.
(iv) In branching programmes, wrong answers may be dealt with by the programme by taking the learner on a *remedial* loop where that particular mistake is clarified.

■ **Disadvantages of programmed learning**

Some disadvantages

(i) Because of the nature of the process, these programmes are suitable only for certain kinds of learning material which lends itself to this sort of breakdown of skills.
(ii) Some critics (e.g. *Ericksen*, 1967) claim that programmed learning addresses only the rate of learning and disregards other equally vital factors that determine the idiosyncratic learning progress of each student.

2. Behaviour modification in the classroom

Behaviour modification attempts to change behaviour in terms of operant conditioning and the patterns of reinforcement which have been associated with the behaviour over time. The main principles behind its use in classroom management are:

(i) It works on the ABC model (*Antecedents* or context of an event, the *behaviour* itself, and the *consequences* of the behaviour).
(ii) The concern is with the external or environmental events that modify behaviour. This focuses the teacher on the role of these external factors in modifying behaviour, rather than seeing the behaviours as emanating from a fundamental disorder within the child.
(iii) Through careful description and recording, teachers can begin to understand the causes of classroom problems, and have a technique by which these factors can be modified (by changing the nature and availability of reinforcers).

■ **Criticisms of behaviour modification techniques**
(i) The approach is often criticised as being narrow and simplistic, and the mechanistic overtones are seen as unacceptable to many in the field.

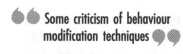 Some criticism of behaviour modification techniques

(ii) The concept of reinforcement is seen as circular. Something is a reinforcer if it reinforces. Teachers may be unaware what it is about a situation that children find reinforcing, therefore their control over it is presumed rather than actual .
(iii) The presumed power of the classroom technology of behaviour change has given rise to ethical objections, particularly when applied to the control of children in schools (*Clarke*, 1979).

EXAMINATION QUESTIONS

1. Discuss how animals might learn in the natural environment. *(25)*
2. (a) Describe the main features of imprinting. *(10)*
   (b) Using evidence, discuss the view that imprinting is distinct from other forms of learning. *(15)*
   (AEB, 1993)
3. Discuss the role of both reinforcement and punishment in the learning process. *(25)*
   (AEB 1993)
4. Discuss how learning may be influenced by cognitive factors. *(25)*

ANSWERS TO EXAMINATION QUESTIONS

OUTLINE ANSWERS TO QUESTIONS 1 AND 4

Question 1

This is a fairly straightforward question to answer, and would possibly take the following form.

1. Description of different types of learning (habituation, sensitization, imprinting etc.)
2. A consideration of the significance of each of these explanations to the adaptation or survival of animals e.g to optimize foraging strategies, find mates, avoid predators etc.
3. A critical consideration of the problems of extrapolating from data obtained in laboratory studies of learning (particularly conditioning) to behaviour in the natural environment.
4. A critical consideration of the interaction between genetics and learning and how what and how an animal learns may be shaped by genetic factors (see previous chapter).

Question 4

As the injunction used in the question is *discuss*, the skills presented should give evidence of both *description* (and understanding) and *critical* discussion.

Strictly speaking, this answer does not ask for learning in *non-human* animals, therefore material relevant to cognitive processes in human learning (e.g. the work of Robert Gagné) would be credited.

Material directly relevant to this question would include:

1. The nature and importance of predictability in conditioning.
2. Cognitive inhibition in conditioning.
3. Blocking and the role of spurious stimuli.
4. Learned helplessness (Seligman).

Also relevant would be a critical consideration of some of the more cognitively based explanations of animal learning (e.g. insight learning, cognitive maps etc.).

Also relevant to critical discussion would be a consideration of cognitive processing against, for example the role of evolutionary factors (see section on biological preparedness in Chapter 11; note that some learning appears to be resistant to cognitive processing).

TUTOR'S ANSWER

Question 2

(a) The term 'imprinting' originally referred to the process by which an animal forms a lasting attachment to some object, normally a parent. The term has been extended to include other types of preference which develop later in the life of the animal. Two basic types of imprinting have been identified, *filial* imprinting, in which the young animal attaches (normally) to a parent, and *sexual* imprinting, for the broader attachment to the species of the imprinting object.

Imprinting is often seen as a type of learning, albeit learning that takes place during the early stages of an animal's life. Unlike most learning, however, it is extremely rapid, takes place only during a brief 'critical' period, is irreversible, and has effects which might be manifested only after a long delay.

One of the characteristics of imprinting is its occurrence within a critical period. The critical period refers to a phase in the animal's development during which it is particularly sensitive to certain stimuli. The onset of the critical period involves two important factors, the developmental stage of the animal, and its post-birth experience. The onset of the critical period may also involve a following response, and as such requires a certain level of physical maturity in the young animal. When it comes to the offset of the critical period, imprinting is more or less a self terminating process. By limiting preferences to stimuli which are 'familiar', it effectively prevents new experiences from modifying them.

Lorenz believed that an attachment, once formed, could not be transferred to a different object, presumably because the critical period had passed. Filial imprinting can be reversed, if the young animal is confined with a novel stimulus and prevented from fleeing. Sexual imprinting appears more permanent, but is not absolute. There appears to be a bias to imprint upon members of the same species, but experience of a different species will lead to a more or less permanent preference for that species as a sexual partner. Sexual preferences for the foster parent species are not restricted to particular individuals, but show generalisation to all members of that species. Sexual imprinting thus involves a preference for the *type* of female that played the parental role. This is in contrast with filial imprinting which is much more likely to result in attachments to particular characteristics of a parent or parental object. This tendency to sexually imprint on the type of female that reared them occurs predominantly in the males of sexually dimorphic birds (male and female plumage different). In sexually monomorphic birds (male and female plumage similar), both males and females sexually imprint. In sexually dimorphic birds the females normally rely on innate recognition of members of the opposite sex, and it is only in the latter case, where both sexes are so coloured to facilitate camouflage, that sexual imprinting takes place. In this way, the young birds can establish precise and detailed recognition of their own species for later mating.

From the point of view of evolution, it is important that parents should care only for their own offspring, and young animals need to stay close to ensure parental behaviour. Many animals have specific mechanisms for ensuring that strange juveniles are not adopted. Thus, most gull chicks develop a specific recognition of their parents' call and vice versa. This is normally facilitated by pre-natal exposure to the sounds of the parents, such that much of the auditory imprinting process takes place before the bird is born.

It also makes sound evolutionary sense that mating should only take place between members of the same species. Matings across species are normally sterile, so recognition of members of the same species becomes vital.

(b) A controversy remains over whether imprinting is a highly distinct phenomenon, or whether it is an aspect of learning which shares many of the principles and characteristics of other aspects of learning. Lorenz's original claims for critical periods and irreversibility have been subjected to considerable modification. Traditional views of learning as conditioning have emphasised the importance of reward in the learning process. No reward is necessary to bring about imprinting, although the mother is a natural source of reward. The imprinting process has been experimentally subverted to bring about imprinting to objects which provide no reward at all. Indeed, research by *Hess* (1958) has shown that far from decreasing the intensity of following behaviour, punishment during the critical period can actually intensify it. The young animal plays an active role in becoming imprinted. It seeks out objects on which to imprint, and its preference for slight novelty during imprinting has been interpreted as a mechanism to ensure that it learns about all aspects of the parent, an integrated perceptual model. Studies of the biology of imprinting (*Horn et al.*, 1981) have shown that there are specific biochemical changes in localized areas of the brain which are consequent upon the specific experience of imprinting. Destruction of these areas after imprinting prevents the animal from showing any preference. Using Garcia's ideas (*Garcia*, 1966) on biological preparedness, it seems possible that imprinting is an example of extreme preparedness, whereby an animal is biologically prepared to learn an attachment quickly and easily, and to remain resistant to future extinction of this attachment. This can then be seen to facilitate survival. This contrasts with the multi-trial, open to extinction types of learning demonstrated in conditioning experiments. In terms of sociobiological principles, imprinting can be seen as an evolutionarily stable strategy that promotes the survival of both the individual and the gene line (Selfish gene theory, *Dawkins*, 1976).

STUDENT'S ANSWER WITH EXAMINER'S COMMENTS

Question 3

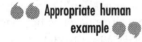 **Accurate opening**

Skinner believed that behaviour is shaped by its consequences – its consequences being either reinforcing or punishing. If a consequence of behaviour is pleasant then this will reinforce behaviour and increase the likelihood of it happening again.

If a consequence of behaviour is unpleasant, then this will weaken the behaviour and decrease the likelihood of it happening again.

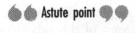 **Manager to avoid the common confusion over negative reinforcement and punishment**

There are two types of reinforcement, negative and positive. A positive reinforcer rewards desirable behaviour. For example, pressing a lever will obtain a reward of food. A negative reinforcer, however, stops or avoids something unpleasant. For example, a rat pressing a lever might turn off an electric shock.

Punishment is again different. For example, if a rat presses a lever, it will receive an electric shock. This has the effect of reducing its tendency to repeat the behaviour.

Skinner found that by using positive reinforcement and rewarding rats with food if they pressed a lever that they would soon learn to press the lever if they wanted food.

Negative reinforcement has ben studied in the context of avoidance learning. Puppies are put in a shuttlebox where they can jump to either side of the box . One half of the box is electrocuted. The dogs jump to the other side of the box to escape the shock. If a bell is sounded before the shock is to be introduced, then through classical conditioning they learn to associate the bell with the shock. The dogs then learn to jump to the other side of the box when they hear the bell and so avoid the shock. Their behaviour is negatively reinforced by the avoidance of the shock. Avoidance learning is very hard to extinguish. The dogs will continue to jump to the other side of the box on hearing the bell even if no shock is administered as they are not able to 'test reality' without risk of a shock. This means that avoidance behaviour is very persistant.

 **Appropriate human example**

This can be seen in phobias. For example, if a person has a phobia against bees, then a state of anxiety is produced when this person comes into contact with one. By running away and avoiding the bee, the anxiety is reduced and so this negatively reinforces the phobic behaviour.

As stated above, unlike reinforcement, punishment weakens behaviour. For example, Skinner found that if a rat received an electric shock when he pressed a lever then he would soon learn not to press the lever.

Astute point

How do we know if something is a reinforcer or a punisher? Skinner states that this decision has to made retrospectively and that a reinforcer is something that has reinforced behaviour, and a punishment is something that has weakened behaviour. This definition may seem circular but reinforcers and punishments may not always have the desired effect. For example, a boy who throws temper tantrums may be smacked by his mother to 'punish' him and weaken this behaviour. However, the boy throws the temper tantrums as he feels neglected and lacking attention from his mother. The attention his mother gives him, therefore, even if it is a smack, actually reinforces his tantrum behaviour. The smack has the opposite effect to the one intended.

Needs some evidence

Skinner argued that punishment should be used in conjunction with positive reinforcement when bringing up children. Punishment would install a child with a conscience, and weaken undesirable behaviour, positive reinforcement would enable the child to learn alternative and desirable behaviour. Skinner believed that punishment was how a child learned to have a conscience. He believed that conscience is a conditioned emotional response brought about by anxious feelings towards figures of authority in childhood who were responsible for punishment, such as parents and teachers.

This is quite a sensible answer to a question that typically yields a great deal of subjective, non-psychological content. The essay is not particularly well supported by research evidence, and the section on punishment is a lot weaker than the section on reinforcement. Overall, though, the answer is characteristic of a grade B.

REVIEW SHEET

1. In what way does learning contribute to adaptation?

_____

_____

2. In what important way is habituation biologically significant?

_____

_____

3. What is biological preparedness?

_____

_____

4. *Garcia and Koelling's* research on food avoidance established a number of differences between food avoidance conditioning and traditional classical conditioning. Give *three*.

_____

_____

_____

5. What is the major difference between classical and operant conditioning?

_____

_____

6. What are the three major types of imprinting?

_____

_____

_____

7. What have cross-fostering experiments told us about imprinting?

_____

_____

_____

8. Is imprinting reversible?

_____

_____

9. What is meant by the following terms in classical conditioning?

   Generalization:

   _____

   _____

   Extinction:

   _____

   _____

10. What, according to *Rescorla* (1972) was the role of the conditioned stimulus?

    _____

    _____

11. Distinguish between negative reinforcement and punishment.

    _____

    _____

    _____

12. Give *three* reasons why cognition is seen as important in learning.

    _____

    _____

    _____

13. Give *one* advantage and *one* disadvantage of programmed learning:

    _____

    _____

    _____

    _____

EXPERIMENTAL DESIGN AND RESEARCH METHODS

GETTING STARTED

This chapter discusses some of the issues relating to research design and statistics. You will, no doubt, have met many of these concepts in the more practical context of your coursework. Although it is possible to cover many of the more 'popular ' areas in the chapter that follows, many questions relating to this part of an 'A' level syllabus also require you to use the skills you have acquired in your coursework. You should try to get as much practice as possible answering past questions to get used to the skill of commenting critically on the design of a psychological investigation.

The two questions at the end of this chapter are taken from recent AEB 'A' level papers (note that the 'A' and 'AS' papers for the AEB share the same compulsory research question). These are presented along with a set of answers provided by the Chief Examiner when the questions were set.

HYPOTHESES

INDEPENDENT, DEPENDENT AND EXTRANEOUS VARIABLES

POPULATIONS AND SAMPLING METHODS

RELIABILITY AND VALIDITY

LEVELS OF MEASUREMENT

MEASURES OF CENTRAL TENDENCY

MEASURES OF SPREAD

PARAMETRIC AND NON-PARAMETIC ANALYSIS

TEST CHOICE

LEVELS OF SIGNIFICANCE

ESSENTIAL PRINCIPLES

HYPOTHESES

The experimental or alternate hypothesis

Hypotheses are *testable* statements of *prediction*. These qualities are very important in hypothesis formulation as not only are you making a statement of prediction to guide research, you are also constructing a prediction that can be tested against reality (an important characteristic of the scientific method). As a rule, **alternate hypotheses** should have the following qualities:

●● Desirable characteristics of the alternate or experimental hypothesis' ●●

1. They should be *specific*, with vague terms avoided and variables operationalised (i.e. instead of saying that subjects will *do better* on a test, you could say that they would *achieve a higher score*). The acid test after writing your hypothesis is to look at it from the perspective of a naive experimenter. Would you know how to operationalise variables (particularly in terms of collecting actual data) from the hypothesis provided?
2. They should contain reference to both the *independent* and dependent variables (if an experiment), or whatever other combination of variables is appropriate.
3. They should make reference to the *significant* difference, correlation, association or whatever, that you expect to find. There is some debate on the need to do this, but it is a safe practice.

●● Very important to practice formulating and stating hypotheses ●●

The null hypothesis

This is a statement that there will be *no* significant difference, correlation, association etc. (any 'effect' is simply attributed to chance factors). It is not necessarily the opposite of the alternate hypothesis (although it is the opposite of a two-tailed hypothesis, the opposite of a one-tailed hypothesis would be a different one-tailed hypothesis). The use of the word *not* placed at the right place in an alternate hypothesis will normally turn it into a **null hypothesis.**

One and two-tailed hypotheses

A **two-tailed** hypothesis will predict that there will be a significant difference, correlation, association etc., but will not predict which condition will do better (difference), whether the correlation will be positive or negative (correlation) or which variable is specifically associated with which other variable (association). In case you have a little trouble with the last one, suppose that an association exists between gender and tabloid newspaper preference. A two-tailed hypothesis might predict a significant association between gender (male or female) and preference for one of two tabloid newspapers (*The Sun* and *The Daily Mail*). It would not say which gender would prefer which paper. A **one-tailed** hypothesis would make a more specific prediction, perhaps suggesting a significant association between gender and newspaper preference, with males preferring *The Sun* and females preferring *The Daily Mail*.

An example: 'Kit-e-Kat makes for happier cats.'

A suitable hypothesis might be:
The **independent variable** [IV] is that aspect of an experiment which is (normally)

●● A suitable hypothesis ●●

Cats regularly fed on Kit-e-Kat will show significantly more purring behaviour when presented with food than cats fed on an equivalent brand. (**One-tailed**, – the hypothesis that is, not the cats!)
　　There will be a significant difference in the amount of purring behaviour upon food presentation between cats fed regularly on Kit-e-Kat and those fed on an equivalent brand. (**two-tailed**)
　　There will not be a significance difference in the amount of purring behaviour upon food presentation between cats fed regularly on Kit-e-Kat and those fed on an equivalent brand. (**null hypothesis**).

INDEPENDENT, DEPENDENT AND EXTRANEOUS VARIABLES

manipulated by the experimenter, although in natural experiments, the IV is manipulated by some other agency. It is predicted to have an effect on the **dependent variable** [DV] (the change in behaviour that is actually measured). In the 'Kit-e-Kat' example, the type of cat food (IV) is being predicted to have an effect on the amount of purring behaviour (DV).

However, nothing is ever that simple, and there are a range of **extraneous** variables that might also have an effect on the DV. These may be *constant* in that they will always affect behaviour in the same way, or *random* in that their effect is less predictable. For example, if the 'non Kit-e-Kat' cats are dragged forcibly out into a rain soaked back yard where food is thrown at them, they are unlikely to show as much appreciation and general happiness than the pampered puss which has its Kit-e-Kat served graciously to it while it reclines lazily in front of a gently flickering log fire. These different conditions would be fairly obvious examples of constant error variables. Random error variables might be how the cat is feeling, how hungry it is , whether it actually likes the stuff and so on.

 Constant errors should be eliminated at the design stage

POPULATIONS AND SAMPLING METHODS

A **population** in a psychological investigation is the group that we are interested in studying. It could, for example be 'A' level students in a college, mothers attending a particular maternity unit, or even a community of chimpanzees. As we don't normally have the resources (time or opportunity) to study the whole population, a representative **sample** is drawn from that population. It has to be representative in order to allow generalisation back to that population. Various sampling techniques exist to ensure such a representation.

1. The random sample

A sample is **random** only if every member of the target population has an equal chance of being selected. Simply picking subjects 'at random' as they walk past you in the refectory is not a random sample by this definition, but is referred to as an *opportunity sample*.

To obtain a random sample normally requires a list of all members of the population under study (target population). This is referred to as the *sampling frame*. Some ways of obtaining a random sample are as follows:

(i) Random number tables. (Each member of the population has previously been given a number).
(ii) Computer generation of subject number choice.
(iii) Names in a hat (or crash helmet, or bucket... .).

Types of sample

2. The stratified sample

If the population is not homogeneous (i.e. it is not made up of very similar people), then the differences between them in terms of e.g. age, gender, race etc. may have a significant effect on your results. The nature of the sample should, therefore, reflect the nature of the population. Thus, if the population is 80% female 20% male, then so should be the sample. The **stratified sample** is achieved by constructing two (or more) sampling frames (in this case one female and one male sampling frame). The same techniques as used in random sampling can then be applied to the frames, but in the desired ratios e.g. for a sample of 10 in the above example, 8 females would be selected and 2 males.

3. The systematic sample

Less desirable from a 'random' point of view, but possibly easier to administer, this involves taking, e.g., every 10th name from your sampling frame in order to get the desired size of sample. This is a **systematic** method of sampling.

4. The quota sample

This involves taking a **quota** of subjects from each of a specified number of target groups (e.g. 16–18, 19–21 and so on). This is rarely random, and may well be subject to considerable investigator bias.

WHAT IS AN APPROPRIATE SAMPLE SIZE?

Small samples tend not to be representative, and unusual responses or scores tend to have a dramatic effect on the overall data. *Larger samples* tend to be more representative of the underlying population (showing **regression to the mean**) and are less affected by unusual scores. Very large samples may be inappropriate on logistical and economical grounds. Many textbooks quote 30 as a suitable compromise, where further increases in sample size are unlikely to have a correspondingly large effect on the data. It does, however, depend largely on the nature and design of the investigation.

EXPERIMENTAL DESIGNS

These are used in an experiment to control for the effect of subject variables. There are three major types:

1. The repeated measures design

In the **repeated measures design** all subjects take part in all conditions.

■ **Advantages:** Overcomes subject variables (same subjects). Economical (same subjects used twice).
■ **Disadvantages:** May be influenced by *order* or *practice effects*. The **order effect** is produced when the *order* in which subjects do conditions has an effect on how well they do them (e.g. through fatigue, boredom etc.). The **practice effect** is produced when performance on one condition has a direct (possibly through learning) effect on performance on the other. These can be largely overcome by **counter-balancing** (half the subjects do Condition A followed by Condition B, the order is reversed for the other half) or **randomization** (the order in which subjects take the conditions is determined randomly). If the order or practice effects are large, or **asymmetrical** (the effect from A to B is not the same as that from B to A) then the design is not appropriate and one of the others is used instead.

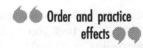 Order and practice effects

2. The matched subjects design

Like the repeated measures design, the **matched subjects design** is described as a *related* design, in that an attempt is made to relate the subjects in some way. Subjects are matched across the conditions in terms of factors that that the experimenter feels might have a strong influence on their performance. For example, previous research may have established that gender, age and personality types need to be controlled in a particular type of investigation. Each subject is thus matched with a similar subject (in terms of those conditions). Allocation to the conditions is then determined randomly.

■ **Advantages:** As subjects are matched in important subject variables, these are less likely to influence the DV.
■ **Disadvantages:** Selection of subjects becomes less random, and the matching process tends to be somewhat cumbersome and imprecise.

3. The independent subjects (groups, samples...) design

From the original sample, subjects are *randomly* allocated to conditions in the **independent subjects design**. It is thus assumed that any subject variables that might influence results are not applied to one condition in a systematic manner.

■ **Advantages:** Allocation to conditions is simpler and quicker, and there is no systematic bias to one condition or the other.
■ **Disadvantages:** This design does not eliminate subject variables, but merely 'hides' them randomly in the two conditions. In order to do that effectively, it requires quite large sample sizes, therefore is less economical than the repeated measures design.

RELIABILITY AND VALIDITY

 Reliability involves consistency

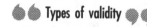 Checks on reliability

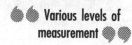 Types of validity

1. RELIABILITY

Reliability refers to the ability of a test, measurement or questionnaire to perform consistently over a number of occasions.

Measurements within psychological experiments are normally repeated a number of times so that average or typical scores might be discovered. When using tests or questionnaires, they may be assessed for their *internal* and their *external* reliability.

Internal reliability refers to the extent to which all items in the test are performing in the same way, in other words is the information they provide consistent? This can be checked by various methods including:

The split halves method

This involves splitting the test into two halves (e.g. odd numbered questions and even numbered questions) in order to test whether subjects performed the same on each.

External reliability refers to a test's consistency over time, and can be measured by, for example:

Test-retest method:

Subjects carry out a test and then after a given period of time carry out the same test again. Results are correlated with high positive correlations indicating high reliability

2. VALIDITY

Validity refers to the ability of a test or measurement to measure what it is supposed to measure. Various *types* of validity exist including:

Construct validity:

The ability of a test to accurately measure an underlying psychological construct (for example, does an IQ test measure intelligence?).

Content validity

A test should adequately represent a given area of skill or knowledge.

Predictive validity

The ability of a test or questionnaire to predict performance on some criterion in the future. This can be tested by correlating performance on the measure with performance on the later criterion.

Concurrent validity

A test may be validated by comparing performance on the test with performance on an existing valid test, or a measurement of the actual behaviour concerned. For example, a test of neuroticism can be validated against clinical reports of neurotic behaviour.

Face validity

The degree to which a test or measurement appears to be an example of the behaviour of interest. For example, in a study of the aggressive behaviour of schoolchildren, hitting and kicking would be examples of the behaviour with high face validity, but sarcasm and name calling might not, de spite the fact that they are also classified as aggressive behaviour.

LEVELS OF MEASUREMENT

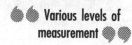 Various levels of measurement

Nominal data

Data here is grouped in categories. The scores in each category are described as the *frequencies*.

Ordinal data

Data here is in the form of ratings or ranks. It has more information than nominal data in that it imposes an *order* or *magnitude* into the data, but the distances between each ranked position are not necessarily the same.

Interval data

Data is measured using discrete units of measurement (e.g. seconds, centimetres etc.) but the scale used does not have an abolute zero point (e.g. a temperature of 0 degrees celsius does not indicate zero temperature).

Ratio data

As for interval data but with an absolute zero point. In other words, '0' means zero of the thing being measured. Because of this fact, *ratio* statements can be made (e.g. 20 seconds is twice as long as 10 seconds, whereas 20°c is not twice as hot as 10°c).

MEASURES OF CENTRAL TENDENCY

1. The arithmetic mean

The **arithmetic mean** is the *arithmetic average* of a set of scores, calculated by taking the total of all scores in a condition, divided by the number of subjects. The main *advantage* of the mean is in its sensitivity caused by using all the data. This is a prerequisite for the more sensitive parametric tests. Its main *disadvantage* is that, particularly in smaller samples, it is influenced by extreme scores, which may then cause the mean to be less representative of the data. It is also less appropriate with skewed data for the same reasons.

    The mean is commonly used in conjunction with interval or ratio data.

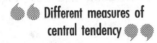 Different measures of central tendency

2. The median

The **median** is the mid point of a set of scores when they are placed in rank order. The *advantages* of the median are that it is unaffected by extreme scores and can also be used when extreme scores are unknown. Its *disadvantages* are that it is cruder than the mean, and is thus unsuitable for parametric analysis, and may be unrepresentative in small sample sizes.

    The median is commonly used in conjunction with ordinal data.

3. The mode

The **mode** is the most frequently occurring score in a set of data. Its *advantages* are that it demonstrates the most 'popular' response, and like the median, is less affected by extreme scores. Its *disadvantages* are that it ignores most of the data (and therefore is a relatively crude measure) and is inappropriate when there are only a small number of scores.

MEASURES OF SPREAD

1. The range

The **range** is calculated by taking the smallest from the largest of a set of scores. Its *advantage* is the ease with which it can be calculated, but its *disadvantages* are its extreme susceptibility to extreme scores and its inability to give information about the dispersion of the scores in between.

2. The standard deviation

The **standard deviation** is a calculation of how scores deviate from the mean. Its *advantages* are that it takes account of all the data and provides appropriate information necessary for decisions about parametric analysis.

PARAMETRIC AND NON-PARAMETRIC ANALYSIS

Parametric tests make a number of assumptions about the population from which the sample was drawn. These are:

Parametric tests make assumptions about the parameters of the population

1. The data must be either interval or ratio.
2. The sample must be drawn from a population in which the dependent variable is normally distributed. (As this cannot be tested directly, it is assumed from the sample statistics provided the sample is representative).
3. The variances obtained in the two (or more) conditions should not be significantly different.

Advantages of parametric tests

Parametric tests are described as being more *power efficient* (better able to correctly reject the null hypothesis) and more *sensitive* (use of all the data to make decisions).

Disadvantages of parametric tests

These tests place greater constraints on the type of data that can be used, and may also be used inappropriately if the assumptions behind their use are abused.

TEST CHOICE

1. TESTS OF DIFFERENCE

(a) Related designs

Related 't' test (parametric) or Wilcoxon signed ranks (non-parametric).

(b) Independent designs

Independent 't' test (parametric) or Mann-Whitney U test (non-parametric)

2. Correlations

Pearson's product moment (parametric) or Spearman's rank order (non-parametric).

3. Associations

Chi-squared test of association.

LEVELS OF SIGNIFICANCE

❝❝ A lower level of significance indicates a lesser likelihood of chance having caused the result ❞❞

To say that a test result is **significant** is to say that the probability of chance causing the results is less than a predetermined minimum level. If 0.05 is set as the minimum level at the start of the investigation, and the statistical test yields a result such that the probability of chance (p) is less than (<) 0.05, then the decision is made to reject the null hypothesis and accept the alternate hypothesis. Remember that the null hypothesis is a statement that the results obtained are due to chance factors. Thus, a significance level of $p = 0.05$ indicates a 1 in 20 probability that the results were caused by chance, a level of $p = 0.01$ indicates a 1 in 100 probability and so on. If the null hypothesis is rejected when the probability of chance causing the results is still quite high (say $p = 0.10$ or 1 in 10) then there is the same chance (i.e. 1 in 10) that a **Type 1 error** (rejecting the null hypothesis when it is true) is being made. If the level of significance chosen at the outset is unduly stringent (say $p = 0.001$), then it increases the chance of making a **Type 2 error** (retaining the null hypothesis when it is false).

EXAMINATION QUESTIONS AND ANSWERS

Question 1

1. A group of researchers decided to investigate whether there is an association between people's age and their ability to tell the difference between music played to them on record, cassette and compact disc. They placed an advertisement in a newspaper asking for volunteers who would be interested in participating in the study. There were 218 respondents. For the purpose of the study the researchers divided respondents into two age groups: those under the age of 40 and those aged 40 and over.

Having first carried out a **pilot study**, the researchers began testing the discriminative listening skills of the two age groups. The procedure that the researchers used was as follows: Participants were asked to which type of music they would prefer to listen in this investigation: rock, jazz or classical. One of the researchers then played each participant a single recording of their preferred type of music three times: once from a record, once from a cassette and once from a compact disc. The order of presentation of the three formats was randomized for each participant.

After hearing the three presentations each subject was asked to identify which of the presentations was from a record, which was from a cassette and which was from a compact disc. Participants' responses were recorded as being correct (all three f ormats correctly identified) or incorrect (less than three formats correctly identified).

The researchers analysed their final data using a chi-squared test (X^2).

The results were as follows:

TABLE 1

	Number of participants who were	
Age of participants	Correct	Incorrect
Under 40 years	85	35
Over 40 years	55	43

N = 218

The chi-squared analysis produced a value of 4.47

The relevant line (df = 1) of the statistical table for chi-squared interpretation was:

TABLE 2

Significance level	.10	.05	.01	.001
Chi-squared value	2.71	3.84	6.64	10.83

Questions and Answers

(a) State an appropriate null hypothesis for the above study.   *(1)*

An appropriate null hypothesis would be that there would be no significant association between the conditions, or that any association would be due to chance.

(b) What is an independent variable?   *(1)*

An independent variable is one which is purposefully or differentially manipulated between the experimental conditions.

(c) What is a dependent variable?   *(1)*

A dependent variable is the means of outcome/response measurement.

(d) What was the dependent variable in the above study?   *(1)*

The dependent variable used in the given study was the respondent's identification of format (record/cassette/CD).

(e) Identify the target population in the above study.   *(1)*

The target population was the total readership of the newspaper for that particular issue.

(f) Identify the sample in the above study. *(1)*

> The sample for the study was the people who responded to the advertisement in the newspaper.

(g) What is meant by the term 'pilot study' (line 7)? *(1)*

> A pilot study means a (usually) small-scale, pre-run of an investigation.

(h) Give *two* reasons why a pilot study was used here. *(2)*

> Less costly; helps to guide the design of the final, more complete, study.

(i) Identify *one* possible uncontrolled variable in the study and describe the effect it may have had. *(3)*

> Potential uncontrolled variables in the given study include:
> The specific nature of the population, the nature of the volunteer sample, lack of verification of hearing acuity and age of respondents, lack of rationale of age banding, lack of verification of respondents' familiarity with the different formats, no assessment of comparability between different types of music played, no assessment of comparability of sophistication or performance capacity between formats.

(j) Describe how you would have dealt with this uncontrolled variable. *(3)*

> The appropriateness of an answer here would depend entirely upon the uncontrolled variable selected.

(k) Give *two* reasons why a chi-squared test was used to analyse the results of the study. *(2)*

> Reasons for the use of chi-squared include, the fact that the data to be analysed were nominal, there was no evidence that any other criteria for parametric analysis were satisfied, that a related design had not been used, that expected frequencies were high enough, that scores were independent.

(l) What is meant in TABLE 2 by the phrase 'significance level'? *(2)*

> Statistical level means the probability/likelihood that an effect can be attributed to random errors/uncontrolled variables.

(m) State the significance level of those given in TABLE 2 at which researchers are most likely to make a type 1 error. *(1)*

> A type 1 error is more likely to be made at the 0.10 significance level.

(n) Explain the reasoning behind the decision you made in question (m) above. *(2)*

> The reason for this lies in the nature of what a type 1 error is (an acceptance that the IV, rather than random errors is causing the observed effect when it is not). This is more likely to occur when a 'liberal' significance/probability level is used.

(o) Explain whether the null hypothesis would be retained or rejected. *(3)*

> The null hypothesis would be rejected at the 0.05 level because the test value of chi (4.47) exceeded the table value (3.84).

(AEB A/AS level 1992)

Question 2

A psychologist was interested in the effect that different techniques of attitude change have on individuals' readiness to change their attitudes. Food preferences in schoolchildren were thought to be a suitable area for study.

The experimental situation involved a total of three classes of 30 children each, one class chosen at random from each of the second, third and fourth years of a secondary school. Seven days before the experiment, the 90 children were pre-tested by being given a 'food preferences' questionnaire. In it they were asked to indicate their preference for eating a range of 'healthy' foods (wholemeal bread, green vegetables, fruit etc.). The highest score which anyone could achieve on the questionnaire was 20 and the lowest was 1. The higher the score, the greater the preference for 'healthy' food. Most of the children had low scores on the questionnaire.

On the day of the experiment, each class was randomly divided into two halves. One of the halves was then allocated to Condition A and the other to Condition B. In Condition A, children were given a 30 minute lecture by an expert in nutrition, who used a variety of attractive presentation aids such as slides, photographs and recipes as well as explanations of healthy eating. In Condition B, children took part in a 30 minute discussion, in which the nutrition expert was also a participant, about the benefits of changing to a healthier diet. The class teacher was present in both conditions but did not offer information or try to influence the children. For practical reasons, second, third and fourth year students received the lecture or took part in the discussion in their year groups so that at no time during the experiment did they mix with other years or other conditions.

All the children were then re-tested using the 'food preferences' questionnaire. The difference in pre-test and re-test scores were then used as a measure of attitude change. The mean change for Condition A and Condition B in each class was calculated. Scores under A and B for each year group were then compared to see if there was any difference between them. A suitable non-parametric test was applied. A significance level of $p < 0.05$ (two-tailed) had been set. A summary of results is given below .

TABLE 1: SUMMARY OF RESULTS OF THE EXPERIMENT

Mean increase (+) or decrease (-) in attitude in favour of healthy food

Class	Condition A (Lecture)	Condition B (Discussion)	Level of significance (two-tailed)
2nd Years	+4.9	+5.4	$p > 0.05$
3rd Years	−0.04	+7.2	$p < 0.05$
4th Years	+0.8	+8.6	$p < 0.01$

Question and Answers

(a) Identify the dependent variable in the investigation. *(1)*

> The change in expressed preferences measured as an increase or decrease in attitude to healthy food.

(b) State an appropriate null hypothesis for the investigation. *(1)*

> There will be no significant difference between conditions/any difference will be due to chance.

(c) State how the classes might have been randomly divided into two halves. *(1)*

> E.g. random numbers from a register, names from a hat.

(d) Give one reason why the 'food preferences' questionnaire was given before the day of the experiment. *(1)*

> To establish a baseline.

(e) Name and explain one method by which the reliability of the questionnaire could be assessed before using it for the study. *(3)*

> The most obvious methods are test–re-test and alternate/multiple forms. In the former, the questionnaire could be given to the same group of subjects with a period of time in between. The results are then correlated, the higher the (positive) correlation, the more reliable the questionnaire. In the latter, an equivalent questionnaire of equal difficulty and asking the same sort of questions can be used. Subjects should respond in pretty much the same way on both.

(f) Give *one* reason why the experimenter chose classes from three different year groups. *(1)*

> To make the sample more representative (or to enable age comparisons to be made, etc.).

(g) Explain *one* way in which the two conditions of the experiment might have differed from the way intended by the experimenter. Explain how this could have been overcome. *(4)*

> Potential uncontrolled variables include differences in subjects due to bias in sampling, situational variables (environment, testing conditions), experimenter effects, different content in discussion and lecture, gender/race of class teacher. Differences between year groups might also have an effect, e.g. inability to concentrate for 30 minute lecture, relationship with teacher.
> Strategies for controlling the specified variable will depend on the particular variable chosen.

(h) State *one* advantage and *one* disadvantage of using the mean over other measures of central tendency. *(2)*

> *Advantage:* Most accurate, uses all the scores in a computation.
> *Disadvantage:* Misleading with skewed data.

(i) Name a non-parametric test which could have been used to establish whether there was a significant difference between the scores on Condition A and B in TABLE 1. *(1)*

> Dependent on whether the test is concerned with differences between year groups, or the 'before and after' nature of the testing, Mann-Whitney would be the most appropriate for the former, and Wilcoxon (or the sign test) for the latter.

(j) Give *two* possible reasons why a parametric test was not chosen to analyse the results. *(2)*

> Reasons might be because the researcher established or had grounds for believing that data would be ordinal measurement, have unequal variances (or be a non-normal distribution).

(k) For each of the three classes, state whether you would conclude that the comparisons between Condition A and B were significant. *(3)*

> 2nd year comparison was non-significant, 3rd year was significant, and 4th year was significant.

(l) Explain why the experimenter adopted a significance level of $p < 0.05$ in planning the investigation. *(2)*

> Reasons might include: to achieve a balance between Type 1 and Type 2 errors, experiment is not well controlled leading to random error, lack of sophistication of measurement, or because it is the commonly accepted level in psychology (this would need to be explained to get the full two marks).

(m) Given the aim of the investigation, explain the overall conclusion that would be drawn from the results. *(3)*

> The results might be interpreted to support the view that group discussion is better than lecture, but this is qualified by the results from 2nd years. There might be good reasons for not expecting a change in attitudes in the younger children.

(AEB A/AS 1993)

REVIEW SHEET

1. What *three* qualities should an alternate hypothesis possess?

   _____

   _____

   _____

2. 'Students who read revision texts achieve significantly higher grades in 'A' level examinations than those who do not.'
   Construct a *two-tailed* hypothesis from the one-tailed one above.

   _____

   _____

   _____

3. What is the difference between an IV and a DV?

   _____

   _____

4. What makes a sample *random*?

   _____

   _____

5. What are the *three* major experimental designs?

   _____

   _____

   _____

6. How does each one attempt to overcome subject variables?

   i) _____

   ii) _____

   iii) _____

7. How might the *internal* and *external* reliability of a test be measured?

   Internal: _____

   External: _____

8. What are the *five* main types of validity?

   i) _____

ii)
_____

iii)
_____

iv)
_____

v)
_____

9. Distinguish between:
Nominal and ordinal data:
_____
_____

Ordinal and interval:
_____
_____

Interval and ratio:
_____
_____

10. Give an advantage of each of the following:
The mean:
_____

The median:
_____

The mode:
_____

11. What is the parametric equivalent of the Wilcoxon test?
_____

12. What is the non-parametric equivalent of Pearson's product-moment correlation test?
_____

13. What test is most appropriate if data is ordinal (non-parametric) and part of an independent subjects design?
_____

14. If a 'p = 0.10' level of significance was chosen at the start of an investigation, would a Type 1 or Type 2 error be more likely?
_____

If a 'p = 0.01' level had been chosen?
_____

EARLY SOCIALISATION

GETTING STARTED

This chapter focusses on **early childhood socialisation**. In particular, it deals with the notions of attachment and deprivation. Notable in this area is the work of John Bowlby, who drew extensively on concepts from ethology and psychoanalysis to develop his theory of attachment. Although Bowlby's theories have been extensively criticised in the last fifteen years, together with the work of James and Joyce Robertson he has focussed our attention on the importance of the early years in the emotional development of the child.

Similar controversy surrounds the idea of enrichment studies (or compensatory education). The development of Project Headstart in the USA was seen by many as an inevitable failure and an example of President Johnson's drive to secure more votes among America's 'forgotten people'. The failure of the original Project Headstart set off an academic argument over the genetics of intelligence and the futility of environmental intervention.

The chapter also discusses the importance of play in the social and cognitive development of the child. The idea of play as vital for the cognitive development of children is often overstated, and in the words of Brian Sutton-Smith has led to the *idealization* of play in psychological literature.

Material in this chapter will enable you to answer questions on the following areas.

- **Attachment and deprivation in human beings**
- **The role of early experience in the development of the child**
- **Psychological theories of play**
- **The role of play in the social and cognitive development of children**

ATTACHMENTS AND DEPRIVATION

ENRICHMENT OF EARLY EXPERIENCE

PLAY

ESSENTIAL PRINCIPLES

'**Attachment** *is an affectional tie that one person forms to another person, binding them together in space, and enduring over time.*' *(Ainsworth,* 1973)

Deprivation can occur when...

1. Insufficient opportunity for interaction with a mother figure (privation).
2. Insufficient interaction with mother (masked deprivation).
3. Repeated breaches of ties with mother figures.

ATTACHMENT

Reason for study of attachment

There appears to be a common tendency for the young of a species to seek proximity of certain other members of their species. This is functional when the young are born helpless, thus requiring the bond between the infant and the caregiver to remain intact.

Reasons for development of attachment

Types of reinforcer

Some early explanations of attachment saw the mother as a **secondary reinforcer** with food as the relevant **primary reinforcer** (see Chapter 12). The mother becomes important because of her continued association with the provision of food. The work of *Harlow* (1962) with rhesus monkeys cast doubt on this explanation.

Later explanations have stressed the importance of *physical contact* in the development of the attachment bond. A study by *Anisfeld et el.* (1990) found that babies who had been picked up and carried a great deal were much more securely attached at age 13 months.

Ethological influences

Bowlby (1965) argued that the formation of an attachment is biologically pre-pro-grammed into the baby. Taking a lot of his ideas from the work on **imprinting** in animals (see Chapter 12), he claimed that babies who were 'programmed' to stay close to their mothers would be more likely to survive in a harsh and sometimes hostile environment. Thus, babies who had the genes for attachment were very much more likely to survive to sexual maturity and pass on those genes to the next generation (in sociobiological terms, attachment would become an **evolutionarily stable strategy** (see Chapter 11).

Types of attachment

Mary Ainsworth et al., using the **strange situation** technique, (which involves the mother leaving the infant with a stranger in a strange place for a brief period of time), identified three different attachment types.

Types of attachment

1. **Securely attached**: These infants seek to interact with the mother following her absence.
2. **Insecurely attached** (*avoidant*): May show avoidance toward the mother on her return, and may be just as easily be comforted by the stranger.
3. **Insecurely attached** (*ambivalent*): Simultaneously show signs of both seeking and resistance to the mother upon reunion.

Attachment and later development

Attachment through the life cycle

In a study of nursery school children *(Waters et al.,* 1979) found that children classified as securely attached at age 15 months were more likely to be social leaders. They were described as self directed and eager to learn, whereas the insecurely attached children were more socially withdrawn and hesitant about participating in activities. However, it is possible that these differences were more due to the continued responsiveness of the parents throughout the childhood years than a direct causal effect of the quality of the attachment bond.

Research by *Hazan and Shaver* (1987) suggests that peoples' intimate relationships in adulthood reflect their attachments in infancy. Adults who had secure attachments in infancy found it easy to develop trusting relationships with others. Those who had been insecure (avoidant) in infancy found it difficult to get close to others and were less likely to develop intimate relationships. Adults who had experienced the insecure (ambivalent) attachment pattern tended to have adult relationships characterised by anxiety and expectations of rejection. Other studies in the area have tended to support these findings (*Collins and Read*, 1990; *Simpson*, 1990).

DEPRIVATION

Bowlby's maternal deprivation hypothesis

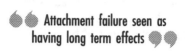
Attachment failure seen as having long term effects

Bowlby believed that the infant should experience a warm, intimate and continuous relationship with its mother. He suggested that prolonged separation from the primary caregiver, or the failure to form an attachment bond (**privation**), would lead to adverse effects in later life including the development of **affectionless psychopathy** (people who have little conception of loyalty or conscience, and have trouble forming two-sided relationships with others).

Bowlby claimed that children deprived of maternal care (or prevented from forming an attachment bond) would nearly always be retarded in some way, physically, socially and intellectually.

Where did Bowlby's ideas come from?

1. His ideas of a sensitive period came from ethological work on imprinting. Bowlby believed that the child was most vulnerable to the effects of deprivation from 6 months to 4 years. As in imprinting, attachment is then followed by a fear of strangers.

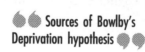
Sources of Bowlby's Deprivation hypothesis

2. Evidence from studies of short-term separation (*Robertson and Robertson*, 1967) showed dramatically how children in hospital could go through a characteristic sequence of *protest*, *despair* and finally *detachment*.

3. Studies of privation (e.g. *Goldfarb*, 1947) had found evidence of retardation in social, linguistic and intellectual development which were extremely long lasting. Goldfarb found that institutionalised children who received a period of care in a foster family, were later more socially and intellectually advanced than another group who stayed behind in the orphanage

4. Research with rhesus monkeys (*Harlow and Harlow*, 1958) demonstrated that young monkeys separated from their mothers shortly after birth and raised in isolation would show irreversible effects. Those females who did manage to mate later on tended not to care for their offspring, abusing them instead. Bowlby saw this as a possible explanation of child abuse in humans.

5. Bowlby's own studies of juvenile delinquents (*Bowlby*, 1946) discovered a pattern of early separation from the primary caregiver in many of the delinquents he studied. He assumed that these patterns of separation were responsible for the later delinquency.

Evaluation of Bowlby's maternal deprivation hypothesis.

1. The nature of imprinting, and the original claims for **irreversibility** have been subject to considerable modification, and would no longer support Bowlby's claims. More recent studies of adopted children (e.g. *Tizard*, 1977) have found that older children can form satisfactory new relationships with adults despite the lack of an earlier attachment.

2. Bowlby's original idea of **monotropism** (attachment to only one caregiver) is challenged by findings by *Robertson and Robertson* (1973) who found that the caregiver can be adequately compensated for by other sympathetic figures during separation.

3. Evidence from orphanages and other long-term institutions (e.g. *Goldfarb*, 1947) have often been subject to methodological flaws. Goldfarb's study, for example, could possibly have involved a **sampling flaw**, in that children picked for fostering were more socially and intellectually advanced than those who stayed behind.

4. Harlow's original claim that the adverse developmental effects he found in his monkeys could not be reversed was found not to be the case. Experience with younger monkey 'therapists' who would provide the missing 'contact comfort'

enabled the isolated monkeys to overcome many of the harmful effects of their isolation.

5. Bowlby's reliance on **retrospective studies** linking caregiver separation with delinquency cannot be seen as establishing a causal link between the two. It is equally possible that factors other than the absence of the mother (lack of parental supervision for example) could have been responsible for the delinquency. *Rutter* (1981) found that it was the circumstances surrounding the loss that was most likely to determine the consequences rather than the loss per se.

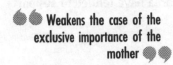

ENRICHMENT OF EARLY EXPERIENCE

The idea that the subsequent development of children could somehow be changed by a period of early **enrichment** stemmed form the early work of researchers such as *Skeels and Dye* (1939, 1966). Such interventionist studies advocated that a period of enriched early experience would be extremely powerful in the later development of the child.

PROJECT HEADSTART

The original **Project Headstart** was set up in 1965. It was designed to intervene in the cycle of deprivation by providing a period of enrichment which would make good the effects of the early deprivation of targetted groups. This was accomplished by providing a period of pre-school nursery education. The failure of Headstart to produce significant gains in the intellectual or educational development of the children concerned was interpreted by *Jensen* (1969) as demonstrating the importance of genetic endowment over environmental influences. Jensen suggested that the success of earlier interventionist studies was largely due to the extreme nature of the deprivation, and that slum deprivation would not depress the inherited cognitive capacity of the children.

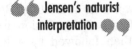

Other criticisms of Headstart

Hunt (1969) suggested that the failure of Headstart was due more to the fact that the whole programme was based on erroneous principles. The intervention was very short, the 'play school' approach offered little educative or cognitive enrichment, and the intervention was outside of the home context (therefore any improvements might be expected to be undermined by the continuing deprivation of the home).

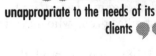

THE MILWAUKEE PROJECT (HEBER AND GARBER, 1975)

This project attempted to overcome some of the shortcomings of Project Headstart. They worked with children *and* their mothers, and produced much greater changes in intelligence and reading ability than had been anticipated at the start of the study. The project started when the children were in their earliest months, and ceased when they were six. Following termination of the intervention, the differences between the experimental group and a control group started to disappear.

These results can be accounted for in one of two ways:

1. The intervention was insufficiently lengthy to enable the children, in their adverse home and school contexts, to maintain their degree of gain.
2. In line with the claims of Jensen discussed earlier, it is possible that the early acceleration merely allowed them to reach their genetic limits earlier, followed by a period of decreasing relative growth when compared to the control group.

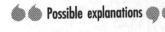

The first explanation is supported by the findings of studies such as *Klaus and Gray*, (1968) and *Karnes* (1970) which involved the training of mothers in their intervention programmes. These studies not only found gains in the children for whom the intervention was intended, but also gains (compared to children whose older siblings had not been involved in the studies) in their younger brothers and sisters.

BRONFENNBRENNER'S ANALYSIS

Bronfennbrenner (1974) summarised 26 of the more 'satisfactory' investigations.

1. There appears to be a more immediate responsiveness to intervention involving structured rather than free play situations. This is consistent with the criticisms of

'play tutoring' interventions which have led to the 'idealization' of play (*Sutton-Smith*, 1984) (see next section on Play for elaboration of this point). Childrens cognitive gains are often misattributed to being caused by play sessions when they might be more appropriately attributed to general adult initiated stimulation (the verbal stimulation hypothesis).

2. Bronfennbrenner states that a decline typically sets in following termination of the intervention. This is consistent with the findings of the Milwaukee project.

 **Importance of the home**

3. The home is seen as having a vital role in maintaining (or more usually undoing) the effects of intervention. The long term involvement of parents, as shown in the *Klaus and Gray* study, is more effective in the maintenance of any improvement.

Bronfennbrenner concluded, however, that the most severely deprived families have '...*neither the energy nor the psychological resources necessary to participate.*' He suggests that only 'ecological intervention' could work. This could take one of two forms. Either there could be a massive and long lasting attack upon the problems of *both* the child *and* the family, or the child could be removed from the pathological conditions (e.g. as in *Skeels and Dye*, 1939) to a complete environmental change followed by adoption.

OTHER FORMS OF ENRICHMENT

The effects of enrichment are not always the product of formal programmes of intervention, nor are they always cognitive/intellectual in nature. *Ball and Bogartz*, (1972) for example, found positive effects on the IQ scores of disadvantaged children who regularly watched Sesame Street on the television.

Baumrind suggests that parents who provide the most enriching environments for their children are those who are non-conformist and authoritative and who expose their children to stress and stimulation (in a moderated amount) from early childhood. Such children are more dominant and purposive in their interactions than other children who are typically shielded from stress and overstimulation which serves to increase preferences for avoidant rather than effective responses.

OPTIMAL MISMATCH THEORY (KUHN, 1979)

An educational programme of enrichment

Educational practices based loosely on Piaget's theory of intellectual development have attempted to accelerate the process through a carefully structured '**optimal mismatch**' programme, which aims to take children through the stages of intellectual development as quickly as possible. It works by 'mismatching' the childs present level of competence with a set of problems which invite cognitive conflict, and give the child the opportunity to discover solutions through their own actions (*Kuhn*, 1979). Such progammes have been mostly successful with moving children into the concrete operational level, but, as critics point out, they are only accomplishing something that would have happened sooner or later anyway, and the strain on teacher resources to accomplish this acceleration does not make it a worthwhile exercise.

PLAY

Definition

Play is difficult to define because the criteria used to classify it are arbitrary. Mood, excitement, type of activity etc. vary enormously from activity to activity. Observers may only guess at the functions of an activity, hence classification is arbitrary.

Smith and Vollstedt suggest a number of ways in which play might be recognised.

1. It is voluntary.
2. It does not lead to an obvious goal.
3. It involves repetitions of activities already mastered.
4. It may be accompanied by 'play signals' i.e. special tones of voice, exaggerated movements etc.

THEORIES OF PLAY

Early theories

1. **Spencer's surplus energy theory:** Spencer proposed a surplus energy theory to accomodate the fact that animals with more complex brains no longer had to use

most of their time for food gathering. Although largely historical in value, the surplus energy theory has, to a certain extent been resurrected by the work of *Berlyne* (1960) who suggested that play restored an organism's arousal to an optimum level when external arousal was too low.

2. **Recapitulation theory:** Around the turn of the century, Hall proposed that the earlier evolutionary development of the human species was created through play. Children went through the fish stage (water play), the monkey stage (climbing) and the gang stage (cooperative play and play with rules). The theory is largely speculative and appears illogical when viewed from a modern understanding of the processes of evolution.

PIAGET'S THEORY OF PLAY

The functions of play in Piaget's theory are twofold.

1. Play can consolidate existing skills through repetition with minor variations.
2. As play is mostly fantasy, with no external goals, it enables the child to achieve a sense of confidence and mastery.

Piaget sees play as an adaptive activity with *assimilation* being more important than *accommodation*. Accomodation is more associated with imitation and purposeful intellectual activity, with assimilative play involving the child repeating actions to display mastery and competence.

Piaget believed that the child went through three stages of play which corresponded to the stages of intellectual development.

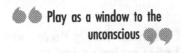 **Stages in Piaget's theory of play**

1. **Mastery play:** The child repeats activities to consolidate and display mastery in different contexts.
2. **Symbolic play:** This involves the child transforming one thing into another for the purposes of play. Through the medium of 'make-believe' the child can control the world around him. Of fundamental importance in this is the role of language (as symbols) and symbolic play is characterised by the extensive use of language.
3. **Play with rules:** This corresponds to the development of concrete operational thought, with the child becoming more logical and rule oriented. The child is also developing socially so that rules are needed to facilitate cooperation and fair play.

Claims for the importance of play in cognitive development

Piaget's theory sees play as being central in cognitive development, but this is not a view shared by many contemporary writers. For example, *Hutt*, (1979), established that children tend to spend more time exploring a novel stimulus than they do actually playing with it. Some studies have focused on the **optimal mismatch** of existing schema and new skills (the presentation of tasks which are optimally 'mis' matched to a child's existing level of intellectual development, so they have a conflict of what they can do, and what the task requires them to do), and have used play to facilitate progress from one intellectual stage to another (*Kuhn*, 1979). However, these studies have assumed that the child is *playing* when under Hutt's terms, they are more likely to be exploring, and hence the adaptive process is *accommodation* not *assimilation*.

FREUD'S THEORY OF PLAY

Through the medium of play, a child can:

1. Repeat pleasant experiences at will in order to achieve mastery in their life (play as fantasy).
2. Display defense mechanisms e.g. **sublimation** (playing with mud and clay may be sublimated manipulation of faeces).
3. Master distressing episodes and use play as a means of dealing emotionally with the issues involved. Play therapy involves the use of play activities for this purpose.

Play as a window to the unconscious

4. Provide evidence of psychosexual stage development and psychosexual conflicts such as the Oedipal conflict. In this context, play may be used as a *projective* technique (as in point 3).

Freud's theory of play succeeds or fails on the strength of the underlying theory of psychoanalysis. Many of the claims (defense mechanisms, psychosexual conflicts etc.) are unsubstantiated by scientific evidence. However, the success of play therapy in the treatment of emotionally disturbed children does lend some support to the insights provided by this theory.

The role of play in social and cognitive development

(See tutor essay at the end of this chapter for a discussion of this area).

EXAMINATION QUESTIONS

1. Evaluate studies which have investigated the effects of separation and deprivation in childhood.
   (25)
   (AEB 1989)
2. Critically discuss the view that the early experiences of children will have a long term effect upon their future development.
   (25)
   (AEB 1990)
3. Use psychological studies to discuss functions of play that may be related to social and cognitive development in children.
   (25)
   (AEB 1991)

ANSWERS TO EXAMINATION QUESTIONS

OUTLINE ANSWER TO QUESTION 1

This question does not really conform to the standard *Skill A and Skill B* format of the AEB examination, as the injunction *evaluate* is only a *Skill B* term. To translate this question into more contemporary 'AEB speak', it would probably read *discuss* or perhaps *describe and evaluate*.

The most effective way of answering it would probably be to describe studies which *support* Bowlby's views on the profound effects of separation and deprivation e.g. Goldfarb, Spitz and Wolf, Bowlby, but then show how most of these early studies have methodological flaws of one sort or another. Goldfarb's study had a sampling error, Bowlby's study of juvenile thieves was a *retrospective study*, and thus cannot tell us much about causality.

Other studies, e.g. Rutter, Clarke and Clarke, Freud and Dann can then be compared to show how the ill effects of separation are not an automatic consequence of the event. It is also important to consider the effects of separation and deprivation separately, as Robertson and; Robertson were quite specific about the modifying factors that were more likely to bring about distress in short term physical separation.

TUTOR'S ANSWER

Question 3

The contribution of play to the development of a child is often unclear owing to the difficulty of knowing *when* the child is playing and when they are engaging in other 'non' play motivated behaviours such as exploration or imitation.

What is and what is not play is difficult to define, as the criteria used to classify play are often arbitrary. *Smith and Vollstedt* (1985) offer the view that play involves activities that are voluntary, contain no clear goals for the child, involve repitition of actions and behaviours previously mastered (a process referred to by Piaget as 'assimilation'), and are often accompanied by 'play signals' (exaggerated movements, special tones of voice etc.).

The role of play in the cognitive development of the child has its roots in the Piagetian view of learning–cognition is seen as developing through the childs own active interaction with their environment, and in Freudian ideas about play as therapy.

This idealization of play has been reflected in the early childhood curriculum of 'free play' in which children are provided with materials and opportunities for play rather than being involved in achievement directed training.

Play theorists such as Piaget and Vygotsky have seen play as having a key role in cognitive development. The functions of play in Piaget's theory are twofold. Play can consolidate existing skills through repitition with minor variations. Also, as play is mostly fantasy, with no external goal, it enables the child to achieve a sense of confidence and mastery.

Vygotsky, likewise, saw the centrality of play in a child's cognitive development. He saw play as the 'leading source of development in the pre-school years'. The nature of pretend play meant that the child was able to liberate itself from the situational constraints of the real world of ideas in an imaginary situation.

More recently, theorists have tended to argue over the importance of play for cognitive development and creative thinking. *Sutton-Smith* (1984), although initially supporting the importance of play for creative processes, now argues against what he calls the 'idealization' of play, and concludes that much of what we define as play reflects the way that adults organise the activities of children rather than describing the actualities of their behaviour.

Reviews of research in this area (*Sylva et al.*, 1980; *Smith and Simon*, 1984) have suggested that play and directed training contribute about the same in the development of convergent problem solving (where there is only one solution to a problem) but play is more effective in the development of divergent problem solving (where many solutions are required). The implication of these findings is that play somehow increases the flexibility of a child's responses. Such studies might be criticised on a number of grounds. It is not clear whether the 'play' children were actually *playing* or rather engaging in typically explorative behaviour which tends to precede play. *Hutt* (1979) established that children tend to spend more time exploring a novel stimulus than they do playing with it. Smith and Simon also express some doubt that play would be as good an inducer of learning as might *any* type of training. In some of the studies reviewed, it was clear that the training used was not optimal for the subjects concerned.

Studies of Oxfordshire nursery schools by *Sylva et al.* (1980) concluded that unstructured, low yield, free play behaviour observed in many instances was less cognitively useful than the more structured, challenging, 'high yield' activities. Depending on one's definition of play, these latter activities, building, drawing, doing puzzles, may not fall into the category of play at all.

Some studies (*Hutt and Bavnani*, 1972) have discovered significant correlations between imaginative play and later measures of creativity. As is the case with all correlations, this does not imply a causal relationship, as it is possible that the child's engagement in imaginative play was a by-product of its creativity.

A number of experimental studies of play have attempted to establish a causal link between play and cognitive development. Typically, children are given a short play experience with objects, and are later compared with another group of children who have been given either an instructional session, or no treatment at all. A number of such studies claimed superiority for the play experience group in areas of creativity, problem solving and conservation. *Smith and Simon* (1984) warn against the possibility of experimenter effects, and the failure to control for familiarity with the experimenter. More ecologically valid studies which involve play tutoring of deprived children over several weeks have claimed a wide range of cognitive, linguistic and social benefits. These typically involve comparison with children who have received little or no extra adult intervention. It is possible, therefore, that general adult intervention and conversation might have been responsible for the gain (this has has become known as the 'verbal stimulation' hypothesis). Later studies which have controlled for adult involvement have not shown any great superiority for play tutoring over other forms of adult involvement. The implication is that it is the stimulation of intervention rather than play per se which gives rise to the observed cognitive improvements.

Many studies which have attempted to show a relationship between socio-dramatic (fantasy) play and cognitive development, have found greater links with social competence.

This implies that cognitive development is linked more to constructive play, and that the benefits of socio-dramatic play may be more social than cognitive.

Childrens' interactions with other children in play activities develop in a set sequence from solitary, through parallel to cooperative play. True cooperative play involves adjustment to rules, and an understanding of the needs of others. This is reflected in the increasing moral development of the child. Through play, children learn to identify the affective states of other children, and can respond to these in an effective and sensitive manner, an ability which challenges Piaget's claims of egocentricity in the pre-school child. Children as young as 2 may show altruism in their play behaviour. They will offer to help another child who is hurt, or will offer a toy in order to comfort another (*Zahn-Waxler et al.,* 1979).

Social play may be used as a medium for expressing developing gender differences in behaviour. Studies of playgroups (*Dunn*, 1983), have found clear gender differences in choice of play activity which lead gradually to increasing self-segregation and mild hostility between the genders. As children get older, this ideology of separation gets stronger. Children of both genders have to conform to the gender-stereotyping of play, or risk the ridicule of their peers.

Children gradually become aware of the relative skills and status of their peers, and stable hierarchies develop. Clear dominance hierarchies are seen in play groups of children as young as 2 (*Strayer*, 1980). In these groups, where the members play together regularly, it is possible to predict which child will win in competitive play encounters. Although position in the dominance hierarchy is not related to their selection as friends in very young children, among 5-6 year olds, more dominant children are likely to be chosen as friends.

The evidence for the supposed benefits of play is still less than convincing. Although it has been less well studied, there seems a clearer link between play and social competence than there does between play and cognitive development. In some societies, children play very little, yet still appear to develop quite normally. Results from empirical studies on the importance of play suggest that while play is likely to have benefits, it is unlikely that they are essential. Rather, these benefits could be achieved in a number of ways, of which play would be one.

STUDENT'S ANSWER WITH EXAMINER'S COMMENTS

Question 2

It has been a long-standing belief among anthropologists that people who belong to the same cultural group, think, feel and act in similar ways because of similarities in the way that they have been treated as infants and young children.

 **An interesting perspective**

This and similar beliefs arose from overreliance on some of Freud's theories. Freud believed that the experiences of early childhood shaped the child, for better or worse, for the rest of their lives, and would thus explain the psychological differences observed in people of different cultures. Although many of Freud's claims about the importance of this early period have not been proved, and critics play down the irreversible contribution to life development of early experiences, the issue is far from settled. Harlow's work with rhesus monkeys, for example, demonstrated that raising an infant monkey without its mother or social companions for the first six months, produces poor levels of social functioning.

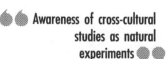 **Awareness of cross-cultural studies as natural experiments**

Although research such as this cannot be carried out on human children for ethical reasons, there are many areas of developmental psychology in which the role of early experience has been addressed. Cross-cultural studies, for example, offer a source of many different forms of child rearing, which would enable researchers to construct natural experiments to interpret the meaning of monkey studies for our own species.

Much of the controversy of the claims surrounding the importance of early experience stems from the work of John Bowlby. Bowlby highlighted the role of the attachment bond in the later social and emotional development of the child. Other researchers have explored the idea of bonding, and tested its significance in the later development of the child. *Klaus and Kennell* (1976) proposed that the first 6–12 hours after birth are a sensitive period for the mother to form a strong emotional bond with her child through physical contact. Lack of this contact, they claimed, would make the bond less strong, and later maltreatment or abuse more likely. Evidence for this claim is somewhat tenuous. The effects of increased contact are somewhat short-term,

 **Good critical awareness**

however, and the long term effects of decreased contact are confounded by many other factors. Research by *Fraiberg* (1975) has suggested that later abuse and mistreatment is not a product of simple 'lack of contact' between parent and child, but more a product of the failure of 'mutuality' between the two. This can occur on either side, e.g. blind children or premature babies may lack the responsiveness that parents need for true mutuality. Parents may also lack attachment skills from their own early experiences, or may approach the task of parenting from an essentially egocentric stance. When these two elements are combined – a child who is less able to respond fully for some reason, and a parent who is less skilful in forming attachments – the likelihood that there will be failure of attachment and possibly neglect or abuse to the child is greatly increased.

❝❝ Good point ❞❞

Bowlby's claims about attachment were focused more on the bond that develops in the middle of the first year. Bowlby proposed that 'mother love in infancy and childhood is as important for mental health as are vitamins and proteins for physical health' . Bowlby also claimed to have discovered evidence that linked delinquency or behaviour problems in adolescence to separation experiences in childhood. Much of what Bowlby claimed has now been discredited. The ethological idea of imprinting, for example, with its claims for a critical period during which the bond develops is not now thought to be characteristic of primates, and evidence exists that children can form attachments with adults well outside the so called critical period. Work by *Rutter* (1980) suggests that the development of psychopathology, or of anti-social behaviour (as predicted by Bowlby) is not an automatic consequence of separation, but is more influenced by the degree of discord at separation.

❝❝ Again, good critical awareness ❞❞

West (1985), found that boys from disrupted or disadvantaged families which provide models of anti-social behaviour in other family members or where discipline of the child is lax, are more likely to become delinquent. However, in this area of development, as in the development of early experience linked psychopathology, it seems that no single cause is sufficient. It is likely that there is a chain of causation whose details will differ from case to case.

❝❝ Awareness of other levels of explanation ❞❞

❝❝ This answer is well researched and deals with material in an informed and critical manner. Its scope is a bit limited, but what is done is done extremely well. It would be well worth a grade A. **❞❞**

REVIEW SHEET

1. Under what *three* conditions can maternal deprivation be said to occur?

    _____

    _____

    _____

2. What are the *three* types of attachment?

    _____

    _____

    _____

3. Bowlby's ideas came from a number of different areas. Identify *three* of these.

    _____

    _____

    _____

4. State *three* criticisms of Bowlby's maternal deprivation hypothesis.

    i) _____

    ii) _____

    iii) _____

5. What are the *three* stages that children might go through at separation?

    _____

    _____

    _____

6. What is *monotropism* and what finding challenges it?

    _____

7. What, according to its critics, was wrong with Project Headstart?

    _____

    _____

    _____

8. The findings of the Milwaukee project could be explained in *two* ways – what were they?

_____

_____

_____

_____

9. Give *three* characteristics of play.

   i)

   _____

   ii)

   _____

   iii)

   _____

10. What according to Piaget, are the *two* major functions of play?

   _____

   _____

11. Give *two* functions of play in Freudian theory.

   i)

   _____

   ii)

12. What did Sutton-Smith mean by the *idealization of play*?

   _____

   _____

15

COGNITIVE DEVELOPMENT

GETTING STARTED

Cognitive psychologists concern themselves with the rational side of human behaviour. Although not applying to all aspects of **cognitive development**, there are a number of issues which are characteristic to most.

1. Cognitive developmental psychologists are more concerned with the rational than the emotional determinants of behaviour.
2. Cognitive theories emphasise the role of the natural environment, seeing formal structured educational experiences as secondary to the self-directed activities of the individual.
3. Cognitive theorists believe in invariant sequences of development which are common to all human beings. These may be shown in terms of fixed *stages* of development.
4. Cognitive theorists tend to ignore gender or cultural differences in cognitive processing.
5. Many cognitive developmental psychologists tend to discount programmes of accelerated development, arguing instead for the importance of **maturational readiness**, i.e. children will only develop when they are maturationally ready to do so. This central belief is in direct contrast to the beliefs held by most behaviourists.

This chapter examines three of the major cognitive theories, those of Jean Piaget, Jerome Bruner and Lev Vygotsky and examines the implications of these theories for education.

Also relevant in this discussion is the study of language acquisition, where cognitive theories are again seen as being in direct opposition to theories based in learning theory.

Information in this chapter will enable you to answer questions on the following areas:

■ **Discussion of theories of cognitive development.**
■ **Application of these theories to education.**
■ **Theories of language acquisition.**

PIAGET'S THEORY

POST-PIAGETIAN RESEARCH

EVALUATION OF PIAGET'S THEORY

BRUNER'S THEORY

PIAGET AND BRUNER COMPARED

VYGOTSKY'S THEORY

APPLICATIONS TO EDUCATION

THEORIES OF LANGUAGE ACQUISITION

ESSENTIAL PRINCIPLES

The following are a number of basic claims made by Piaget.

1. CHILDRENS DEVELOPMENT GOES THROUGH DISTINCT STAGES

(i) The sensori-motor stage

During the **sensor-motor** stage, the child learns to coordinate its sensory input with its motor actions. At the start of the stage the childs behaviour is largely reflexive, but toward the end it is increasingly symbolic. The key development of this stage is *object permanence*, which develops when the child recognises that objects continue to exist even when they are out of sight.

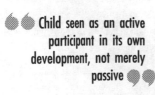
Stages in Piaget's theory of child development

(ii) The pre-operational stage

Children's thought in the **pre-operational stage** is increasingly symbolic, yet they are, as yet, unable to *conserve*. In other words, they are not aware that the physical properties of an object remain the same despite changes in its appearance. This, Piaget thought, was due to the child's reliance on perceptual based rather than logical reasoning. They display various 'curiosities' in their thinking, for example, *egocentrism* (the inability to take anothers perspective), *irreversibility* (the inability to envisage reversing an action) and *animism* (an inability to tell animate from inanimate objects).

(iii) The concrete operational stage

In the **concrete operational** stage, children start to acquire the rudiments of logical reasoning, and can display skills of *reversibility*, (an ability to mentally undo an action), *decentration* (seeing things from more than one perspective) and other skills of *conservation*. However, children in this stage can only solve such problems if they apply to actual objects or events. They cannot solve such problems when they are in the absract.

(iv) The formal operational stage

Children in the **formal operational** stage tend to reason in a more abstract, systematic, logical and reflective way. They are more likely to plan their activities carefully, using logic to reason out the possible consequences of each action before carrying it out.

2. MATURATION VERSUS INTERACTION

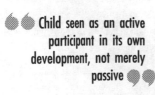
Child seen as an active participant in its own development, not merely passive

Piaget believed that a child developed as a result of two different influences, **maturation**, and **interaction with the environment**. The child develops mental structures (*schemata*) which enables him/her to solve problems in the environment. Adaptation is brought about by the processes of **assimilation** (solving new experiences using existing schemata) and **accomodation** (changing existing schemata in order to solve new experiences). The importance of this viewpoint is that the child is seen as an active participant in its own development, rather than a passive recipient of either biological influences (maturation) or environmental stimulation.

Since Piaget's original claims about the nature and timing of intellectual development, a number of researchers have provided evidence which undermines many of the central propositions of the theory.

Seriation

Piaget claimed that pre-operational children would not be able to display the skill of **seriation** (the correct ordering of different sized objects). *Bryant and Trabasso (1971)* found that such children *could* solve these problems, and that Piaget's result reflected more a failure of *memory* than an ability to demonstrate seriation.

Conservation

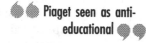

Performance is seen as determined largely by the context of the investigation

Using the infamous 'naughty teddy', *McGarrigle and Donaldson* (1974) were able to show that children as young as 4 years were able to **conserve** when the transformation (the change in conditions in a conservation experiment that is normally brought about by the experimenter) is accidental. This finding emphasises the *context* of investigation.

Moore and Fry (1986) repeated the 'naughty teddy' experiment on the conservation of number, but with two conditions. The first condition was the same as that of McGarrigle and Donaldson in that it had only a few counters in each row. The other condition had lots in each row. After naughty teddy's 'accidental' tranformation of the rows, children *were* able to conserve in the few counters condition, (as in the McGarrigle experiment) but could not in the lots of counters condition (as in the Piaget experiment). Moore and Fry claimed that in these experiments, the children are distracted by naughty teddy, so need to count the counters to make a decision. This is relatively easy in the former condition (so they get it right) but harder in the latter condition, so they resort to reporting *the way they look*, judging the longer row as containing more (which is what Piaget originally claimed).

Support for Piaget's original claims

Egocentricity

Challenges Piagets claim for egocentricity in pre-operational child

Using the 'three mountains' experiment, Piaget demonstrated that children below the age of 7 could not take the viewpoint of another person. However, *Hughes* (1976) constructed an alternative test of **egocentricity** involving a policeman doll and a naughty boy doll which could be placed anywhere in the four quadrants made by two intersecting walls of a dolls house. Most of Hughes' subjects between the ages of 3–5 could successfully place the naughty boy doll where he would not be seen by the policeman, thus demonstrating the ability to *decentre*. *Donaldson* (1978) explains this finding by saying that this experiment drew on the familiar game of hide and seek, therefore children were able to understand the problem that Hughes placed before them. Piaget's three mountains experiment was less familiar to his subjects, therefore they were less likely to provide the right answer.

EVALUATION OF PIAGET'S THEORY

Stage theory challenged

Piaget seen as anti-educational

1. According to many critics, Piaget underestimated young children's abilities. Some researchers have found evidence of object permanence earlier than claimed by Piaget (*Harris*, 1983), and earlier decentrism (*Bullock*, 1985).
2. *Flavell* (1982) criticised the concept of stages. People often display simultaneous patterns of thinking that are characteristic of different stages. This mixing of stages poses problems for a theory that relies on development being organised into discrete stages.
3. Some critics (e.g. *Bandura*, 1965) claim that the steps in intellectual development are not discrete but that development is a steady progression.
4. *Ausubel* (1980) suggested that Piaget excluded the role of verbal instruction in bringing about transition between stages. In this sense, Piaget's theory is seen as 'anti-educational' in that it describes a sequence of events not readily alterable by education and training.
5. Piaget has frequently been criticised for his use of the **clinical method**. The method's sensitivity (children's replies to initial questions determine the line of questioning taken by the experimenter) is seen as detracting from its ability to fulfil the need for standardised procedures.

BRUNER'S THEORY

Development in terms of modes of representation

Bruner claimed that children develop three distinct ways of internally *representing* the world. Bruner proposed a model of development from **enactive representation** (thinking based on physical actions) to **iconic representation** (thinking based on the use of mental images) to **symbolic representation** (the representation of the environment through language).

The development of symbolic representation increases the flexibility of thought, allowing the individual to both represent and manipulate reality. Research by *Bruner and Kenney* (1966) also showed the superiority of symbolic thought over earlier modes of thinking. Children were asked to rearrange a previously viewed arrangement of glasses. Symbolic thinkers were able to complete the task correctly, whereas iconic thinkers could not.

Bruner claimed that different cultures tend to produce different modes of thought because of the differences in the 'tools' they use. He argued that Western cultures are highly symbolic and linguistic, whereas some other cultures are more iconic, relying on images rather than words. *Lamb* (1986) suggested that this fact could explain why some rural African children cannot do conservation tasks, even though they were extremely used to handling objects and liquids.

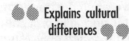 **Explains cultural differences**

PIAGET AND BRUNER COMPARED

Similarities

Both theories agree on the fact that children are biologically organized to understand the world, their cognitive structures maturing over time. They are seen as curious, explorative, and capable of adapting to the world through interaction (*Gross*, 1987).

Differences

Piaget uses a stage sequence of development. Bruner defines development in terms of three modes of representing the world. Piaget does not emphasise the role of language but stresses personal activity. Language is a mere tool to be used in the course of operational thinking. However, evidence from *Bruner et al.* (1966) showed that training in the use of symbols speeds up cognitive development. Bruner stresses that cognitive growth is significantly influenced by culture, family and education. For Piaget, these are of secondary importance to the influences of maturation and the childs own experimentation with the environment.

Importance of language

VYGOTSKY'S THEORY

Vygotsky emphasised the role of the social environment in the cognitive development of the child. Unlike Piaget, Vygotsky rejected an individualistic view of the development of the child. Vygotsky believed that children are born with basic perceptual, attentional and memory abilities. These develop throughout the first two years of life as a result of direct contact with the environment.

As children develop mental representation, particularly the skill of language, they start to communicate with themselves in much the same way as they would communicate with others.

In Piaget's theory, this **egocentric** speech gradually disappears as children develop truly social speech, in which they monitor and adapt what they say to others. Vygotsky disagreed with this view, arguing that as language helps children to think about and control their behaviour, it is an important foundation for complex cognitive skills. As children get older, this self-directed speech becomes silent speech, referring to the inner dialogues that we have with ourselves as we plan and carry out activities.

Research evidence (e.g. *Berk*, 1992) has tended to support Vygotsky's claims for the importance of this inner speech. Children seem to use this type of speech more when tasks are difficult or when they are unclear about their next moves. There is also evidence (*Behrend et al.*, 1992) that those children who displayed the characteristic whispering and lip movements associated with private speech (as it came to be called) when faced with a difficult task, were generally more attentive and successful than their 'quieter' classmates.

Vygotsky believed that this private speech developed as a result of shared dialogues with adults and peers. If children can accomplish difficult tasks with the help of these skilled others, then these dialogues become internalised within their private speech and are used in the future to guide their own efforts in similar tasks. Vygotsky was rather vague about the nature of these social dialogues, although it is generally believed that they have two important features. The first is **intersubjectivity**, where two individuals who might have different understandings of a task, arrive at a shared understanding by adjusting to the perspective of the other. The second feature is referred to as **scaffolding**. Adults may begin an interaction by direct instruction, but as children's mastery of a task increases, so the adult tends to withdraw their own contributions in recognition of the child's success. Research evidence (e.g. *Behrend et al.*) supports the importance of both intersubjectivity and scaffolding in the problem-solving behaviour of children.

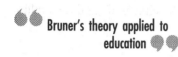

APPLICATIONS TO EDUCATION

❝❝ Piaget's theory applied to education ❞❞

❝❝ Bruner's theory applied to education ❞❞

PIAGET

1. Piaget is concerned solely with the development of thought as opposed to comprehension. Much of what he says about development lacks real relevance for what happens in the classroom.
2. Piaget places a great deal of emphasis on endogenous motivation (maturation) thus ignoring the active role of education.
3. Piaget denies the role of education in accelerating cognitive development from one stage to another. *Kuhn*, (1979) discovered that acceleration was possible using the **optimal mismatch** method (see chapter 14).
4. Language is seen as having only a communicative role with no operative or process role in thought. Education, however, emphasises the importance of linguistic skills (compare this point of view with that of Bruner).

BRUNER

Bruner is best known in the field of education for his contributions to the idea of **learning by discovery**. This method is characterised by a belief in (among others) the following principles.

1. All real knowledge is self-discovered.
2. Problem-solving ability is the primary goal of education.
3. Discovery organises learning effectively for later use.
4. Discovery is a unique generator of motivation and self-confidence.

Evaluation of Bruner's views on discovery learning

Critics of discovery learning (e.g. *Ausubel*, 1980) make the following claims:

1. Most of the articles cited in support of discovery learning consist mainly of theoretical discussion and assertion rather than actual research evidence.
2. Most of the reasonably well-controlled studies report negative findings.
3. Most studies that report positive findings either fail to control other significant variables or employ questionable techniques of statistical analysis.

VYGOTSKY

Vygotsky's approach to cognitive development is exemplified in two different approaches to collaborative learning.

1. Reciprocal Teaching

In this technique, a collaborative learning group is formed, comprising a teacher and a small number of pupils. Typically these groups have been used to improve reading comprehension. Group members take turns at being the dialogue leader, leading the group through four stages of dialogue. They begin by asking questions about the content then **summarising** the material in the passage. Group members then clarify ambiguous or unfamiliar content, and finally the dialogue leader encourages other group members to predict what will happen next in the passage. Reciprocal teaching is seen as forming a **zone of proximal development**, that is a range of tasks that an individual child cannot accomplish on their own, but can accomplish with the help of others.

2. Co-operative Learning

This process, which emphasises the role of knowledgeable peers rather than adults in collaborative groups, has much in common with ideas also proposed by Piaget. Piaget believed that peers may well be more influential in the acquisition of cognitive change because children often may simply accept the perspective of an adult without critical examination. The process of **intersubjectivity** as described earlier, is important in this context. Research by *Azmitia*, (1988) suggests that children benefit most from collaborative learning when their peer is an 'expert' at the task concerned.

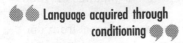

THEORIES OF LANGUAGE ACQUISITION

👂👂 Language acquired through conditioning 👂👂

BEHAVIOURIST THEORIES

Skinner (1957) argued that children learn their language in much the same way as they learn any other skill, through imitation and reinforcement. Language consisted of verbal responses that would be learned through the processes of **conditioning**. Parents would, therefore, shape the verbal responses of their children by providing reinforcement for vocalisations that were clear and accurate. Vocalisations that were not reinforced would then gradually decline in frequency. Skinner claimed that there were three main ways in which children acquired words.

1. Tact

Here the child produces a sound which is close to the correct sound for a given stimulus and is thus rewarded. Through this reinforcement, the child is more likely to repeat the word in the future.

👂👂 Three ways by which children acquire words 👂👂

2. Mand

This refers to words that are acquired by the child because their meaning is important to him. The words are associated with significant events in the child's life and the child thus learns through this association.

3. Echoic

The acquisition of words through imitation of adult speech, which leads to reinforcement from the parents (smiles, approval, etc.).

👂👂 Development of syntax through reinforcement 👂👂

Behaviourist theories also explain how children acquire an understanding of syntax. This too is a product of imitation, with parents providing reinforcement by responding appropriately to questions and statements made by their children.

Evaluation of behaviourist theories

1. Language is creative, its speakers can produce and understand an infinite number of sentences that have never been reinforced.
2. Research by *Brown and Hanlon* (1970) casts doubt on the claim that syntax is learned through reinforcement. They found that parents tend to respond to meaning and factual accuracy rather than grammatical rules.
3. Behaviourist theories do not seem to be able to explain the phenomenon of **virtuous errors** (overgeneralisations of grammatical rules, e.g. 'We seed the mouses') which are unlikely to have been heard by the children, therefore cannot have been reinforced.
4. Reinforcement and shaping are simply too slow and too inconsistently applied to be effective influences in a child's acquisition of language.

NATIVIST THEORIES

Alternative theories to the Behaviourist approach have tended to stress the 'inborn' nature of language. *Chomsky* (1975) proposed that humans possess a **Language Acquisition Device** (LAD) which is an innate mechanism that facilitates the learning of language. Thus, humans learn language because they are biologically equipped for it. The LAD processes input (spoken language) and enables the listener to develop the rules of grammar on the basis of that input.

👂👂 The language acquisition device 👂👂

Reasons for Chomsky's belief in an innate capacity for language

1. Children learn language quickly and effortlessly.
2. Language develops at approximately the same pace and in the same sequence for all children. This suggests that language is more to do with biological maturation than personal experience.
3. Evidence from cross-cultural studies (e.g. *Slobin*, 1971) supports this view of the universality of language.

Unlike Skinner, who stressed the *performance* of verbal responses, Chomsky focused more on the *competence* displayed in the production and comprehension of language.

Chomsky suggested that children quickly develop **transformational rules** which enable them to extract the same meaning (**deep structure**) from different word orders (**surface structure**).

Evaluation of nativist theories

1. The LAD concept is vague. There is no knowledge of how it works, or how it is organised neurally.
2. More recent research (*Bohannon et al.*, 1988) has established that parents do provide their children with subtle corrective feedback about grammar.
3. Support for Chomsky comes from the biolinguistic theory of *Lenneberg* (1964) who points out that human beings have evolved highly specialized organs for the production and reception of language, and that nearly all human beings develop language regardless of their level of intellectual ability.

More contemporary theorists have tended to adopt an interactionist view to language acquisition. **Interactionist** theories tend to stress *both* maturation *and* experience.

Cognitive interactionist theories (e.g. *Maratsos*, 1983) put forward the view that children's use of the rules of grammar is an indication of their understanding of the state implied by the rule (e.g. the use of the suffix -ed at the end of a word implies an understanding of the past).

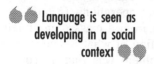 **Language is seen as developing in a social context**

Social communication theories stress the role of interpersonal communication and the social context of language learning (*Bohannon et al.*, 1985). The child interacts with mature language users in a social context, and thus learns basic rules through that interaction. Social exchanges with others are thus seen as playing a crucial role in moulding language skills.

EXAMINATION QUESTIONS

1. Outline *two* theories of cognitive development and evaluate these theories in terms of empirical evidence.
   (25)
   (AEB 1992)
2. Evaluate some theories of cognitive development in terms of their applications to education.
   (25)
   (AEB 1988)
3. Critically consider the role of learning and experience in the development of language.
   (25)
   (AEB 1993)

ANSWERS TO EXAMINATION QUESTIONS

OUTLINE ANSWER TO QUESTION 3

The requirement in this question is for you to offer a description of learning/experience in the development of language, and then to evaluate the same.

There are two main ways in which this could be attempted although the former way does lend itself better to the evaluative requirement of the question.

The first way is to offer an account of theories and evidence which are embedded in the idea of language development through experiential learning (e.g. the behaviourist theories). The use of nativist theories could then be used as evaluation of t hese viewpoints provided that their inclusion is made explicit to the question.

The second way is to present the largely empirical work that has been carried out on language stages and the influence of social dynamics. This approach has not been covered in this chapter, and can be found in *Gross* (1992).

TUTORS ANSWER
Question 2

The developmental theory proposed by Jean Piaget is largely concerned with the development of thought as opposed to comprehension, and as such cannot be considered a 'theory of instruction' (*Ginsberg*, 1981). However, others have interpreted Piaget's theory in terms of its educational implications. The main implication appears to be the concept of readiness, whereby the child is not seen as being able to deal with the cognitive demands of a task until he or she is maturationally ready to do so. *Ausubel* (1980) criticises this concept of *maturational* readiness and replaces it with the idea of cognitive readiness. Cognitive *readiness* is defined as the adequacy of existing cognitive capacity or level of functioning in relation to the demands of a given learning task (*Ausubel*, 1980). In most circumstances, Ausubel claims, it is solely a function of cumulative prior learning experience, although this may depend on varying proportions of maturation and learning. Ausubel also claims that 'lack of maturational readiness' may be a convenient available scapegoat when children show insufficient developmental readiness to learn.

Ausubel's theory thus focuses more on the active role of education rather than Piaget's emphasis on the endogenous motivation of maturation.

Early attempts to accelerate children through Piaget's stages through carefully controlled educational stimulation did produce some encouraging results in that preschool children were able to attain the stage of concrete operations (*Kamii*, 1972; *Lavatelli*, 1970). However, these result were not derived from a classroom situation therefore cannot be considered to be a valid representation of what happens in the more social context of classroom learning. Another problem was that as concrete operational reasoning is attained by nearly all children, it is difficult to know whether the attainment was caused by the intervention.

Kamii and DeVries (1977) based their educational programme on the Piagetian view that intellectual development only comes about as a result of the individual's own constructive activity. The role of the educator in such a programme, they claimed, was to provide opportunities for activity. This has led to the development of learning environments in which the child is more left alone to develop their own competencies, rather than being a part of a highly structured and formalised learning environment. The effectiveness of this approach has been recently criticised in the light of statistics provided from primary school assessment tests (*Alexander*, 1992).

Optimal mismatch theory (*Kuhn*, 1979) was developed to provide a child with activities that challenged their thinking, but did not invite failure. However, the aim of providing learning experiences which are *optimally* mismatched with each individual childs present competencies does appear somewhat idealistic and impractical in the crowded primary classroom.

For Jerome Bruner, he has been a supporter of discovery learning. Central to the idea of learning by discovery is the belief that all real knowledge is self-discovered and through the medium of language is effectively organised for later use. Bruner believed that the development of problem solving ability was the primary aim of education. As the child works towards the development of symbolic representation he develops a more flexible problem solving strategy. The role of education was thus to foster such self-motivated discovery.

Critics of the 'learning by discovery' technique (e.g. *Ausubel*, 1980) have stressed that most of the assertions about its effectiveness have largely theoretical rather than empirical, and those which are based on empirical investigations generally have reported negative findings.

STUDENTS ANSWER WITH EXAMINER'S COMMENTS
Question 1

There are two major theorists in the area of cognitive development, and whilst they agree on a number of aspects, they also have a certain amount of dissimilarity. Jean Piaget is the man whose theory was the one single theory to have such a great impact on cognitive development. He influenced many theorists, one of the most noteworthy being Jerome Bruner.

Piaget, like many others, believed that a child's thinking is different not just qualitatively but quantitatively from an adults. His theory consisted of four stages through which children develop and the first of these he named the sensori-motor period. As he was obliged to put an age range on his stages, he unwillingly did so and so the first stage was estimated to last from birth to 18–24 months. During this time, the child is completely pre-occupied with itself and will learn to connect things to each other, e.g. making a certain movement will cause a string of toys to rattle. However, this association is sometimes not understood in that the child may expect the hand movement to produce the rattling even when the toys are not present. The child also lacks object permanence, once something is out of sight the child thinks it no longer exists and will not search for it. Towards the end of this period, the child starts to develop speech.

The second stage lasts from 2–7 years, the pre-operational stage. The child is beginning to develop physically and Piaget believed that the use of language indicated the ability of more complex thought towards the end of this stage. The child beg ins to realise that other people can see things differently from themselves i.e. a two year old child shown a card with a dog on one side and a cat on the other will presume that a person sitting opposite will see the same as they do. Piaget also used the three mountain experiment to show that the child was egocentric. These mountains each had a different distinguishing feature, one had a house, one a cloud and the last a cross. The child would be sat in front of these and a doll sat opposite the child. T hen the child would pick the view they themselves had. Piaget also used experiments to prove that the pre-operational child could not conserve, show class inclusion or reversibility, before the age of seven which was when Piaget believed there was an 'enlightening period' for the child.

The third stage of cognitve operations lasted from seven to twelve years and was the time when the child was able to do many tasks not accomplished in the previous stage. Not only could the child correctly predict the order three different coloured balls would come out of a tube, they were now able to correctly predict the reverse order.

The final stage of Piaget's developmental theory was from twelve years onwards. At this formal operational stage the child no longer needed concrete examples, but was capable of the most complex forms of abstract thinking. However, Piaget's theory was not simply accepted and although it played a very great part in education particularly in discovery learning, it prompted a lot of research, most of which did not support his views. However, it must be said that in the light of some criticisms, Piaget did amend some of his beliefs in the 1970s.

Criticisms of Piaget ranged from his belief in four rigid stages which supposedly showed a very clear progression from one stage to the next, whereas in actual fact whilst in one stage certain cognitive abilities may still be in in the previous stage, to his sample size being far too small and elite, he actually used three of his own children. Of course we cannot simply discard the whole of Piaget's theory because some of it has been criticised in research, but it is difficult to place a vast amount of value on it since it has been partially not supported.

In the first stage, Piaget supposed 'object permanence' to be a fact but further research criticises this in saying that the way in which an object disappears does have an effect, i.e. studies show that a one month old baby will show surprise if a toy behind a screen disappears when the screen is moved. Also if the lights are switched out the baby will continue to reach for a toy for over one minute. Similar criticisms are made for Piaget's pre-operational period. *McGarrigle et al.* (1985) found that children were capable of class inclusion when asked of a set of a few white cows and more black cows, all sleeping 'Are there more white cows or sleeping cows?' The standard Piagetian task would ask if there were more red beads or beads when there were a few red and many black. However, the child is perhaps showing a lot of intelligence by simply inserting the word black before beads which would make the sentence more usual. Donaldson also criticised Piaget's belief of conservation. Piaget would have a row of equal buttons, then squash one row together and each time ask the child which group contained more or were they both the same. The child would answer the same for the first part, and then that the row contained more. However the child may have felt dominated by the experimenter, and given the answer they felt they were expected to. *Donaldson* (1984) used a naughty teddy to push the buttons together, thus removing the element of the experimenter performing 'magic tricks' and resulting in over half being able to conserve.

66 A little vague here 99

66 Why is this seen as so important 99

66 Appropriate use of examples 99

66 In what way? 99

66 A little vague again 99

66 More needs to be made of this—What does it show? 99

A second theory is that of Bruner, and although he agreed with Paiget that seven years was a very important time, his theory consisted of three 'modes' : Enactive, iconic and symbolic. This allowed much more flexibility than Piaget's stages as he admitted that one third never reached formal operational reasoning. The enactive mode was described as 'muscle memory' e.g. tying shoelaces. Iconic was more studying and symbolic as it suggests describing. An experiment which allows each mode to be understood is that in which *Sonstroem* (1966) took children who failed the standard Piagetian clay conservation task and had four groups. One moulded, studied and described the new shape they had made, using each mode in turn. Two studied and described. Three moulded and studied, and Four were the control group. This time, when tested for conservation, group one showed a marked improvement because they'd used all three modes, particularly symbolic.

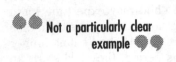 Not a particularly clear example

Bruner's theory was not without its problems though. While Bruner believed that training in language could help development of cognitive thought, Piaget believed speech indicated the capability of deeper thought. Neither theory alone can hope to be completely correct, but together they do form a strong bais of beliefs about cognitive development.

A competent if not spectacular essay. It is always difficult in these sorts of questions to do both theorists full justice, and this candidate was no exception, spending the lions share of the essay on Piaget. Discussion of Piaget did yield some relevant evaluative points, but description of the theory did not fully elaborate some of the key features. Treatment of Bruner was rather weak, better use could have been made of the examples. However, a lot of information presented, so a grade of B/C would be likely.

REVIEW SHEET

1. Briefly outline the main characteristics of Piaget's four stages of intellectual development.

    Sensori-motor

    _____

    _____

    _____

    Pre-operational

    _____

    _____

    _____

    Concrete operational

    _____

    _____

    _____

    Formal operational

    _____

    _____

2. Distinguish between assimilation and accomodation.

    _____

    _____

3. What did McGarrigle and Donaldson find out about the conservation competencies of young children?

    _____

    _____

4. Offer three criticisms of Piaget's theory

    i) _____

    ii) _____

    iii) _____

5. What are Bruner's three modes of representation?

    i) _____

    ii) _____

    iii) _____

6. Suggest one similarity and one difference between Piaget and Bruner's theories

Similarity

_____

_____

Difference

_____

_____

7. Piaget's theories are often described as anti-educational. Give two reasons which might support this claim.

i)

_____

ii)

_____

8. Offer three claims of discovery learning.

i)

_____

ii)

_____

iii)

_____

9. Give two criticisms of discovery learning

i)

_____

ii)

_____

10. Distinguish between the tact, mand and echoic responses in a child's acquisition of language.

i)

_____

ii)

_____

iii)

_____

11. Give two criticisms of the behavioural view of language acquisition.

i)

_____

ii)

_____

12. What is the Language Acquisition Device?

_____

_____

13. Why does Chomsky believe language to be innate? Give two reasons.

i)

_____

ii)

_____

14. Offer two evaluative points (for or against) concerning Chomsky's theory.

i)

_____

ii)

_____

16

SOCIAL BEHAVIOUR

GETTING STARTED

This chapter explores two of the major issues in the development of social behaviour. All societies tend to define gender roles, with some assigning them in a quite rigid way. The vast majority of societies tend to assign **instrumental roles** (the *doing* roles) roles to males, and the **expressive roles** (the more *nurturant*, caring roles) roles to females. Gender role differentiation has traditionally been occupationally linked, with the greater physical strength of men making them more likely to take on heavier, more physically demanding work. Womens mobility has always been constrained by pregnancy and the need to care for children when they are young. However, technological, educational and societal changes have meant that such divisions in role (with some notable exceptions!) are no longer necessary. Yet traditional gender roles continue to exist. Some of the theories that follow try to explain why this is the case. More recent work on androgyny, however, has suggested that many young people are rejecting traditional gender roles and are displaying evidence of both male and female gender traits.

According to the traditional view, moral judgements cannot be objectively investigated, (therefore cannot be studied scientifically), and the purpose of scientific psychology is to explain behaviour, rather than to judge it. There are several reasons why this view is no longer acceptable. Firstly, to ignore the moralistic considerations that underlie much of our behaviour is to ignore one of the most significant influences on our actions. Secondly, Moral development is seen as especially important to the child development specialist because of the orderly and systematic changes that take place with age.

Material presented in this chapter will enable you to answer questions on the following topics:

■ **Discussion of the social influences on the development of gender role.**
■ **Discussion on theories of moral development.**
■ **Compare and Contrast major theories of moral development.**

GENDER ROLE

BIOLOGICAL INFLUENCES ON THE SOCIALISATION OF GENDER ROLES

THEORIES OF GENDER ROLE DEVELOPMENT

MORAL RELATIVISM AND MORAL UNIVERSALISM

THEORIES OF MORAL DEVELOPMENT

CHARACTERISTICS OF KOHLBERG'S THEORY

THEORIES OF MORAL DEVELOPMENT COMPARED

ESSENTIAL PRINCIPLES

The term **gender role** refers to the collection of attitudes, behaviours, perceptions and affective reactions that are more commonly associated with one sex than the other. (*Lamb*, 1978).

BIOLOGICAL INFLUENCES ON THE SOCIALISATION OF GENDER ROLES

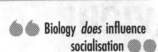 Biology *does* influence socialisation

Biology may be seen as contributing to the socialisation of gender roles in two important ways:

1. It provides critical cues (identification of the child as male or female) that elicit appropriate training by others.
2. The age at which a child reaches puberty shapes the ways that others view the adolescent. Early maturers are seen as more self confident, more socially skilled, more conservative and are more highly regarded by their peers (*Medinnus and Johnson, 1969*)

THEORIES OF GENDER ROLE DEVELOPMENT

Identification with the aggressor

1. PSYCHOANALYTIC THEORY

The main premise of the **psychoanalytic** theory is that identification with the parent of the same sex proceeds out of the **Oedipal conflict**. As a result of the resolution of this conflict, boys adopt 'masculine' behaviours and girls 'feminine' behaviours. The process is seen as being more difficult for boys as it involves a discontinuation of earlier attachment processes. Boys, according to the original theory, must identify with their father to forestall the possibility that the father might punish them as retribution for the child's feelings toward the mother. Girls according to Freud, discover, during the Oedipal period, their lack of a penis. This causes them to reject their mother (whom they blame) but, fearing maternal rejection, they change their wish for a penis into the wish for a child. In this way, according to Freud, traditional gender roles are established in a culture. Females who did not conform to this path of development were seen as deviant, and displayed *penis envy* if they tried to assume the role more normally adopted by males.

Criticisms of psychoanalytic theory

1. Freud's view of 'deviant' feminine development has been criticised by *Horney* (1939) and *Mitchell* (1980) who argue that penis envy is actually understandable envy of the status that men have in traditional patriarchal cultures.
2. Freudian theory is extremely difficult to prove or disprove. Any failure to produce the predicted findings in interpreted as the use of defense mechanisms such as repression or reaction formation, which prevent an individual from being aware of the real motivation for their behaviour.
3. From a strict Freudian perspective females are seen as morally inferior to males. *Garol Gilligan* (1982) has proposed that females possess a different moral orientation than males, not an inferior one.

2. LEARNING THEORY

Learning theory explanations of gender role can be conveniently divided into three different types.

(a) Socialisation theory

This proposes that parents and significant others shape behaviour through the direct use of reward and punishment.

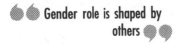 Gender role is shaped by others

Evidence for this point of view comes from *Condry and Condry* (1976) who found that parents tend to have strong gender based expectations of their children's behaviour. *Rheingold and Cook* (1975) found that parents do discourage their children (particularly sons) from engaging in gender inappropriate behaviour.

However, in a review of evidence on differential treatment by parents of boys and girls, *Maccoby and Jacklin* (1974) found little evidence that parents treat children differently with respect to behaviours that are typically gender typed.

(b) Observational learning

This proposes that parents act as *models* so that boys imitate their fathers and girls their mothers. Gender role learning is considered easier for girls than it is for boys, as girls continue their attachment with the mother, whereas boys must distance themselves from the mother in order to emulate the father.

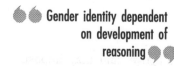

A more parsimonious explanation than the psychoanalytic one

Evidence from *Lamb* (1977) showed that fathers might make themselves more available and relevant to their sons at a certain point in their development, and this encourages boys to imitate. *Bandura et al.* (1963) showed that models that are more powerful are more likely to be imitated.

However, this does not explain why girls to not imitate their fathers (it may be that relevance and availability is importance in both genders).

Studies of children from households where mothers were frequently engaged in non-traditional household and child care tasks, have shown that the children themselves were less gender typed in their own choice of activities and occupation (*Serbin et al.*, 1993).

(c) Reciprocal role theory

This proposes that male and female roles are complementary in most cultures and that boys and girls learn their roles by interaction with the opposite sex (notably their mothers and fathers) as well as by imitation of those with similar roles.

Evidence for this perspective comes from *Hetherington* (1965) who discovered that the femininity of girls tends not to be related to the femininity of the mother, but more to the attitude to femininity of the father. *Hetherington* (1972) also discovered that girls who were deprived of their fathers seemed to experience later difficulties in their interactions with men. Those who, at an early age, had lost their fathers through death tended to be abnormally respectful and shy toward men, and those who had lost their fathers through divorce tended to be unusually aggressive toward men.

However, caution is suggested in the interpretation of Hetherington's research, as it does not explain why the *reason* for the father absence had such an effect. It is possible that the effect was determined by, among other things, the attitude of the mother to the loss.

3. COGNITIVE-DEVELOPMENTAL THEORY

Gender identity dependent on development of reasoning

This theory proposed by *Kohlberg* (1966) proposes that children go through three stages in the development of the gender concept. At the age of 2 they label themselves based on physical characteristics. This is called *gender identity* At 3–4 they move into *gender stability*, where they believe that boys will remain boys throughout life and girls will remain girls. They do not however, understand that this is true across all *situations*. This knowledge called *gender constancy* develops between 5–6 when children begin to understand that gender is not threatened by clothes worn or activities undertaken. Gender roles are then seen as inviolable by the child, Kohlberg claiming that conformity to these roles is seen as a *moral imperative*.

Evidence in favour of this proposition comes from *Slaby and Frey* (1975) who found, using a split screen technique that the degree of gender conservation in 6 year olds could be used to predict what they watched (male or female).

The theory is attractive because it proposes that children seek out any appropriate models, therefore it can explain the fact that many researchers have found no great similarities between sons and their fathers, or daughters and their mothers . However the theory predicts that gender knowledge is established far later than evidence suggests. A study of pre-school children by *Martin and Little* (1990) showed that children who had not achieved gender stability nonetheless still showed a strong preference for gender-typed toys and activities.

Gender labelling and gender knowledge

Some of Kohlberg's critics have suggested that he underestimated the importance of gender labelling, that is the ability to recognise gender consistently and divide up the world on the basis of these labels. *Fagot and Leinbach* (1993) suggest that children will prefer gender appropriate friends and activities almost as soon as they acquire the ability to label.

Being able to label, however, is not the same as acquiring gender knowledge. As children get older, they acquire more complex and more detailed knowledge of their own gender. *Shank and Abelson* (1977) suggest that such knowledge is based around the development of **scripts**, which are sequences of actions associated with particular behaviours. It is possible that children acquire greater knowledge of the scripts associated with their own gender than with the other gender. *Bauer* (1993) suggests that gender labelling may well expose the child to greater same gender activities which in turn gives them a greater opportunity for gender-appropriate learning.

Vygotsky's theory likewise has a number of applications to education. The importance of the social context of learning is emphasised in the technique of reciprocal teaching. In this technique, a small group of children work with a teacher, taking turns to be the dialogue leader, who helps the group to question, summarise and clarify subject content, and from this predict what will happen next. The group thus provides what Vygotsky referred to as a zone of proximal development, that is a range of tasks that an individual child cannot accomplish without the help of others. The social dialogue that develops during such activities is then used by all members when next trying to accomplish a similar task. Although Vygotsky's education ideas might be seen as being directly opposite to those of Piaget, it is difficult to disentangle the relative effects of natural development (as emphasised by Piaget) and the social environment (as emphasised by Vygotsky).

EXTRAFAMILIAL INFLUENCES

Schools are seen as having a powerful influence on the development of gender roles for the following reasons:

1. Teachers may have gender related expectations of behaviour which may be communicated to pupils in subtle ways.
2. When children start school, or change school, they come into an unknown environment with unknown expectations of behaviour. The child thus tries to choose the most appropriate behaviour for the new social context. Doubt and uncertainty (not to mention the extremely powerful impact of their peers) will lead the child to choose what is seen as the safest course, conformity to traditional gender roles.

ANDROGYNY

Bem (1975) felt that traditional gender role, may be maladaptive, and may impose unwarranted restrictions on the aspirations and attainments of (particularly) women.

Androgynous individuals, then, are those who are high in *both* male and female traits. Research by *Massad* (1981) showed that amongst both males and females, the frequency of androgynous individuals was higher than that of those possessing only the traditional single gender traits. This tendency was more obvious in girls than boys. *Bee* (1984) feels that this is because in Western cultures, male traits are associated with status and occupational prestige, and therefore are considered more desirable.

In the 1990s, however, psychologists have been reluctant to measure masculinity and femininity as simple traits. *Spence* (1993) argues that such simplistic notions tell us little of value when considering gender differences in social behaviour.

> ❝❝ Androgynous individuals display *both* male and female characteristics to a high degree ❞❞

MORAL DEVELOPMENT

Morals are that part of our value systems which are concerned with the 'proper' ends of our behaviour, with questions of right and wrong, and with accountability for our actions (*Ausubel*, 1980).

MORAL RELATIVISM AND MORAL UNIVERSALISM

❝❝ In moral relativism, no one culture is seen as morally superior to another ❞❞

❝❝ The existence of moral universals ❞❞

It is possible to classify theories of moral development according to their interpretation of the concept of **morality**. Psychoanalysis and social learning theory tend to equate morality with the values, standards etc. that are part of a particular culture. Morality, therefore, is **relative** to the culture under study. There are no grounds for identifying one culture as more or less 'moral' than any other. This point of view is supported by evidence from anthropology and sociology, which has shown that differences do exist across cultures in what we might regard as 'moral' judgements and behaviour.

On the other hand, cognitive-developmentalists, especially Kohlberg, make the claim for **moral universalism**. According to this idea of morality, there are certain universal moral principles, in terms of which the values of any culture may be judged. Prominent among these values would be the concepts of justice and the value of human life. There are two main problems with this point of view. First of all, there appears to be little agreement on what the universal moral principles actually are, nor does it follow that if a large proportion of people share a similar value, then that value is necessarily any more 'right'.

THEORIES OF MORAL DEVELOPMENT

❝❝ Importance of the Oedipal conflict ❞❞

1. PSYCHOANALYTIC THEORY

The **psychoanalytic** explanation of moral development is based on the idea that conflict is aroused in the child during the phallic stage (*Oedipal conflict*). Successful resolution of this conflict results in identification with the same sex parent, and the internalisation of parental values into a superego.

The implications of psychoanalytic theory are that this conflict is inevitable, being produced by unconscious impulses. The manner in which the child resolves the conflict determines their attitude to authority, strict superegos being associated with excessive compliance to authority, and weak superegos with hostility to authority.

Evaluation of psychoanalytic theory

1. According to the theory, discipline which promotes fear of punishment or loss of parental love should motivate children to behave in a morally desirable manner. Evidence from *Kochanska* (1991, 1993) suggests that children exposed to this kind of discipline may actually develop weak consciences.
2. Other research (e.g. *Miller and Swanson*, 1958) has demonstrated that there are different types of guilt (as opposed to the unitary superego proposed by Freud). In a classic study by *Hartshorne and May*, (1928), childrens' moral conduct was found to be situationally determined (i.e. not consistent across situations).
3. More recent psychoanalytic ideas (e.g. *Emde et al.*, 1991) have emphasised the importance of positive and nurturant emotions in the development of morally desirable behaviour. Although acknowledged by Freud, the influence of positive caring emotion was seen as less important than the fear of punishment.

2. SOCIAL LEARNING THEORY

Social learning theory sees moral behaviour as being learned through direct reinforcement and through the observation of models. It is maintained through:

(i) Expectations of future reward and puinishment, and intermittent reinforcement.
(ii) The self monitoring reinforcement system, by which we correct our behaviour in line with personal standards.

The main features of the social learning theory of moral development are:

❝❝ Moral learning is the learning of moral behaviour ❞❞

(i) Moral learning is indistinguishable from any other form of learning, i.e. it is learned in the same way. In a sense, this means that there is no such thing as a social learning theory of moral development, but merely a theory which explains the learning of all socially influenced behaviour, of which moral behaviour is but one example.
(ii) Moral development is seen as the learning of moral *behaviours* (as opposed to Kohlberg's perspective of moral *reasoning*).
(iii) It is an extreme moral relativist position (see earlier section).
(iv) Children tend to acquire their initial morally desirable behaviour through modeling. Once they have acquired a moral response, it is maintained by the frequent praise of significant others (*Grusec*, 1989)

Evaluation of social learning theory

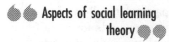
Aspects of social learning theory

(i) In the same way that the *Hartshorne and May* (1928) study appeared to contradict psychoanalytic theory, it supports the social learning perspective. A particular behaviour will be not be performed if it is likely to lead to punishment. Hartshorne and May found that children would be less likely to cheat if they thought they would be found out and punished. If they thought they could get away with it, they were likely to cheat.

(ii) Many terms (e.g. reinforcement, which is circular i.e. something is a reinforcer only if it reinforces) are ill-defined.

(iii) The social learning theory has a peculiar attitude to psychoanalysis, rejecting the terms and concepts of the theory. However, the **Self monitoring reinforcement system** which monitors behaviour and administers 'self-rewards' and 'self-punishments', appears to have the same functions as the Freudian notion of the **Superego**.

3. COGNITIVE-DEVELOPMENTAL THEORY

Piaget's theory of moral development (*Piaget*, 1964) proposed that the moral development of children reflects their level of intellectual development. Piaget claimed that changes in the intellectual abilities of children (e.g. decentrism and the later development of formal operational reasoning) had a direct influence on their moral reasoning abilities. Younger childrens' reasoning about morality is based on *adult* constraint whereas older childrens' moral reasoning is based more on an understanding of the importance of cooperation, mutuality and rationality in morality.

Developments after Piaget

Piaget's theory has largely been superceded by the theory of Lawrence Kohlberg. Kohlberg claimed that moral reasoning is dependent on intellectual development *and* social experience.

CHARACTERISTICS OF KOHLBERG'S THEORY

Aspects of Kohlberg's theory

(i) Moral development consists of age-linked sequential reorganizations in moral attitudes and reasoning.

(ii) Major aspects of moral development are culturally universal.

(iii) Moral principles are viewed as structures that arise through the experience of social interaction with others.

(iv) The extent of environmental influences is determined by the general quality of cognitive and social stimulation over time.

KOHLBERG'S LEVELS OF MORAL DEVELOPMENT

(i) The Pre-conventional level

Levels of moral development in Kohlberg's theory

The child is seen as responsive to the moral rules of others, either in terms of the power of other people, or the hedonistic (seeking pleasurable events and avoiding unpleasant ones) consequences of their actions (i.e. doing things because they stop you getting into trouble or enable you to gain reward).

(ii) The conventional level

Moral reasoning is determined by an attitude of loyalty to interpersonal expectations and the social order (i.e. doing things because you are expected to do them by others).

(iii) The post-conventional level

Morality is based on universal ethical principles. These are seen to include unconditional respect for individuals, the value of human life and an appreciation of justice based on the moral equality of all individuals. (i.e. doing things because they are *right*).

EVIDENCE ON KOHLBERG'S THEORY

(i) Older and more intelligent children are more advanced in their moral reasoning than younger and less intelligent ones (*Rest*, 1986).

(ii) The progression of change does proceed upwards but with occasional regression (*Kuhn*, 1976)

(iii) A number of studies have confirmed the invariance of Kohlberg's stages. In other words, *all* people go through the stages in the *same* order (*Rest*, 1986; *Walker*, 1989).

Cultural bias in theory

EVALUATION OF KOHLBERG'S THEORY

(i) Kohlberg's conception of moral maturity is culturally biased, other equally valid conceptions of moral maturity are not accounted for by his theory.

(ii) His theory had a very limited data base (approx 50 American males) for the claims of universality.

(iii) Data about the moral judgement/moral behaviour relationship are neither extensive nor strongly positive. *Rest* (1974) found only modest positive relationships between the moral reasoning scores of children and their moral conduct as perceived by others. *Kohlberg* (1971) claimed that when people reach postconventional morality, they are more likely to behave consistently with their moral principles.

(iv) *Carol Gilligan* (1982) believes that Kohlberg's theory devalues the *ethic of care* shown by many females when considering moral dilemmas. Kohlberg's postconventional level stresses abstract and rational commitment to moral ideals. Such ways of thinking are more often stressed in males. She claims that *care for others* is a different rather than a less valid base for moral judgement.

THEORIES OF MORAL DEVELOPMENT COMPARED

Cognitive Developmental (Kohlberg)	Social Learning Theory (SLT)	Psychoanalysis
1. Age related changes in moral thought	Changes in moral behaviour	Changes in moral behaviour
2. N/A	Concerned with *how* moral actions are learned	Concerned with *what* is learned rather than *how* it is learned
3. Certain moral principles exist that are common to all humankind and which transcend culture (i.e. moral universalism)	Concerned with the rules, norms and values that prevail in a particular culture (i.e. Moral relativism)	As SLT
4. Moral development is largely pre-programmed (linked to intellectual development)	Moral development is seen as reponses to external stimuli (other people). Development is stimulated by what other people do. Maturity means having *more* responses	Moral development is largely pre-programmed. Development is the unfolding of inevitable tendencies
5. Development proceeds in stages. Maturity is the acquisition of the highest stage	Development is cumulative and continuous rather than being stage related	Development proceeds in stages. Maturity is the acquisition of later stages
6. Conscience is seen as a process of reasoned judgement about what is right	Conscience is characterised by the need to avoid punishment through self reproach or to seek approval through expectations of external or internal reinforcement	
	(*Self monitoring reinforcement system*)	(*Superego*)
7. Allows for intergenerational change as adolescents may discover corruption and hypocrisy in the world, particularly in those who originally taught the concepts of conventional morality. Some may react by seeking higher levels of moral development, others by regression to moral cynicism	Concerned with the passing on of traditional norms and values – 'status quo' explanations of moral transmission	

EXAMINATION QUESTIONS

1. Critically consider the view that gender roles are socially constructed. *(25)*
   (AEB 1992)
2. Discuss psychological theories of moral development. *(25)*
3. Compare and contrast the cognitive-developmental and social learning theories of moral development. *(25)*

ANSWERS TO EXAMINATION QUESTIONS

OUTLINE ANSWER TO QUESTION 3

This question might be approached in one of two ways. Either these two theories could first be described (Skill A in AEB terms) and then points of contrast and comparison could be drawn between them, or the description and the compare/contrast parts could be integrated as the essay develops. Relevant similarities and differences between the two theories include the following:

1. Cognitive developmental theory (Kohlberg) concerns itself with moral *reasoning* whereas social learning theory concerns itself more with moral *behaviour*.
2. Kohlberg's theory stresses the importance of *universal moral principles* which transcend culture therefore is a theory embedded in the idea of *moral universalism*. Social learning theory is more concerned with the transmission of the rules and values that prevail in any given culture, therefore is more concerned with *moral relativism*.
3. Cognitive-developmental theory sees moral development as proceeding in stages, whereas it is seen as gradual and continuous in social learning theory.
4. Conscience to the mature thinker is a process of reasoned judgement about what is right and wrong in cognitive developmental theory, but a system to monitor behaviour and compare it with expectations of reward or punishment in social learning theory.
5. Social learning theory is seen as an explanation for the transmission of traditional values, whereas Kohlberg's theory is an explanation of intergenerational change as adolescents may discover hypocrisy and moral shortcomings in those who they had previously looked up to. This may then result in either a development toward a higher level of moral functioning, or the development of moral cynicism.

TUTOR'S ANSWER

Question 1

The term gender role refers to the collection of attitudes, behaviours, perceptions and affective reactions which are more commonly associated with one gender than the other.

Freudian psychoanalytic theory proposes that each child passes through a conflict (the Oedipal/Electra conflicts) in which they fear punishment or rejection from the parent of the same sex. They are motivated to overcome the resultant anxiety by identifying with the parent of the same sex, thus internalising many of the attitudes and behaviours of that parent, including their gender role. This process is considered (by Freud) to be easier for boys than for girls, because girls need only continue a previous attachment, whereas boys must forge a new attachment with the father. Subsequent evidence (*Lamb*, 1977) has cast doubt on this claim, as both boys and girls appear to form pre-Oedipal attachments with the father.

Freudian theory has not, on the whole, attracted empirical support, and failure to support hypotheses has often been dismissed as evidence of defence mechanisms such as repression or reaction formation.

A theory that conforms more to the need for scientific validation is learning theory. This view on gender role development was originally attributed to *Bandura* (1969) and

Mischel (1970). Central to this theory is the idea of reinforcement, with parents and others (teachers or even siblings) rewarding gender appropriate behaviour and discouraging gender inappropriate behaviour. *Langlois and Downs* (1980), for example, found that parents and same sex peers did tend to do just that. However, *Maccoby and Jacklin* (1974), in a review of literature in the area found little evidence of differential treatment by parents in some areas which have traditionally been sex typed (for example, in autonomous and dependent behaviour). *Lamb* (1978) in a postscript to this review, suggested that most research in this area had been conducted on a very narrow age range, and there was no way of knowing whether differential treatment occurred at all ages.

This theory also proposes that children may observe the gender role behaviour of significant others, and imitate it. The role of such differential observation and observation is also less than clear cut. If differential observation were important, it could be rightly suggested that the majority of children would acquire a female gender role, as the majority of early caregivers are female, therefore exposure to female gender roles is far more than the corresponding exposure to male gender roles. Bandura did suggest that boys acquire the male gender role because fathers make themselves more prominent in the lives of their sons, particularly as the boy himself develops a male gender identity and actively seeks to identify with things that are male.

Bandura also suggested that models which are seen as being powerful are more likely to be identified with than those who are not.

An interesting twist to this argument comes out of research in the Southern states of the USA, where generations of unemployment among working class blacks has sometimes resulted in an undermining of the perceived power of the male gender role, wi th the result that some males appear actively to identify with their mothers rather than their fathers. A problem with this 'power' explanation of identification is that it begs the question of why girls fail to identify with the same power figure that boys do. It is clear that the warmth and nurturance of a model, as well as its prominence in the life of the child will determine the likelihood of identification taking place.

A third major theoretical approach is cognitive-developmental theory (*Kohlberg*, 1969). Kohlberg argued that the child's growing sense of gender identity is crucial to gender role development. Children attend to same gender models and imitate their behaviours because they realize that this is what a child of their gender usually does. This theory is attractive because it places no special responsibility on the parents (thus providing a persuasive explanation of the successful gender socialization found in one-parent families), allowing the child instead to imitate gender appropriate models from television, school and so on. This theory also explains the observation that, as several researchers have found, young boys still develop the rather rough and noisy male gender role *despite* the fact that female carers (mothers, playgroup leaders and teachers) tend to often reward the quieter more 'feminine' behaviour in both girls *and boys.*

However, Kohlberg's whole theory rests upon the notion that children develop their gender identity at a much later age than research suggests is actually the case. It is a central requirement of this theory that children do not develop gender identity before they are able to conserve (an intellectual requirement, the development of *gender conservation*). The fact that they clearly do must inevitably weaken the tenability of the theory. Kohlberg's theory is unique in explaining intergenerational change, in that upon attaining formal operational reasoning, children may question what they feel are outmoded gender stereotypes and adopt newly defined roles for themselves.

The idea that gender roles continue to develop throughout life receives support from the research of *Livson* (1975), who found that the most psychologically healthy individuals at age fifty were those who had learned to integrate the opposite gender part of their character into their own gender roles. Livson referred to these individuals, rather tellingly as 'improvers'.

Such research also questions the relevance of 'traditional' gender roles. Research by *Mussen* (1962), and *Webb*, (1962) has found that high masculinity scores in males and high femininity scores in females often tend to be inversely related to anxiety and adjustment in later life. Bem's work on androgyny has lent support to the idea that people with more flexible gender roles are generally more adaptable to the demands of modern living (*Bem*, 1975).

There are a number of often subtle socialising influences in the gender-role development of the child. In school for example, the child is exposed to pressures from his or her peer group. These peers often have an absolute idea of masculinity and femininity, and may treat deviation with considerable ridicule. As peers provide the school age child with most of their opportunities for interaction, their prescriptions and reactions are highly significant. If the expectations and reinforcements offered by tecahers and peers are ambiguous, then it seems likely that children will choose the safest course and stick to the traditional roles which are readily supported by the rest of society.

This essay has dwelt exclusively upon social determinants of gender role. This is not meant to underestimate the importance of biological factors in this developmental process. Biological characteristics tend to provide cues for differential treatment and training by others, and secondly they often set up behavioural predispositions which, although they can be overidden by society are usually reinforced by them.

STUDENT'S ANSWER WITH EXAMINER COMMENTS

Question 2

"A good idea to open with a definition of the area"

Moral development, according to *Eleanor Maccoby* (1980) is the child's acquisition of rules which govern behaviour in the social world and, in particular, the development of a sense of right and wrong, and how the child begins to understand the values that guide and regulate behaviour within a given social system. There are three major psychological theories of moral development; cognitive-developmental theory, social learning theory, and Freud's psychoanalytic theory. Cognitive developmental theories will be concentrated on in this essay.

There are two main researchers of cognitive developmental theory, Piaget and Kohlberg, but it is the work of Kohlberg that is referred to most in the present day as his work is more refined and elaborate and up to date than the work of Piaget.

"Good research support"

Cognitive developmental theory is based on the idea that children's cognitive abilities, together with their social experiences, determines their moral reasoning. Two researchers who support Kohlberg's idea of a child's acquisition of moral develo pment are *Rest* (1974) who, found that it is age-related, and that older children are more likely to be in higher stages , and *Tomlinson-Keasey and Keasey* (1974) who found that moral development is linked to cognitive reasoning ability generally. The 'stages' which Rest talked about are the stages of development through which children shift as they get older (Kohlberg). They start at the intial stage, pre-conventional, which is characterised by responsiveness to moral rules of others, in terms of the power of others, or the hedonistic consequences of moral actions. The next stage is conventional morality, which is characterised by an attitude of loyalty to interpersonal expectations and the social order, and finally, post-conventional where there is an effort to define moral values and principles independently from the authority of the people who made them.

"Good evolution"

There are criticisms, however, of the cognitive-developmental theory. This theory seems to show a lack of cross-cultural evidence to support claims of unive rsality, also the ideas of moral maturity may be culturally biased, and the levels of maturity shown by an individual may vary with the nature of the task. Therefore morality may not be unitary through adolescence and beyond.

"A little unclear as to why children identify"

Freud's psychoanalytic theory of moral development is based on the idea that conflict is aroused in the child during the phallic stage (3–5 years, the Oedipal conflict). Children, as they go through the phallic stage, associate their behaviour wit h that of their same sex parent; girls identify with their mother's behaviour, and copy it, and boys identify with their father's behaviour and copy it. However, two implications of Freud's theory are that the manner in which the child resolves the confli ct will determine their attitude towards authority and also research has shown that conflicts are inevitable as they are a product of unconscious impulses. There is evidence to support Freud's theory but it is very limited. The main researchers who do support the theory are *Whiting and Child* (1953) who found that love-oriented societies produce guilt prone adults and that identification with parents is necessary for the development of conscience. However, in modern times, there is an increasing number of fa milies who defy the traditional norm of the stereotypical family unit e.g. homosexual parents, one-parent families etc. This challenges Freud's theory that the traditional family is imperative for a child's moral development to develop 'correctly'. *Miller and Swanson* (1958) found that there were different types of guilt and there is no evidence to suggest there is a unitary superego.

There has been lots of research done on Freud's psychoanalytic theory, and the majority of these studies do not support Freud's theory. A common criticism of Freud is that his evidence was considered to be too clinical in that it was based on case studies of his patients who were all, with the exception of one, adults. No valid theory of the development of children can be based solely on studies of adults, therefore the majority of Freud's work is probably invalid.

❝❝ A sweeping condemnation ❞❞

A general evaluation of Freud's psychoanalytic theory is suggested by *Hartshorne and May* (1928) who say that children's moral conduct is situationally controlled and it is not consistent across all situations. People behave differently in different situations and often their moral values are different.

❝❝ This is a competent answer to this question. Note that the question asks for theories of moral development, and this candidate has chosen to write about two. This is perfectly acceptable, as two theories described in depth can get the same number of marks as more theories described in less depth. The essay never really explained how and why progression occurs through the levels (not stages) of pre-conventional, conventional and post-conventional reasoning. With Freud, there were some sweeping generalisations made, particularly in the rather sudden condemnation of the theory as 'invalid'. However, there was a lot of information which was treated critically, so the answer would probably be characteristic of a grade B. ❞❞

REVIEW SHEET

1. Define gender role.

   _____

   _____

   _____

2. In what ways might biology influence the socialisation of gender role?

   _____

   _____

   _____

3. State two criticisms of the psychoanalytic theory of gender role.

   i)

   _____

   _____

   ii)

   _____

   _____

4. What are the three subdivisions of learning theory as it applies to moral development?

   i)

   _____

   ii)

   _____

   iii)

   _____

5. In what two ways does school influence the development of gender role?

   i)

   _____

   ii)

   _____

6. What does androgyny mean?

   _____

   _____

7. Why are girls more likely to develop it than boys?

   _____

   _____

8. What is meant by the following?

   Moral relativism

   _____

   Moral universalism

   _____

9. How, according to social learning theory, is moral behaviour maintained?

    _____

    _____

    _____

10. State three features of social learning theory as it applies to moral development.

    i)

    _____

    ii)

    _____

    iii)

    _____

11. State three criticisms of social learning theory.

    i)

    _____

    ii)

    _____

    iii)

    _____

12. Give three features of Kohlberg's theory

    i)

    _____

    ii)

    _____

    iii)

    _____

13. What are the three levels in Kohlberg's theory and how are they characterised?

    i)

    _____

    ii)

    _____

    iii)

    _____

14. State two criticisms of Kohlberg's theory.

    i)

    _____

    ii)

    _____

ADOLESCENCE, ADULTHOOD AND SENESCENCE

GETTING STARTED

This chapter focuses on the issues relating to **adolescence** and **adulthood**. These are areas which, traditionally, psychology has tended to leave alone, being more concerned with child development, and to a lesser extent psychological changes in old age. This was the case for a number of reasons, not least of which was the need for understanding in order to make policy decisions. The importance of adolescence as a period of rapid psychological development is now generally acknowledged.

The chapter also discusses the psychological changes that take place in mid to late adulthood, and examines the common belief that this period is more a period of decline rather than a period of psychological growth. Those who have confronted the period in between adolescence and old age have tended to stress the pathology of development in this period, as if major personality change in adulthood were a sign of somewhat dubious maturity. Two factors in particular have contributed to the need for a more constructive view of adulthood. Firstly, social phenomena such as the change in attitudes toward birth control, divorce, redundancy etc., as well as a prolonged life cycle have created the need for often wholesale change in mid-life, presenting the adult with a whole series of challenges to which they must respond. Secondly, the social and technological change in modern societies means that childhood is no longer a period of preparation for what is a predicatble and highly stable set of roles in adulthood. Todays individual encounters a world which is totally new and often unpredictable, and as such, has heightened the need for a continuous re-adaptation throughout life.

It is now a common assumption in psychology that psychological disturbances can be caused by environmental stresses. It is a popular argument that the increase in psychiatric consultation is a consequence of the increasing stresses and strains of modern living. Psychologists have now begun to examine the possibility that psychological distress or disorder can result from stress brought about by adverse circumstances. These events, which often necessitate major life re-adjustments have been tellingly labelled *Critical life events*.

The chapter finishes by examining some ideas on the nature of psychological development in late adulthood (**senescence**), and propositions for successful ageing.

Material in this chapter will enable you to answer questions on the following topic areas:

- **Social, cultural and individual factors affecting development in adolescence.**
- **Social, cultural and individual factors affecting development in adulthood.**
- **Social, cultural and individual factors affecting development in old age (senescence).**
- **The impact of critical life events.**

ADOLESCENCE

STORM AND STRESS IN ADOLESCENCE

SOCIAL INFLUENCES IN ADOLESCENCE

ADULTHOOD

IDENTITY DEVELOPMENT IN ADULTHOOD

CRITICAL LIFE EVENTS

SENESCENCE

ESSENTIAL PRINCIPLES

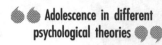

⬤⬤ Adolescence in different
psychological theories ⬤⬤

There is no one, generally accepted definition of **adolescence** in psychology. Instead, different theorists assign a developmental place for the adolescent in their theories. For Freud, the onset of the genital stage and the re-emergence of the Oedipal conflicts characterise adolescence. For Erikson, the adolescent is faced with the psychosocial task of establishing a true identity, and avoiding role (identity) confusion. In Piaget's theory of intellectual development, adolescence is a time where the individual develops **formal operational reasoning,** or the ability to think abstractly, and to Lawrence Kohlberg, adolescence marks the beginnings of post-conventional morality where the adolescent starts to challenge the moral conventions of his culture as he moves toward an understanding of justice and other universal ethical principles.

THE DEVELOPMENT OF IDENTITY IN ADOLESCENCE

⬤⬤ Developing a sense of
identity ⬤⬤

The central task of adolescence might be seen as the development of a **sense of identity.** *Erikson* (1968) believes that a coherent and unique identity emerges out of all the successive identifications of childhood. In childhood the need to develop a sense of identity is less important, young children are protected by others, have limited cognitive abilities, and few critically important choices to make.

Erikson also suggests that events at earlier stages of a child's life have a cumulative and often profound effect on their ability to develop a positive, complex and successful identity in adolescence.

Erikson notes the following variations in identity formation:

⬤⬤ Normative v deviant
identities ⬤⬤

1. Identities may be **normative** (prescribed by the adolescents background) or **deviant** (at odds with the background). Reasons for adopting a deviant identity may be positive (as in the case of a political activist) or negative (as in the counter-culture of *non-achievement* which Erikson feels may be indicative of a disturbed parent-child relationship).
2. Identity formation may be prematurely terminated or indefinitely extended. *Douvan and Adelson* (1966) suggest that premature identity formation may arise out of an effort to avoid the anxieties inherent in identity confusion. In other cases, individuals are in a 'pathologically prolonged identity crisis', and may struggle to establish consistent loyalties and commitments (*Weiner*, 1970).

⬤⬤ Turmoil in identity
formation ⬤⬤

Based on psychoanalytic interpretations of the adolescent period, it is often asserted that adolescents must go through a period of intense turmoil. Thus, adolescence is seen as a state of transient disturbance and maladjustment. Some writers (e.g. *Hirsch*, 1970) feel that an adolescent who does not experience this turmoil is likely to experience premature identity formation and is more likely experience psychopathological illness later on.

However, this view of adolescent turmoil as *normal* or even *desirable* has the inherent danger that *really* disturbed individuals may simply have their disturbance dismissed as 'adolescent turmoil' and appropriate treatment withheld. This is supported by the work of *Rutter* (1976) who followed up groups of 'normally disturbed' adolescents. 50% of these cases, they needed later psychiatric treatment.

RESEARCH EVIDENCE ON THE 'STORM AND STRESS' CLAIM

Offer and Offer (1974) found evidence of three different types of adolescent with respect to emotional turmoil. (This study was carried out over an eight year period.)

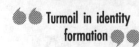
⬤⬤ Some research results on
the role of emotional
turmoil ⬤⬤

1. The Continuous growth group

These showed no evidence of an identity crisis or of emotional turmoil. They were described as psychologically healthy and happy people.

2. The surgent growth group

These were reasonably well adjusted, but did have greater difficulties in reacting to unexpected trauma. They showed a tendency to use less mature defense mechanisms (projection, anger etc.).

3. The tumultuous growth group

Only members of this group (approximately 21% of Offer's sample) showed the symptoms associated with the turmoil (depression, anxiety, shame and guilt, etc.) anticipated by the *storm and stress* theorists.

Evaluation of Offer's work

The conclusions reached by Offer that adolescent turmoil was neither necessary nor commonplace are challenged by Douvan and Adelson. They argue that absence of turmoil is a worrying sign, and is indicative of 'premature identity consolidation'. Offer disagrees, claiming that all their findings pointed in the opposite direction. His *continuous growth* group were well adjusted, in touch with their feelings, and developed meaningful relationships with others.

SOCIAL INFLUENCES IN ADOLESCENCE

1. The family

The rapidity of social change means that children and parents have often grown up in worlds that are substantially different: This has resulted in:

- A decline in adult authority, now a product of individual skills and resources rather than 'going with the job'. The development of post conventional morality in adolescents means that they are no longer reliant on the need to conform to the moral expectations of others.
- The parental task being made more difficult by the influence of peer groups, symbolized by a 'youth culture'. Peers groups are perceived as providing a oppposite set of influences to those provided by the family. This false dichotomy will be discussed later.

Cooper (1970) in his book *The Death of the Family* saw the family as a 'malignant force that acts only to frustrate the fulfillment of the needs of its members.' This theme was echoed in the work of *Mead* (1970) who suggested that as we live in a 'country of the young', parents cannot offer models or guidance which are relevant to the adolescent. Instead, they turn to the peer group.

2. Peer influences

Peer influences take on increasing importance as the dependence on the family decreases. *Conger* (1971) suggested that the parent/peer group conflict was, in fact, a false dichotomy because:

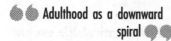 **Values of peer group and parents often similar**

(i)   There is often considerable overlap between parental and peers values (because of common background etc.).
(ii) Adolescents actively appraise influences. Parental influences are still likely to predominate in moral and social values.

Lamb (1978) suggested that identification with the peer group was more likely to be due to parental disregard than any inherent attraction of the peer group.

Berk (1994) suggests that the peer group is especially useful in providing a temporary identity while adolescents work on developing their own.

ADULTHOOD

Adulthood as a downward spiral

Traditional theories of **adulthood** have often stressed the more inevitable organismic direction of development, and have underestimated the role of socio-cultural factors. Many studies (e.g. *Chown*, 1961) have suggested that as people get older, they become more rigid and dogmatic in their outlook on life. They also appear to demonstrate an increasing egocentricity with age. This latter characteristic in particular means that the older person often suffers from a decreasing ability to display competence in adapting their behaviour to the changing demands of their social environment.

THE KANSAS CITY STUDIES (NEUGARTEN, 1965)

Examined significant psychological changes in the age range 40 to 60. They discovered that whereas 40 year olds saw themselves as possessing energy congruent with the opportunities of the outside world, 60 year olds saw the world as 'complex and dangerous'. Neugarten described this as a move from *active* to *passive* mastery.

A parallel conclusion to that of the Kansas City studies was that individuals gradually disengage, in that social interaction lessens with age. This is generally considered a functional and adaptive process (*Cumming and Henry*, 1961). *Kuhlen* (1964) similarly noted that as individuals age, the 'growth motives' of youth (achievement, creativity and self actualization) begin to contract as the individual begins to see him/herself more negatively and with less self confidence.

In the 1970's, this view of ageing as inevitable decrement was challenged on a number of grounds.

● ● **Disengagement seen as an adaptive process** ● ●

● ● **A contrary view to the impact of age on psychological development** ● ●

1. The evidence that socio-psychological changes inevitably reflect biological changes was acquired from subjects in which the pathologically elderly were over-represented (*LaBouvie-Vief*, 1977). Such decremental changes were, it appears, related to *pathology* rather than ageing.
2. LaBouvie-Vief argues that the disengagement that occurs in later adulthood is often the product more of the fact that society increasingly withdraws from the individual rather than the reverse.
3. Perceived decremental changes with age are often so defined in terms of youth-centred theories where the positive changes and developments in adulthood are less appreciated.

The view that growth and development is possible is now represented in a number of research findings. A longitudinal study by *Livson* (1975) examined how a sample of psychologically healthy men and women had changed from age 40 to age 50. She found two patterns, stability and improvement. Stable men and women had maintained their traditional gender role. By contrast, the *improvers* were those who had managed to integrate the opposite side of their gender role into their existing personality structure.

Such research has shown the need to view crises as sometimes being incremental and positive, rather than the regressive steps implied in earlier research.

● ● **Later androgyny** ● ●

IDENTITY DEVELOPMENT IN ADULTHOOD

Sheehy (1976) suggests that the sense of identity carved out in early childhood is only a preliminary and somewhat limited one, largely defined by outside pressures. Within the age period 35–45, she claims, many people choose to rework the narrow identity defined in their emergent adulthood. In this **authenticity crisis**, life's priorities are re-examined and a new sense of personal equilibrium and happiness becomes possible.

Sheehy's findings, like those of Livson before her, emphasise the error of equating psychological changes as mere parallels of biological changes. Evidence from *Livson*, (1975) suggests that changes in adulthood are more sociological than psychological, being created by major role transitions and conflicts rather than by maturation. Such a view is emphasised in work on 'social timetables' (*Havighurst*, 1972). Adults appear to internalise 'social clocks' by which they judge their life position. Learned norms of age-appropriate behaviour then act as 'prods' or 'blocks' on their development, and their perception of their own life position relative to these norms affects their behaviour and their self-image.

A final proposition on the inadequacy of biological theories of ageing concerns the effects of cultural change. Many studies using cross-sectional age samples have attempted to explain the 'decrement' of age by referring to maturational deterioration. *Schaie and LaBouvie-Vief* (1974), however, suggest that such apparent decrement can be better explained in terms of patterns of generational change. Schaie found that age differences in rigidity reflected cohort changes (the effect of groups born at the same time and thus exposed to the same historical influences) rather than age changes as such.

● ● **Adulthood influenced by perception of social timetables** ● ●

CRITICAL LIFE EVENTS

Any life event that causes a major readjustment is described as a **critical life event**. Examples would include; widowhood, divorce, retirement and so on.

THE SOCIAL READJUSTMENT SCALE (HOLMES AND RAHE, 1967)

The **Social Readjustment Scale (SRE)** was one of the earliest attempts to examine the impact of life events on possible psychological disorders. The SRE comprises 43 life events which are graded in terms of the amount of readjustment needed to accomodate to them.

Typically, it shows a higher rate of critical life events in the period preceding the onset of different types of pathology.

Criticisms of the SRE

1. The scale assumes that the disruptive effects of life events are the same for all people, yet this seems unlikely.
2. The SRE does not take any account of the significance of events (i.e. some events are clearly pleasurable, some are not).
3. The SRE assumes a particular direction between event and disorder whereas the opposite may also be true (e.g. diagnosis of depression following redundancy may be interpreted as the former being caused by the latter).
4. A tendency exists, following the onset of some major psychological problems, to enter a 'search for meaning', i.e. searching the memory for things that could explain the present state. Depressed patients are more likely to recall negative memories than they are positive memories.

Critical life events implicated in the development of psychopathology

Criticisms of SRE

THE BROWN AND HARRIS STUDY (1978)

Female subjects were assessed psychiatrically and then interviewed in depth about what had happened to them in the previous year, and their reactions to those events. A proportion of the women were diagnosed as suffering from depression. Results showed that events rated as severe (in terms of their threat to the woman) were four times more common in women with depression than in those who did not suffer from depression.

Examination of the data from the Brown and Harris study showed that critical life events appear to have a formative link in the development of depression, whereas they only have a triggering effect in the development of other psychopathological disorders.

Brown and Harris also identified **vulnerability** factors that might increase the potency of particular life events. These were:

Importance of the close, confiding relationship

1. The absence of a close confiding relationship with another person.
2. Three or more children living at home.
3. Lack of employment.
4. Loss of the woman's own mother in early life.

Criticisms of the Brown and Harris study

1. Biological psychologists claim that they have ignored the role of biochemical, genetic and other physiological factors in the onset of depression.
2. Some of the measures used in the study (e.g. of the threat to the woman) were never checked or validated (*Tennant*, 1981).
3. Cross-cultural studies (e.g. *Costello*, 1982 in Canada), have failed to agree on the vulnerability factors, but have supported the claim for the importance of the main factor from the Brown and Harris study, the absence of a close, confiding relationship.

Problems of retrospective studies

4. Brown and Harris, like most other studies in this area, relied on **retrospective studies**, where the previous life history of a subject is examined in order to see what antecedent events could be responsible for the present disorder. *Tennant* (1983) has pointed to the problems inherent in such studies, and has stressed the need for more prospective studies, where samples of patients are followed for appreciable lengths of time.

RESOURCES AND DEFICITS

An important factor in determining the psychological effect of certain life events is the degree to which an individual finds them threatening, and also the *balance* of resources

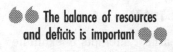
The balance of resources and deficits is important

and deficits that an individual can apply to the adaptive process. Many different variables serve to mediate the effects of life events, including biological, psychological and social characteristics of the individual. Generally, the better the individual's resources, the better he or she is able to adapt to critical life events, although the impact of resources and deficits varies over the life span. Thus, what may be a resource at one stage of life, may be a deficit at another (*Leiberman*, 1975).

Past behaviour is a useful predictor

Probably the best predictor of an individual's future behaviour following life crises is the past behaviour of the individual to similar events. Generally it can be argued that successful adaptation in the past enhances the ability of the individual to deal with future events. Past experiences may create affective responses (e.g. reducing anxiety) or effective coping strategies (e.g. goal setting and decision making).

SPECIFIC LIFE EVENTS

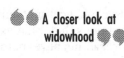
A closer look at widowhood

One prominent area of research is on the effects of widowhood. This is commonly associated with depression. Some studies (e.g. *Parke*, 1964) have established such a link, whilst others have found the link somewhat more tenuous, although most seem to agree that where there is a relationship between widowhood and psychiatric disorder, the disorder tends to be depression. There are indications that loss of a partner through divorce does not have the same impact as widowhood. *Briscoe and Smith* (1975) compared three sets of depressed patients, one group had been recently widowed, one recently divorced, and one was a control group with no recent critical life events. The latter two groups contained subjects with a much higher incidence of previous depressive episodes or a family history of depressive illness. This indirect evidence tends to suggest that widowhood had a direct formative influence on the development of depression, whereas divorce did not.

However, a problem in the interpretation of these findings is whether the depression following bereavement is the same as that found in clinical depression. Several researchers have suggested that it is not.

SENESCENCE

Senescence refers to the psychological developments in late adulthood.

Developmental tasks

One way of looking at old age is to examine the **developmental tasks** of old age (*Havighurst*, 1972). These are:

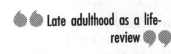
Some developmental tasks of old age

1. Adjusting to declining physical strength and health.
2. Adjusting to retirement and reduced income.
3. Adjusting to the death of the spouse.
4. Establishing an explicit affiliation with one's age group.
5. Adopting and adapting social roles in a flexible way.
6. Establishing satisfactory living arrangements.

Personality development

Late adulthood as a life-review

A common reaction in late adulthood is to engage in a **life review** (*Butler*, 1971). This is a chance to review and relive past experiences. It may culminate in wisdom and peace, or in anger and depression.

This theme is echoed in Erikson's theory of **personality development** (*Erikson*, 1963). Late adulthood is seen as the psychosocial crisis of integrity versus despair. Integrity is achieved if individuals are able to view their lives with satisfaction and contentment, life has had a purpose. Despair brings a sense of regret and a fear of death.

ERIKSON'S THEORY (IDENTITY AND THE LIFE CYCLE, ERIKSON, 1980)

To Erikson, integrity in old age is achieved by an acceptance of one's own life for what it has been, rather than regretting that it has not beem different. It also involves an acceptance that one's life is one's own responsibility. There is also a recognition that one life has but a small part to play in history, and that the individual's place in the universe is likewise a minor one.

Failure to develop such ego integrity leads to despair, a sense that life is too short to change anything. Despair may be hidden behind disgust, either with institutions or with poeple. This signifies the individual's disgust with him or herself.

Although rooted in the psychoanalytic tradition, Erikson's theory differs from Freud's in three major ways.

❝❝ Some criticisms of disengagement theory ❞❞

(i)   Erikson focuses on the conscious mind whereas Freud's theory deals more with the unconscious mind.

(ii) Erikson sees the personality as developing throughout life, whereas Freud sees adult personality as being shaped by childhood experiences.

(iii) Whereas Freud concerned himself more with the biological influences on individual development, Erikson stressed the social and cultural determinants of development.

Criticisms of Erikson's theory

1. Some critics have claimed that Erikson has a 'naive and accepting attitude towards the family' which is not always as conducive to psychological development as Erikson appears to suggest (*Buss*, 1979).

2. Buss also claims that Erikson's theory makes a serious value assumption, namely that 'psychological growth and health is possible only to the extent that the individual is not out of step with society'. This view demands a benign view of society, denying that social reality may be psychologically or physically repressive or constricting. Under such conditions, argues Buss, shame and doubt, guilt rather than initiative and identity diffusion rather than identity may be the appropriate responses. 'Unqualified acceptance of one's total life history, and by implication of the external forces that have helped to shape that life, is too heavy a price to pay for the comfort of integration (*Buss*, 1979).

PATTERNS OF SUCCESSFUL AGEING

1. Disengagement theory (Cumming, 1963)

Disengagement is seen as a natural and gradual process. Several events contribute to disengagement e.g. retirement, death of a spouse.

Criticisms (Rose, 1968)

(i)   Disengagement is not a type of adjustment in old age, but a continuation of an earlier life-style.

(ii) Adults who remain active are happier than those who withdraw.

(iii) Social changes e.g. lowering the retirement age, better health care, may discourage disengagement in the future and encourage more active involvement.

2. Activity theory (Blau, 1973)

Contrary to disengagement theory, activity theory suggests that withdrawal causes a lowering in self-esteem and happiness. It proposes that individuals need to find substitute roles for those that have been terminated. The greater the role resources (active involvement) the better the adjustment.

Criticisms

Activity theory is criticised as an over-simplification. Meaningless role adjustments may not help the individual but research suggests there is a relationship between morale, personality adjustment and activity levels (*Hendricks and Hendricks*, 1977).

EXAMINATION QUESTIONS

1(a) What is meant by the term adolescence?   *(4)*

(b) Discuss one psychological study concerned with adolescence.   *(7)*

(c) Critically consider whether adolescence must inevitably be a period of 'storm and stress'   *(14)*

(AEB 1993)

2. 'For people in middle age and onwards there are many opportunities for positive psychological development.' Use psychological studies to discuss this claim.

(AEB 1991)

3. Discuss the role of personal and cultural factors in senescence.   *(25)*

4. Discuss what psychologists have learned about the impact of critical life events during adulthood.   *(25)*

(AEB 1989)

ANSWERS TO EXAMINATION QUESTIONS

OUTLINE ANSWERS TO QUESTIONS 2 AND 4

Question 2

As the injunction in this question is *discuss*, it is necessary to both describe and evaluate material . Using the material presented in this chapter, a suitable way of answering this question would be:

1. An examination of the traditional 'decremental' views of adulthood, and a critical examination of the claims of these theories.
2. Livson's research studies on identity change in adulthood, and the view that crises may be incremental rather than decremental.
3. Sheehy's work on the 'authenticity crisis' saw adulthood as an opportunity to rework the narrow identity defined in their emergent adulthood.
4. Havighurst's social timetables which explain adult development in terms of major role transitions and conflicts rather than be maturation.
5. Schaie and Parham (1974) suggested that changes in age are more a product of cohort changes than age per se.

Question 4

This is a fairly straightforward question where the results of studies and theories relating to critical life events can be described and evaluated.

1. Early attempts using the Social Readjustment Scale demonstrated a link between critical life events and depression but was flawed in its interpretation.
2. Later research by Brown and Harris also demonstrated a link and identified vulnerability factors which would determine the impact of life events for different people.
3. Studies of specific life events have not always found that they are linked to the onset of psychopathological disorder. Briscoe and Smith's study suggested that widowhood was linked to depression but that the depression was not necessarily the same as clinical depression.
4. The degree of impact of a critical life event may be determined by the resources and deficits of the individual. Research by Leiberman has established the role of such resources and deficits in the adaptation to life events.

TUTORS ANSWER

Question 1

(a) *Stratton and Hayes* (1993) define adolescence as the period between childhood and adulthood. They suggest that in some societies the period is very brief, being characterised by a *rite of passage*, whereas in Western culture the period extends over a much longer period. Different psychological theorists have tended to see adolescence as reflecting different stages of development. Erikson sees adolescence in terms of the need to develop a sense of identity, Kohlberg in terms of the development of post-conventional reasoning.

(b) Based on *Marcia's* (1980) claim that individuals pass through a number of different identity statuses which reflect their degree of crisis and resultant commitment to a specific role, *La Voie* (1976) studied ego identity in American high school students. La Voie found a significant positive relationship between self esteem and established ego identity. Using a questionnaire designed to measure the degree of basic trust (the result of Erikson's first developmental stage, trust versus mistrust), La Voie was able to demonstrate that a positive relationship also existed between the degree of basic trust and the establishment of later identity.

However, two critical points can be emphasised here. Firstly, the relationships demonstrated do not show a causal relationship. Secondly, the nature of the sample (American high school students) represent a rather restricted sample given Marcia's belief that identity development is a universal process. On a more positive point, La Voie's results have been replicated in a number of other studies.

(c) The idea of an identity crisis in adolescence has been a feature of a number of theories of adolescence. *Erikson* (1959) suggested that the physical, mental and social changes experienced in adolescence would throw the adolescent into an identity crisis. Erikson claimed that to resolve this crisis, the adolescent needed to develop three aspects of identity, a sexual identity, an occupational identity and an ideological identity. Failure to develop these identities successfully would result in what Erik son referred to as role confusion.

Evidence from *Waterman and Nevid* (1977) supported Erikson's claim that these different types of identity did exist, and that they perhaps developed at different times during adolescence. However, the resolution of these issues of adolescence, an establishment of a 'synthesised' identity, does not appear to be achieved during the adolescent period, as claimed by Erikson, but probably some time in early adulthood *(Bee and Mitchell, 1984)*. Whether or not this identity crisis is as traumatic for the adolescent as claimed in the writings of Hall in the early 1900s and *Anna Freud* (1969), is a matter of debate. Freud claimed that such disturbance in adolescence was normal and that its absence was a cause for concern. It is a commonly held belief among many theorists that not to experience the *storm and stress* of adolescence is to show evidence of a *premature crystallization of identity*.

Research by *Offer and Offer* (1974) established three distinct patterns of growth in adolescence. Only one classification (the tumultuous growth group – 21% of Offer and Offer's sample) showed any evidence of the turmoil proposed by many other theorists. Offer's other two groups, the continuous growth group and the surgent growth group either showed no significant evidence of emotional turmoil during adolescence or showed reasonable signs of being well adjusted despite the use of more immature defense mechanisms such as projection and regression. This led Offer and Offer to conclude that normal development was possible without such turmoil being experienced. Their studies, carried out over an eight year period showed that adolescents who did not experience any significant degree of turmoil grew into mature adults, they were 'in touch with their feelings, and developed meaningful relationships with others. Their conclusions have been criticised by others (e.g. Douvan and Adelson) who feel that lack of turmoil was a bad prognostic sign, and could only prevent the adolescent developing into a mature adult. They suggested that absence of turmoil in adolescence was a sign of 'premature identity consolidation, and ideological constriction'). *Douvan and Adelson* (1966) had carried out a study of 3, 000 adolescents, and despite discovering similar trends to those of the Offer and Offer research, they expressed considerable dismay at the relative absence of turmoil they found in the average adolescent.

One problem of accepting adolescent disturbance as a normal feature of development is that by accepting disturbed behaviour as normal simply because it occurs in adolescence might mask the existence of other manifestations of disturbance that require prompt attention. *Rutter et al.* (1976) demonstrated that a significant number of young people who had originally showed evidence of 'situational adjustment reaction of adolescence' required later psychiatric treatment.

STUDENT'S ANSWER WITH EXAMINER COMMENTS

Question 3

❝❝ Good; brief definition and scene set for further development of essay **❞❞**

The study of senescence (old age) has traditionally been equated with decrement, both physically, mentally and socially. For example, *Chown* (1961) suggested that as people age, they become more dogmatic and rigid in their views. These ideas are now widely challenged.

The reactions of individuals to age related changes vary from person to person. These changes are not all within the individual (such as changes in mental capacity), but may also be 'external', such as retirement.

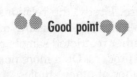

Havighurst (1972) saw the adjustment to these changes as two of the six developmental tasks of late adulthood. These tasks also include adjusting to declining physical strength and health, and establishing an explicit affiliation with ones age group. This last task may also be linked with *Cummings* (1963) disengagement theory, as the affiliation with one's age group may result in (or may be caused by) withdrawal from society (e.g. reduced social activities). Cummings sees this disengagement from society as a natural process, which may be triggered by events such as widowhood.

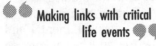

This idea of an individuals withdrawal from society may in fact be the withdrawal from society may in fact be the withdrawal of a 'youth oriented' society from the elderly person. Society's disengagement may be brought about by a number of things such as media influences and cultural expectations, and also by more physical factors such as income reduction. Disengagement may be due to the supposed 'withdrawal' being seen through the eyes of 'youth centred' psychologists. The changes in lifestyle may be due to personal changes in priorities not to disengagement.

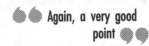

The idea of personality development in old age was put forward by Erikson in 1963, who described the psychological crisis of integrity (satisfaction and contentment) versus despair (regret and fear of death). Whether people experience integrity or des pair may be caused by a number of, mainly personal' factors such as feelings of self-confidence and self-esteem, and previous experiences.

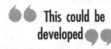

Other factors affecting the adjustment to ageing and related changes may include personality, health, finances and prior attitudes. The last factor is especially related to retirement, one of the major personal and social changes in later adulthood. Compulsory retirement means that many people find themselves out of work when they don't feel ready. The loss of power associated with this may result in people having to change a lot of their attitudes. The accompanying reduction in income may result in a withdrawal from society. The health of many people deteriorates after they have retired, especially if they were given no choice). This follows Blau's activity theory (*Blau*, 1973) which suggests that withdrawal causes a lowering in self-esteem and h appiness due to the decrease in the number of 'roles'. This theory has, however, been criticized by *Havighurst* (1968) who points out that many people are satisfied with disengagement, so succesful ageing cannot simply be based on this theory.

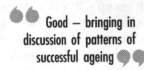

One criticism of most of the studies that all these theories have been based on was put forward by *LaBouvie-Vief* (1977) who noted that many of the subjects used were elderly people suffering from mental disorders, and often in nursing/residential homes, so any conclusions would be unreliable.

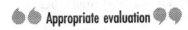

Research by *Neugarten* (1965) also suggests that as people age, they begin to see the world differently. Neugarten found that 60 year olds saw the world as more complex and dangerous than did 40 year olds. However, this may be due to the different situations they were brought up in. In 1965, the 60 year olds would have been born in the 1900–1910 decade, and the 40 year olds in the 1920–1930 decade.

Livson (1975) suggests that the changes in adulthood are created by major role transitions (such as retirement or widowhood) rather than by biological ageing. This view is also taken by *Havighurst* (1972), who suggests that adults tend to follow internal 'social timetables', and to follow these as to when they should do things (such as starting a family, or, in later adulthood, retiring). These timetables are often based on societies expectations of what is the correct timing.

One final theory of adult development was put forward by *Levinson* (1978). Late adult transition is where older adults may become concerned with the nearness of death, and the realization of the need to relinquish 'centre stage'.

Personal and social factors have a major role to play in senescence, in particular to the adjustment to age changes, both biological and emotional, and those which are culturally imposed. These factors can include the individual's experience, and their reaction to societies expectations of them, so everyone will adjust differently, and will therefore age successfully or not depending on these vital factors.

This is a good example of how a student has made an effective attempt to answer the question as set. They have integrated material on both personal and cultural factors affecting the older person. Evaluation of material (e.g. Erikson's views on the later psychosocial crises) is not always well developed, but overall this is an excellent essay and would fully deserve a grade A.

REVIEW SHEETS

1. What is the notion of adolescence in each of the following theories:

   Freud:

   _____

   Erikson:

   _____

   Piaget:

   _____

   Kohlberg:

   _____

2. What is the difference between a normative identity and a deviant identity?

   _____

   _____

3. What were the conclusions from Offer and Offer's (1974) work on adolescent identity crisis?

   _____

   _____

   _____

4. Why is parental influence seen as decreasing in adolescence?

   _____

   _____

   _____

5. What, according to Chown are the major decremental changes with increasing age?

   _____

   _____

   _____

6. What is meant by disengagement?

   _____

   _____

7. How does LaBouvie-Vief view disengagement?

   _____

   _____

8. Who were Livson's improvers?

_____

_____

9. What happens in the authenticity crisis?

_____

_____

_____

10. What is meant by cohort change?

_____

_____

11. What, according to Brown and Harris were the vulnerability factors affecting the impact of critical life events?

_____

_____

_____

12. Give two criticisms of the Brown and Harris study.

    i) _____

    ii) _____

13. Give three of Havighurst's developmental tasks of old age.

    i) _____

    ii) _____

    iii _____

14. What is activity theory?

_____

_____

18

ABNORMALITY

GETTING STARTED

This chapter explores the main issues around the explanation of **abnormal** behaviour, particularly the models proposed by the mainstream perspectives. The model of abnormality adopted by a psychologist also has important implications for the treatment of abnormal behaviour. Biomedical models, for example, propose that abnormal behaviour is the result of malfunctions or injury to physical processes, therefore appropriate treatment would also be physical. Behavioural models see abnormal behaviour as being the result of faulty learning, therefore the appropriate treatment is to provide opportunities for unlearning. Psychoanalytic models of abnormality see abnormal behaviour as an indication of unconscious impulses or conflicts, and propose a variety of methods for putting the client more in touch with the original causes of the maladaptive behaviours that they now display.

Any classification or treatment of abnormal behaviour has important ethical and practical considerations. These are discussed at the end of the chapter.

Material in this chapter will enable you to answer questions on the following topic areas.

- **Discussion of the models of abnormality including the treatments used.**
- **Problems of evaluating the effectiveness of treatments of abnormal behaviour.**
- **Practical and ethical implications of defining behaviour as normal.**

CONCEPTIONS OF ABNORMALITY

THE BIOMEDICAL MODEL OF ABNORMALITY

BIOMEDICAL TREATMENTS

THE BEHAVIOURAL MODEL OF ABNORMALITY

BEHAVIOURAL TREATMENTS

THE PSYCHOANALYTIC MODEL OF ABNORMALITY

PSYCHOANALYTIC TREATMENTS

ESSENTIAL PRINCIPLES

Stratton and Hayes (1993) suggest five definitions of the term **abnormality**.

1. Behaviour which is different from the norm (i.e. unusual).
2. Behaviour which does not conform to social demands.
3. Statistically uncommon behaviour (based on assumptions of normal behaviour).
4. Behaviour which is maladaptive or painful for the individual.
5. Failure to achieve self-actualization (the humanistic view).

The **biomedical model** of abnormality proposes that psychological disorders have underlying biological or biochemical causes. Psychological disorders are referred to as *mental illnesses*. These mental illnesses are seen as arising from one of four main sources:

(i) Infection

The action of germs or viruses may lead to a cluster of symptoms, or **syndrome**. Early work on general paresis established that this condition was brought about by the action of the syphilis germ.

(ii) Inherited systematic defect

A number of mental disorders run in families and may be transmitted from generation to generation. It is possible that schizophrenia may result from an inherited neural dysfunction.

(iii) Neurochemical factors

Some disorders appear to be caused by the action of neurochemicals in the brain. Schizophrenics, for example show a characteristically high level of *dopamine* (a transmitter substance). Treatment of schizophrenia normally involves using drugs that block the action of the dopamine, thus limiting the symptoms of the disorder.

(iv) Effects of trauma

Trauma may be physical (e.g. brain damage, poisoning) or psychological (e.g. bereavement, rape). Alcohol and drug abuse are examples of poisoning which might lead to psychological disorders. Korsakov's syndrome is an alcohol related condition that might lead to memory disturbances, confusion and apathy. Psychological trauma such as bereavement are increasingly associated with the development of depression.

Evaluation of the biomedical model

(i) The medical approach has led to a relatively humane and effective treatment of the mentally ill.

(ii) Its 'scientific' status, and its association with the medical profession means that the model enjoys more credibility and popularity than other models.

(iii) Anti-psychiatrists such as Szasz, Laing and Goffman object to the use of the medical model in the area of mental disorders. Szasz in particular, sees the use of labels such as *mentally ill* as a form of scapegoating so that *normal* people can see themselves as good and *mentally ill* people as somehow bad and deviant.

(iv) The use of classification systems of mental illness such as DSM III-R or the ICD-10 enable practitioners to narrow down the range of possible treatments and therefore makes treatment more effective.

(v) These classification systems, however, may suffer from a lack of *inter-observer reliability* in that different practitioners may interpret symptoms in completely different ways. *Cooper et al.* (1972) found that American psychiatrists were between two and ten times more likely to diagnose schizophrenia following videotaped diagnostic interviews, than were their British counterparts.

(v) Classification systems also suufer problems of *validity* in that there is frequently a great deal of overlap between the symptoms of different disorders (thus making accurate diagnosis *and* treatment more difficult).

BIOMEDICAL TREATMENTS

Biomedical therapies are physiological interventions intended to reduce symptoms associated with psychological disorders (*Weiten*, 1992).

(a) DRUG THERAPIES

Therapeutic drugs fall into three major groups:

- **Anti-anxiety** drugs which relieve tension and nervousness.
- **Anti-psychotic drugs** which are used to reduce psychotic symptoms such as mental confusion and delusions.
- **Anti-depressant drugs** which are used to elevate mood.

Evaluation of drug therapies

(i) Drug therapies may produce clear therapeutic gains for many patients, and may be particularly effective with severe disorders that have not responded to other types of treatment.

 **Drug therapies evaluated**

(ii) Some critics argue that drug treatments offer only short term release from symptoms, and do nothing to attack the cause of the problem.

(iii) Drug treatments are an example of the *reductionist* approach to the treatment of abnormality. Their simplicity may lead practitioners to overuse them in place of more extended psychotherapies. By making extensive use of such treatments, attention may be diverted away from the real cause of the problem behaviour.

(b) ELECTROCONVULSIVE THERAPY (ECT)

ECT is a treatment where a (sub-lethal) electric shock is passed through the temporal lobes of the brain to produce a cortical seizure and convulsions. The use of ECT declined in the 1960s and 1970s but has been used more and more in the treatment of severe depression since the 1980s.

ECT has also been effective in the treatment of secondary affective (mood) disorders of schizophrenics.

Evaluation of the use of ECT.

(i) ECT *may* produce death in one in 200 patients over the age of 60, and irreversible cerebral damage can arise from consistent use of the treatment.

(ii) *Small et al.* (1986) in a review of the ECT controversy, found that ECT does produce short and long-term intellectual impairment, but that this is not inevitable, and rarely permanent.

Memory loss overestimated

(iii) *Sachs et al.* (1988) found that most former ECT patients do overestimate their memory loss.

(iv) Some proponents of ECT maintain that it is very effective as a treatment (e.g. *Fink*, 1988) but others claim that it acts merely as a placebo (*Small et al.*, 1986). These contradictions may be due to methodological weaknesses in studies that have

Lack of control group in studies

explored the ECT effectiveness issue. *Barton* (1977) found only six studies (from hundreds) that had used a control group to compare the effects of ECT treatment.

(c) PSYCHOSURGERY

Although rarely used today, the use of surgical techniques (such as leucotomies or electrode implants) remains highly controversial. *Heather* (1976) regards such techniques as *crimes against humanity* and as such they raise interesting ethical points about the use of psychosurgery as a form of social control rather than a type of treatment.

THE BEHAVIOURAL MODEL OF ABNORMALITY

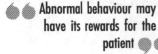 Mental disorders are learned

The **behavioural model** of abnormality makes two major assumptions.
a.   All behaviour is a product of learning.
b.   What has been learned can be unlearned.

The implication is thus that there is no differences in the *ways* that normal and abnormal behaviours are learned. Unlike psychodynamic models, which see symptoms as an indication of the underlying problem, behavioural models see the symptoms *as* the problem, therefore treatment is focused on the alleviation of those symptoms. The acquisition of abnormal behaviour is predominantly attributed to the following three types of learning:

(i) Classical conditioning

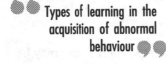 Types of learning in the acquisition of abnormal behaviour

In the **classical conditioning** process, a neutral stimulus is paired with one which naturally causes anxiety, and thus also becomes capable of eliciting anxiety. Classical conditioning models have been used to explain the acquisition of many irrational fears, phobias or emotional reactions. *Hinde* (1970) suggests that our fears of particular animals may be acquired in this way, but that we are *biologically prepared* (see chapter 12) to fear animals with particular perceptual characteristics and that learning is much more rapid and resistant to change in these cases.

(ii) Operant conditioning

Explanations of behaviour acquisition using **operant conditioning** models emphasise that behaviour is influenced by its consequences such that behaviours that result in desirable outcomes are more likely to be repeated than those which lead to undesirable ones. Abnormal behaviour is thus subject to the same laws as normal behaviour. An agoraphobic, for example, may find that their phobic behaviour has rewarding consequences in the shape of extra care and attention from others.

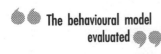 Abnormal behaviour may have its rewards for the patient

(iii) Observational learning

The work of Bandura in the 1960s demonstrated that behaviour could be acquired as a result of **observing and imitating** significant others (models). Bandura argued that behaviour could thus arise without any direct need for reinforcement in the individual concerned.

EVALUATION OF THE BEHAVIOURAL MODEL

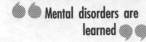 Behavioural model only concerned with the symptoms

(i)   This approach might be described as *parsimonious* it that it proposes simple, testable explanations for behaviour. As the current state of the individual is all that matters, there is no need to probe further.
(ii) It is able to explain the **neurotic paradox** in that although neurotic behaviour may be seen as self-destructive, it pays off for the neurotic individual in the form of attention from others.
(iii) Within the behavioural approach, some practitioners tend to use medical classification systems and their approach is essentially **nomothetic** in nature, whereas others reject these systems, treating all cases as unique (the **idiographic** approach).
(iv) As much of the behavioural model stem from laboratory work with animals, it makes assumptions about the validity both of the use of animals themselves and of the context in which they were studied. Both of these assumptions might be seen as questionable.
(vi) Behavioural techniques are often criticised as being **dehumanizing** (*Heather*, 1976) and mechanistic. This is a difficult point to debate, but if the object of behavioural intervention is to **rehabilitate** clients, then it appears more **humanizing** than *dehumanizing*. Similarly, if the processes of learning are mechanistic in the first place (a point emphasised by behaviourists) then it makes sense that the *unlearning* process is likewise mechanistic.

The behavioural model evaluated

BEHAVIOURAL TREATMENTS

(a) SYSTEMATIC DESENSITIZATION

The technique of **Systematic desensitization**, is based on the principles of classical conditioning, aims to reduce an individual's anxiety through counterconditioning. It has three main stages:

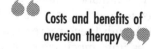
Stages in systematic desensitization

- **preparation of a hierarchy of anxiety** (i.e. a list of stimuli related to the source of the anxiety prepared in order of their ability to produce fear in the client)
- **training in relaxation**
- **working through the hierarchy whilst remaining relaxed.**

The aim of the techniques is to reverse the original classical conditioning so that the feared object is now associated with relaxation rather than fear.

(b) AVERSION THERAPY

In this highly controversial technique of **aversion therapy**, an aversive (unpleasant) stimulus is paired with a stimulus that elicits a response which for whatever reason is considered undesirable. Because of its use of aversive stimuli it attracts a great deal of ethical problems.

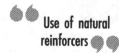
Costs and benefits of aversion therapy

Evaluation of Aversion therapy

It is often considered to be unethical (because of its use of aversive stimuli) yet its use must always be considered in the totel context of rehabilitation (see chapter 3). Evidence from *Lang and Melamed* (1969) demonstrated its effectiveness in this respect.

(c) TOKEN ECONOMIES

Secondary and primary reinforcers

Working on the principles of operant conditioning, these techniques involve rewarding clients with *secondary reinforcers* that might then be exchanged at a later time for *primary reinforcers* such as food, visits etc. **Token economies** have been used in prisons, schools and hospitals, and in the treatment of schizophrenics, delinquents as well as in the treatment of those suffering from eating disorders such as anorexia nervosa.

Evaluation of Token Economies

Use of natural reinforcers

(i) The success of the programmes is extremely variable. Some clients do not respond, others become dependent on the rewards. Recent developments in this area have tended to move away from the provision of artificial rewards to the use of more naturally occurring social reinforcers.

(ii) Their use, particularly in the USA, has been criticised on ethical and legal grounds. Some programmes used basic human rights (food, privacy etc.) as primary reinforcers because of the effectiveness of the programme in working toward them. Such procedures were ruled illegal by State authorities.

(d) BIOFEEDBACK

In **biofeedback**, some bodily function is monitored and information is amplified and fed back to the individual by auditory or visual means. This facilitates increased control by the individual, (for example, by relaxing, they might lower their heart rate), this is fed back to them and they are thus rewarded for their efforts.

Evaluation of biofeedback techniques

Claims for its success do seem to have been exaggerated. Although it can help people exert a greater control over a number of activities (e.g. blood pressure, muscle tension etc.) other techniques such as relaxation training may be just as effective.

(e) MODELLING

Based on the idea of observational learning, the technique of **modelling** involves the client being exposed to a model who, through a series of graded steps 'conquers' the individual's feared object e.g. fear of spiders.

Evaluation of modelling

Bandura claims a 90% success rate for this type of treatment (higher than that claimed for systematic desensitization).

The use of modelling is not restricted to the treatment of specific items, it can be used in group therapy where active participation is seen as valued such that the individual imitates the effective behaviour of other group members.

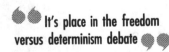

THE PSYCHOANALYTIC MODEL OF ABNORMALITY

❝❝ Types of anxiety ❞❞

❝❝ Mental disorders as unresolved conflicts ❞❞

The essence of the **psychoanalytic model** is that behaviour is influenced by unconscious forces.

Central to psychoanalysis is the idea of **anxiety**. Anxiety is seen as a warning of impending danger to the individual. This may be **moral anxiety**, which results from the ego's conflict with the superego, or **neurotic anxiety** which results from the ego's conflict with the instinctual urges of the id. To cope with these conflicts, the ego resorts to a number of coping strategies. Key amongst these defensive strategies are the **defence mechanisms** such as regression, repression and sublimation. Repression typically develops in early childhood when the child's ego is seen as being weak and unable to deal with the anxiety experienced by the child. Although these repressions develop in early childhood they may not manifest themselves until much later when they are usually precipitated by some personal crisis.

Reactivation of repressed anxiety then causes a neurotic conflict which the patient experiences as a symptom. These symptoms might then interfere with normal functioning so that psychoanalysis becomes necessary.

Evaluation of the psychoanalytic model

(i) The model is often criticised as being unamenable to scientific testing, and by the overuse of *reaction formation* explanations if contrary findings are obtained (i.e. it is claimed that the ego reverses real conlicts and feelings before they reach the level of conscious awareness).

(ii) Freud's view of the origins of abnormal behaviour is seen as deterministic and therefore pessimistic. Normal development is thus seen as a struggle against inevitable biological forces.

❝❝ It's place in the freedom versus determinism debate ❞❞

(iii) Freud established the *case study method* as a source of insight into the nature and processes of human development. Because of the rather unrepresentative nature of his clients, however, there must be some doubt about the validity of his claims for a universal theory of development.

PSYCHOANALYTIC TREATMENTS

The objectives of psychoanalysis are threefold:

a. To free healthy impulses.
b. To strengthen the ego and re-educate it so that it approves more of the id.
c. To alter the superego so that it is more humane and less punitive.

❝❝ Objectives of psychoanalysis ❞❞

To bring about these objectives, psychoanalysts employ the following techniques.

(i) Free association

❝❝ Interpretation is a key feature of psychoanalytic treatment ❞❞

The client is encouraged to mentally **free-wheel**, to talk freely about anything. This is not, however, a totally free process, as repressed impulses press to be released. The patient feels, therefore, a *compulsion to utter* but the ego tries still to repress unacceptable impulses by creating *resistance*. The therapist uses this struggle to offer *interpretation*.

(ii) Dream analysis

Dreams are seen as an avenue to the unconscious, and are taken to be an indication of *wish fulfilment*. However, unacceptable impulses are displaced onto contemporary objects. It becomes the job of the therapist to interpret the references provided by the client.

(iii) Transference

Clients frequently **transfer** their feelings onto the analyst. The therapist becomes like an authority figure or parent through which repressed feelings can be expressed. Analysis of transference in the psychoanalytic session provides important insight and encourages more adaptive social behaviour following interpretation.

EVALUATION OF PSYCHOANALYTIC THERAPIES

❝❝ Lack of efficacy of the treatment ❞❞

1. *Eysenck* (1952) delivered the most damaging indictment of psychoanalysis when he reviewed studies of therapeutic oucomes for neurotic patients. He found that about two thirds recovered within two years. What was so damning for psychoanalysis was that for similar patients who received no treatment at all, the figure was also two thirds.
2. Critics of Eysenck's findings discovered that he had made a number of rather arbitrary judgements about 'recoveries' that were unfavourable to the groups that that received psychoanalytic treatments. *Bergin*, (1971) estimated that the recovery rate for untreated patients was closer to 30%.
3. It has been claimed that only certain kinds of patients would benefit from psychoanalytic treatment. Schofield suggested that such patients would be the YAVIS clients (*Young, attractive, verbal, intelligent and successful*). Although a recent review of studies (*Luborsky et al.*, 1988) did not find any evidence for the first three of these descriptions, they did find, in addition to the latter two factors, that psychoanalysis worked better with highly motivated clients who had a positive attitude toward therapy.

EXAMINATION QUESTIONS

1   Describe and evaluate some of the ways in which psychologists have defined abnormality.
(25)
(AEB 1992)

2(a) Describe one type of therapy or treatment for mental illness or behavioural disorder.
(10)

 (b) Discuss the difficulties of evaluating this type of therapy or treatment.   *(15)*
(AEB 1992)

3   Consider the ethical and practical implications involved in defining behaviour as abnormal.
(25)
(AEB 1988)

ANSWERS TO EXAMINATION QUESTIONS

OUTLINE ANSWER TO QUESTION 2

The first part of this question is a straightforward description of and one therapy or treatment for a mental or behavioural disorder. The list of potential treatments is almost endless, and could include; psychoanalysis, behaviour therapy, drug therapy, cognitive therapy etc. Note that you are only asked to *describe* the treatment, so don't waste time evaluating it because there are no marks being offered for that skill in part (a).

The second part of this question is more difficult but might address the following issues:

Assessing the effectiveness of therapy.

(i) It is a fundamental requirement to establish suitable control groups. Because of the ethical problems of witholding treatment, this is not always a straightforward process. A control group may receive *attention* as a placebo rather than the therapy being assessed. Clients can also act as their own controls, being tested before, during and after therapy.

(ii) Measuring the outcome of the treatment may also present problems in defining what is meant by *cure*. Changes in the symptoms may be alright for behaviourist techniques, but projective tests may be necessary for the more psychoanalytic treatments.

(iii) Individual differences in patients and therapists, and the relationship between them might confound attempts to measure the effectiveness of a particular type of treatment.

2. Evaluating the therapies.

(i) Eysenck's claims against the effectiveness of psychoanalysis showed the difficulties of evaluation in this area.

(ii) *Smith and Glass* (1977) analysed the results of 25,000 experimental and 25,000 control clients for over eight hundred different effects, and concluded that the average psychotherapy client was better off 75% of the time.

(iii) *Shapiro* (1980) suggests that the effectiveness of a therapy is due partly to the inherent characteristics of the therapy itself, and partly to other factors that might be common to all therapies (the qualities of the therapist, the quality of the therapy session, client expectations regarding the outcome and so on).

TUTORS ANSWER

Question 3

The success of the biomedical model in the explanation and treatment of abnormal behaviour is due to three main factors. Firstly, because of the success of physical medicine, psychiatry which makes use of similar 'sickness' analogies, shares a similar status. Secondly, there was the discovery that certain medical conditions had physical origins. Thirdly, the medical approach promised great improvements in the treatment of the insane.

More recently, however, there has bee an increasing resistance to the suitability of the medical approach in the treatment of abnormal behaviour. This resistance focuses on two main areas, the practical and ethical implications of adopting such a 'sickness' analogy.

To adopt the 'sickness' model of abnormality assumes that behaviour can be identified and classified in a systematic way. Classification systems such as the ICD-9 and the DSM III-R have a number of advantages in that they give mental health professionals the means to tie together diagnosis and treatment in a more precise way. However, the very act of classifying is fraught with potential problems. Problems relating to reliability may be experienced due to the subjective interpretation of symptoms that exists within the mental health field. If different psychiatrists reach different diagnoses after exposure to the same information, then it presents serious problems for the accuracy of the system. *Cooper et al.* (1972) discovered that psychiatrists in the USA were far more likely to diagnose patients as schizophrenic than their equivalents in the UK.

Classification systems may also have problems relating to validity, where the overlap between the symptoms of many disorders means that accurate distinctions between them are often difficult to distinguish. Accurate diagnosis often requires the intuition and experience of the skilled practioner, therefore is a product of subjective judgement despite the precision and objectivity of the classification system being used. Such problems have far reaching implications for the effective treatment of these conditions.

The medical approach to abnormality is often attacked on the grounds that it ignores the question of cultural relativity. Anthropological evidence shows that definitions of 'mental illness' appear to differ from culture to culture. Although physical illnesses appear the same wherever they occur, the same is not true for psychological disorders. *Cochrane* (1985) makes the point that although depression is the commonest psychological disorder found in the UK, its occurrence in many other cultures is less well established. Schizophrenia does appear to be universally present in all cultures, and occurs at approximately the same rate, but conceptions of its status differ from culture to culture. In the UK it is seen as a lifelong disability with periods of remission, but in Mauritius it is viewed rather like a physical infection which can be cured.

The biomedical definition of abnormality as illness has led to a number of ethical concerns. The problem of *labelling* means that people who are considered mentally ill carry with them a stigma which has far reaching consequences for much of the rest of their life. *Scheff* (1966) explains that the mentally 'ill' person is seen as breaking a set of 'residual rules' of society which are rather vague and unspecified, having to do with 'decency' and 'reality'. As the breaking of these rules can be strange and frightening for those observing it, the fear can be reduced by labelling such unintelligible behaviour as 'mental illness'. The label not only reduces uncertainty, but also enables the person possessing the label to seek reinforcement by seeking help for the labelled condition. The label thus stabilises and reinforces the role of being 'mentally ill'.

Rosenhan's classic work 'On being sane in insane places' (*Rosenhan*, 1973) demonstrated the ease with which people were labelled should they present initial symptoms of mentall illness yet follow these symptoms with subsequent normal behaviour. Once the label had been applied, Rosenhan found, there were considerable difficulties in losing it during his 'stooge' patients' stay in hospital. A follow up study where Rosenhan informed hospitals in advance that the could expect a number of 'stooge' patients led to a number of incorrect diagnoses of genuine patients.

Spitzer (1975) defended the psychiatric profession by claiming that psychiatrists had trouble not with telling the sane from the insane, but in telling the genuine insane from those feigning insanity. The roles played by Rosenhan's subjects (hearing voices, seeking admission, an apparent lack of concern at their condition and their hospitalization), Spitzer suggested, indicated a rather more abnormal pattern of behaviour than Rosenhan had anticipated.

An added ethical problem of labelling is that because of differences in status, education or race, some people are more likely to have their symptoms labelled as abnormal than others. The greater prevalence of mental disorders in the lower socioeconomic groups may have more to do with both the greater resistance (through intelligence and personal influence) of the middle classes toward labelling and the financial constraints placed upon the lower class groups in seeking early treatment of abnormal behaviours.

It is a contention of labelling theory that the act of labelling will lead to an entrenchment of symptoms as the mentally ill person fits into the mentall illness role. This is not necessarily the case. *Warren* (1974) pointed out that assuming the label 'alcoholic' helps alcoholics to recover. However, *Doherty* (1975) points out that those who reject the mental illness label tend to improve more quickly than those who accept it.

Opponents of traditional psychiatric models suggest that rather than being a supportive and positive intervention in the life of the client, classification as 'mentally ill' can be seen as a form of social control. *Szasz* (1972) claims that many me ntal disorders have no known physical cause yet are labelled as 'mental illness' on the subjective judgement of a psychiatrist, simply because they offend some criterion of 'normality'. The process is then formalized by the provision of mental hospitals where the 'deviant' can be 'treated'. Szasz suggests that many disorders are not illnesses in the same way as we experience physical illnesses, but rather they are problems of adjustment to the stresses of living in a particular environment. Treatment should therefore be social psychological (adjusting the environment) rather than physical (adjusting the individual).

Goffman (1968) sees the mental patient as being involved in a 'career' where they go a series of rituals, starting with diagnosis, hospitalisation, and the 'mortification of self'. In this latter 'ritual', the patient may have personal clothes and possession removed and their private life becomes public. Goffman feels that patients respond to this attack on their identity by becoming 'institutionalised'. They become passive and apathetic to all around them. The institution then, rather than improving the quality of a person's life may be seen as having the opposite effect.

STUDENTS ANSWER WITH EXAMINER'S COMMENTS

Question 1

The way in which a psychologist defines abnormality depends very much on their approach to psychology, whether it be biological, psychoanalytic, behaviourist and so on. The first definition of abnormality is that of deviating from statistical norms. This is when a person's behaviour is not the same as the vast majority of people in the world. However, the problem with this is that just because a person's behaviour is not the same as everybody elses does not mean that they are abnormal. Also there are many behaviours which are statistically the norm but are seen as abnormal behaviour (such as anxiety).

Good – shows awareness of different conceptions of abnormality

The second definition is deviation from social norms, in that they are not doing the same behaviour that is seen as acceptable by the rest of society. This is very much the same as statistical norms in many respects as it is the majority of people doing a particular behaviour which makes it acceptable. The problem with this definition is that different societies have different norms. Does it mean if its acceptable then its normal behaviour, or if its not acceptable then its abnormal behaviour, and what is normal?

The medical (biological) definition of abnormality is that the person who is carrying out the abnormal behaviour has some sort of illness to the brain which is causing it, hence mental illness. The medical model is based on the fact that if something is wrong with the person physically, an illness. This is reflected in the way the people who believe in the medical model, doctors, treat it in the way that they do.

Now DSM III-R

There are five types of mental illness/abnormal behaviour that have been put forward to describe the patient e.g. neurotic, organic, psychotic and so on. These are the names that the medical model uses to describe the patients. In order to discover what is wrong with a patient, there is a classification system that is used to put each patient into a group of illnesses. In the UK the present system is called ICD 9 and in the USA it is called DSM III.

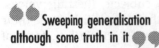
Sweeping generalisation although some truth in it

However, these methods of classification have been heavily criticised as being hopelessly inaccurate, unreliable and so on. For example, Rosenhan proved how inadequate the classification system is in two major experiments. The first experiment involved eight subjects who pretended to be schizophrenic in order to be admitted and to see whether or not they would be admitted to hospital. All the subjects were admitted in different hospitals and waited to find out whether they would be seen as stooges. They were not. It was the other patients of the hospital who knew that they were faking it, and the staff of the hospital paid no attention to them. Rosenhan found he could walk about the hospital with a clipboard happily making notes without drawing attention to himself.

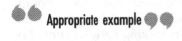
Appropriate example

The next experiment involved doctors being told that several patients were going to be sent to be tested that were actually stooges. In reality there were no stooges, but the doctors found 44 stooges. Rosenhan was heavily criticised for the ethics of this experiment but still it highlights the severe problems of trying to classify a patient.

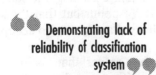
Demonstrating lack of reliability of classification system

Cooper found that a person was 10 times more likely to be classed as a schizophrenic, even though they may not be, in the USA than in the UK. However, the new classification system ICD 9 and DSM III, is hoped to cure this problem. For example, under the previous classification system, many doctors gave different classifications to a patient. In a study with the ICD 9, 80% of doctors agreed on patients' illnesses.

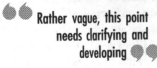
Rather vague, this point needs clarifying and developing

Other problems with the medical model come from Szasz who said that people are classified for convenience. Also, rather than understand a particular type of abnormal behaviour, the patient is seen as being mentally ill. He said mental illness is just a convenient label used by society to name something that it doesn't understand. Abnormal behaviour is caused by thoughts and is not an illness. This is a view held by Freud, who said that the cause of abnormal behaviour is a conflict between the id and the superego.

This is a well informed, if at times rather confusingly presented essay. There is a good breath of information discussed, with some evidence of evaluative discussion. For that balance of material, it is characteristic of a grade B.

REVIEW SHEET

1. What, according to Stratton and Hayes, are the five definitions of abnormality?

    i.
    _____

    ii.
    _____

    iii.
    _____

    iv.
    _____

    v.
    _____

2. What are the four general causes of abnormal behaviour according to the biomedical model?

    i.
    _____

    ii.
    _____

    iii.
    _____

    iv.
    _____

3. Offer two evaluative points relating to the biomedical model.

    i.
    _____

    ii.
    _____

4. What are the three major biomedical types of treatment?

    i.
    _____

    ii.
    _____

    iii.
    _____

5. Offer one evaluative comment on each.

    i.
    _____

    ii.
    _____

    iii.
    _____

6. The behavioural model of abnormality makes two major assumptions, what are they?

   i. _____

   ii. _____

7. What are the three types of learning that explain the acquisition of abnormal behaviour?

   i. _____

   ii. _____

   iii. _____

8. Offer two evaluative comments on the behavioural model.

   i. _____

   ii. _____

9. Suggest two types of behavioural treatment.

   i. _____

   ii. _____

10. Offer an evaluative comment for each of these.

    i. _____

    ii. _____

    iii. _____

11. What, according to psychoanalysis is neurotic anxiety?

    i. _____

    ii. _____

12. Offer two evaluative comments on the psychoanalytic model of abnormality.

i.

ii.

13. What are the three aims of psychoanalytic treatment?

i.

ii.

iii.

14. Offer three evaluative comments on psychoanalysis as a treatment of abnormal behaviour.

i.

ii.

iii.

Index